THE GREAT WHITE WAY

CRITICAL STUDIES IN
BLACK LIFE AND CULTURE
(VOL. 28)

GARLAND REFERENCE LIBRARY
OF THE HUMANITIES
(VOL. 1669)

CRITICAL STUDIES IN BLACK LIFE AND CULTURE
C. James Trotman, Advisory Editor

THE GREAT WHITE WAY
African American Women Writers and
American Success Mythologies

Phillipa Kafka

GARLAND PUBLISHING, INC. • NEW YORK & LONDON
1993

Library of Congress Cataloging-in-Publication Data

Kafka, Phillipa, 1943–
    The great white way : African American women writers and
American success mythologies / Phillipa Kafka.
        p. cm. — (Critical studies in Black life and culture ; vol. 28)
(Garland reference library of the humanities ; vol. 1669)
    ISBN 0-8153-1160-5 (acid-free paper)
    1. American literature—Afro-American authors—History and
criticism. 2. American literature—Women authors—History and
criticism. 3. Women and literature—United States. 4. Afro-American
women in literature. 5. Afro-Americans in literature. 6. Success in
literature. 7. Myth in literature. I. Title. II. Series. III. Series: Critical
studies in Black life and culture ; v. 28.
PS153.N5K34   1993
810.9'9287—dc20   93-21789
                                                                               CIP

Printed on acid-free, 250-year-life paper
Manufactured in the United States of America

To my beloved mentor, Dr. Charles T. Davis,
late Director of Black Studies, Yale University.

CONTENTS

vii

The Great White Way

INTRODUCTION

Since I contend throughout this work that Booker T. Washington was the mediator for African Americans of the European American success mythology as personified by Benjamin Franklin, I will explain this position here. I will also explain how I use the terms "signifying," "European American," and "African American."

The title of this work "signifies" on a rumination about Broadway by the Invisible Man, the nameless protagonist of Ralph Ellison's novel of that name. This Black everyman's experiences drive him underground where he "signifies" on the European American term "great white way" in relation to African American experience: "I doubt if there is a brighter spot in all New York than this hole of mine, and I do not exclude Broadway. Or the Empire State Building on a photographer's dream night. . . . Those two spots are among the darkest of our whole civilization—pardon me, our whole *culture*. . . . Though invisible, I am in the great American tradition of tinkers. That makes me kin to Ford, Edison and Franklin" (*Invisible Man* 1962:9, 10, 11).

From the European American perspective, dazzling technological and material supremacy illuminates itself while putting the rest of the world in the dark. However, from the African American perspective, the image conveys a second dimension of meaning invisible to the rest of the culture, as is the Invisible Man himself.

For African Americans, the term "signifying" has a double meaning. Signifying is an ancient African rhetorical and aesthetic technique characterized by flexibility, power, versatility, and range. It utilizes wit, sarcasm, humor, and irony. Thus Ellison's appropriation and subversion of the popular European American sobriquet for Broadway as "the great white way" to make his own point about European American culture is itself an example of signifying. So subtle and unobtrusive is the technique that bullies and oppressors are generally oblivious when they are being "signified on."

Signifying can be employed with bitter irony, as in my example from Ellison (on which I have signified the title of this book), or in pastiche and parody, to satirize through laughter. It can be used to insult and/or praise. It is a complex, highly developed duel of wits, of word-sparring, involving formal and time-honored formulas and rituals. In this sense, signifying might best be likened to classical Spanish bullfighting, another complex ritual. Like signifying, it is performed primarily in a public arena on an unconscious but dangerous and powerful opponent. When successful, signifying is so subtle and masterful that only the audience realizes what and who this signifier is signifying on and can fully appreciate the time-honored sequence of steps, the grace of style, all the fine points that go into the performance.

When used by such skilled writers as Charles W. Chesnutt and Alice Walker, this powerful ironic technique evokes bitter laughter among those who are aware of the in-joke. These authors often consciously play with unwary readers, reinforcing them in their tendency to mistake illiteracy for ignorance, as Maya Angelou maintains. In short, these authors are signifying on their unwary readers.

Henry Louis Gates, Jr., who has done monumental work on African/African American signifying techniques, asserts that signifying is "a strategy of black figurative language use" which includes "marking, loud-talking, testifying, calling out (of one's name), sounding, rapping, playing the dozens, and so on," as well as call and response (Gates, *Signifying* 1988:52).

Certain coded sequences of tone and language signal the initiated that signifying is occurring, especially when the signifying is formal and serious. In signifying:

1. The signifier consciously talks over the head of his/her opponent to the audience/reader, so that only the latter alone is in on the joke. Generally, the audience understands the ironic point, but not always. Sometimes the opponent is fully conscious of the challenge. For example, the opponent might be another African American who is capable of responding in kind.

2. The signifier succinctly repeats/mimics the opponent's thesis, perspective, or belief. Such repetition/mimicry is done in an exaggeratedly innocent manner and tone, with as straight, as masklike a face as possible.

3. Finally, the signifier, by means of powerfully condensed use of witty language (which can be obscene), rounds on or twists the opponent's belief into its reverse, thus achieving a double and double-edged voice. When this technique, known as "trope of chiasmus," is clever enough, the opponent (especially when European American) does not even realize that he or she has been signified on.

If the opponent is aware of what is going on, the gauntlet is taken up and the opponent "caps" or "riffs" on the challenger, attempting to outperform the original signifier in scathing mockery, humorous insults and invective, or on occasion, with compliments and praise songs. Jazz musicians habitually "riff" in this manner when they perform among themselves. The duel of wits goes on until one opponent has clearly outwitted the other with the most outrageous, imaginative "lie" of the game. The technique demands an audience familiar with the rules of this game and that knows what's going on. This makes it a form of spectator and participant sport, which is why it so easily adapts itself to written and musical forms.

The problem in the United States is that readers and critics have been trained solely in European American rhetorical and aesthetic techniques. Consequently, they read African American literature without comprehension, awareness, or appreciation of those "Black text specific" elements, as Gates defines them, like signifying. These elements make African/African American literature different from both European American literature and other ethnic American literatures.[1]

In my chapter on Phillis Wheatley, I will illustrate her quiet mastery of signifying. Born and raised in Africa, she yet retained her African identity as an individual and as an artist, utilizing African rhetorical and aesthetic devices. At the same time, Wheatley used the discourse and aesthetic techniques then in vogue in England and her colonies, and throughout Europe. Wheatley was also a sincere and devout convert to Christianity and European customs and values. The result was a synthesis of cultural aesthetic techniques. However, Wheatley's signifying would be apparent only to readers capable of simultaneously reading across African, Christian, and eighteenth-century European American techniques and discourse.

When this is done, Wheatley's poetry can be read much as we read Charles Waddell Chesnutt's stories like "The Goophered Grapevine," for example. In this satire within a satire, Uncle Julius is depicted as a survivor whose success can be attributed to his covert shrewdness which he manifests by signifying. If his signifying is ignored or incomprehensible, if he is read from a European American perspective, the character appears to be merely a stereotypical simple, carefree, superstitious Uncle Tom type. However, he is actually a Brer Rabbit or signifying monkey type.

Some years after the Civil War in which his master was slain, Uncle Julius tries to convince a Northern couple who are prospective purchasers of the plantation that it has been the object of conjuring. Who knows how many previous buyers he has frightened away with this tale expressly designed for the purpose of signifying on European Americans? And indeed, Uncle Julius must have had some success at his manipulative game. Up to this point (the story's opening), he has succeeded in being left to himself. Unmolested for years, with free access to the scuppernong vines, he has also secretly and cleverly supported himself financially. He has done this by selling the fruit of the vines in both natural and fermented form.

Traditionally trained scholars (myself included) are products of an elitist European American educational tracking system. This system focused entirely on European, English, and American literature, and at its broadest, added Greek and Latin literature and two (West) European languages. Accordingly, we have an entirely European American perspective and are therefore unaware of, or at best, limited in terms of other perspectives. Similarly, students who are products of a rank and file system of education (where they study only a minimum needed to meet basic requirements except in their area of specialization) are also limited.

Most of us, students and teachers alike, are like fish in water. We do not know what components define what seems to be so natural and instinctive to us: our culture, our world view, our perspectives. We do not even know there are other cultures, much less what components define them. Many of our students do not know what religious components comprise the value system of even our own culture: that it is defined as Judaeo-Christian. They do not know how Judaism differs from Christianity, or even if it does. They cannot discuss the salient features of other significant world religions or views. When questioned, they consistently respond that it is Christianity which has the most adherents throughout the world.

Therefore, both American students and their professors know very little, if anything, about any culture other than their own. For example, what does our education teach us about African American culture, or any other hyphenated American culture? Or for that matter, what does our education teach us about any cultures beyond our own shores? We have been taught and thus assume that there are not any worth worrying about; that other cultures are so many *tabula rasa* waiting for us to come along and teach them how to do it the right way, the American way. "Such a picture," according to R. Radhakrishnan, "is falsely universal since it is the exclusive expression of the dominant point of view that in speaking for all humanity denies its own ideological perspectivity and ends up with an oppressive and repressive totality that does not reflect the interests of all the components that make up that totality. For too long a time, theory has been the executor of such a Colonialist and Imperialist will" (1987:17).

In this work, instead of analyzing from a European American perspective *alone* how selected African American women writers confront European American (male) success myths and what they make out of them, I also take into account, and have already pointed out, the fact that African American writers are African American and European American writers simultaneously. In most cases they have actually been "Americanized" for more centuries than newer Americans. European American culture is part and parcel of the African American consciousness, perhaps more so than with European Americans because of the greater length of time it has been inscribed in them. As Alice Childress quips in the persona of a female house servant: "We always some 'problem' and people takin' pot-shots at us is always called 'tension' and why you and me who have been citizens for generations should be called 'minority' is more than I can see" (1986:83).

For readers to fully appreciate the richness and complexity of African American literature, European American training simply does not suffice. True, our students will receive a solid European American grounding in terms of referents whenever the texts they study reflect European American rhetorical and aesthetic traditions, "influences," etc. But how can students recognize the African/African American aspects of these texts if neither the students nor their professors know about their existence? If they don't know what to look for or where? If the African/African American perspective is invisible to them?

For example, take Zora Neale Hurston's *Their Eyes Were Watching God* as taught by "traditional" white male professors whom Margot I. Duley sees as "hidebound disciplinarians" hampered by "comfortably tenured mind[s]" whose "many forms of resistance" to canonical expansion can be traced to a training in "popularized sociobiology masquerading as objective fact" (1989:649). Such an academic, in reading the following passage from a European American perspective (and unaware of the technique of signifying), will teach it as "universal." In other words it could be replicated in any American novel:

"... Don't stand dere rollin' yo' pop eyes at me wid yo' rump hangin' nearly to yo' knees! ..."

"Stop mixin' up mah doings wid mah looks, Jody. When you git through tellin' me how tuh cut uh plug uh tobacco, then you kin tell me whether mah behind is on straight or not."

"Wha—whut's dat you say, Janie? You must be out yo' head."

"Naw, Ah ain't outa mah head neither."

"You must be. Talkin' any such language as dat. You de one started talkin' under people's clothes. Not me."

"Whut's de matter wid you, nohow? You ain't no young girl to be gettin' all insulted 'bout yo' looks. You ain't no young courtin' gal. You'se uh old woman, nearly forty."

"Yeah, Ah'm nearly forty and you'se already fifty. How come you can't talk about dat sometimes instead of always pointin' at me?"

"T'ain't no use in gettin' all mad, Janie, cause Ah mention you ain't no young gal no mo'. Nobody in heah ain't lookin' for no wife outa yuh. Old as you is."

"Naw, Ah ain't no young gal no mo' but den Ah ain't no old woman neither. Ah reckon Ah looks mah age too. But Ah'm uh woman every inch of me, and Ah know it. Dat's uh whole lot more'n *you* kin say. You big-bellies round here and put out a lot of brag, but 'tain't nothin' to it but yo' big voice. Humph! Talkin' bout *me* lookin' ol'! When you pull down yo' britches, you look lak de change uh life."

"Great God from Zion!" Sam Watson gasped. "Y'all really playin' de dozens tuhniht." (Hurston 1978:122–123)

Because the professor is incapable of seeing this passage as an example of African/African American signifying, the students fail to learn about the tradition. Further, the significance of what Watson terms "playin' de dozens" is also lost: that the author did not choose a European American term to describe the situation, but an African/African American one. Tragically, much else is lost as well. For example, how and/or why the author used the term to comment on and describe the quick and cutting word play; what "playin' de dozens" means and its origin. Also absent is any comprehension of whether or not the situation reflects the rules and rituals of a culture different from that which the European American trained academic had learned (namely, a tradition called "playin' the dozens" rather than one called "Southern local color folk humor").

Zora Neale Hurston, trained at Columbia University under Franz Boas as an anthropologist, was quite capable of making distinctions between European American and African/African American rhetorical and aesthetic techniques if she so chose, and was also capable of employing both. Yet Hurston used and referred to only this one technique as "playin' the dozens." By disregarding both Hurston's chosen terminology and the African/African American system of rhetoric (which Hurston went to great lengths to convey to her readers not only in this example but in many others), traditionally trained professors perpetuate the African/American system as nonexistent, as invisible. Since that system is not taught, it does not exist for students—even though it does.

Moreover, such traditionalists see and teach the earlier repartee strictly from a European American aesthetic and rhetorical perspective. They define it as ironically humorous on the following grounds: Since the only model for irony in the world which is unique and yet universal is the European American model, it therefore follows that all examples of irony are forged in the European American mold. To anyone familiar with the configurations of the ritualized activities involved in doing or "playin' the dozens," such a contention is patently absurd. In fact, *any* hyphenated example of American literature—Asian American or Native American or Chicano or Jewish American or whatever—contains unique rhetorical and aesthetic devices that are not European American alone. And the same goes for any example of any text from any other culture with other than a European American world view—African literature, Indian literature, Chinese literature, etc.

In relation to African American literature specifically, Henry Louis Gates, Jr., Houston Baker, Jr., and Molefi Kete Asante, among others, have attempted to expand European American interpretations of African American texts. They do this by examining the rhetorical and aesthetic techniques used by the writers to express an African/African American world view, or perspective, in addition to a European American one. These critics have taken the courageous step of explaining how much richer a reading of African American literature becomes when undertaken from an African/African American perspective *in addition* to a European American perspective, instead of applying *only* European American perspectives to such texts.

Asante argues, in fact, that "centric" perspectives should apply to any texts from any culture; that to read them solely from the perspective of a European American value system is insufficient, if not flawed. "We all have the capacity to see," he points out, "and usually this is from the vantage point of our culture. In the West and elsewhere, the European has propounded an exclusive view of reality that creates a fundamental human crisis. In some cases it has created cultures arrayed against themselves" (1987:18).

So it is for those who persist in viewing African American literature and oratory entirely from traditional European

American rhetorical and aesthetic perspectives. It is as simplistic as what European Americans hear and read in the phrase "great white way." From that perspective, as with any one-dimensional perspective, all is invisible of which we are unaware. Asante further states in this regard that the West only "tolerate[s] diversity of viewpoints" in order to "establish a single set of criteria for what constitutes validity." The problematic in such a "formulation" which takes into account "neither African nor Southern Hemisphere thought" is twofold. First, it exhibits "ignorance in the sense of ignoring the ways in which people in the cradle of humanity and civilization have dealt with communications or transcendence." Second, and "more seriously," it perpetuates the "Western imposition" of a certain given "view of the world," and the assumption that that particular view is "real." Surprisingly, Asante views the problem not so much "in the expounding of Western categories but in the absolute manner in which they are assumed to constitute the whole of human thought." He therefore dismisses such totalizing essentialism as "unacceptable, in any field, on intellectual and cultural grounds" (1987: 181).

In this work, the term "European American" means a combined Western European (primarily English) and American world view. Once European American readers become aware of the technique of signifying—that there is a double meaning and a double voice in African American material, then they experience a shift in perspective. These readers can then simultaneously perceive *two* dimensions in material where before there appeared to be only one, the European American.

According to Michel Foucault, such insight shifts our hitherto unconscious one-dimensional perception within a culture's "regime" or "general politics" into another dimension so that we experience a double vision or double consciousness. From this perspective, we come to realize that the hegemony has chosen "the types of discourse" which it "accepts and makes function as true." Also exposed is how our culture has trained us "to distinguish true and false statements," as well as "the means by which each is sanctioned." We are thereby empowered to see through "the techniques and procedures accorded value in the acquisition of truth," as well as "the status of those who are charged with saying what counts as true" (1980:131).

Once armed with such an awareness, readers trained solely in European American perspectives are empowered to perceive yet another perspective: one which perceives itself as "other" than the European American perspective, even though it is written from well within European American cultural boundaries. For example, these readers can see two meanings in the phrase "the great white way." They simultaneously see its meaning from a European American perspective and from Ellison's Black everyman perspective.

African American readers, however, are also reading within European American cultural boundaries. Therefore, the total range of expression within the American cultural environment is European American. Within that range, hyphenated Americans are "Othered" and perceive themselves as such. But at the same time they are European American by culture, no matter what Other cultural Otherness enters into their perceptions. Thus European American (trained) critics who define other Americans than themselves only in their characteristics of Other are employing limited definitions. Accordingly, hyphenated American *and* European American writers are Other also. This applies not only to African American writers like Ellison and Wheatley, but to other hyphenated American writers like Native American or Asian American writers who consciously Other themselves from European American culture.

However, in perceiving themselves as Other, these writers distance themselves from and critique that part of *their own* European American cultural construction which does not conform to their notion of the ideal hyphenated American. In expressing their disappointment, in their rage or bitterness at the betrayal of values they cherish, they use dichotomous (we/they, us/them) language which conveys separation from European American cultural gatekeepers, or those who set themselves up as such. Yet despite this oppositional stance to the culture, these writers are also simultaneously writing from within the culture, in the culture's language, and reflecting the culture's values. From their perspective, in fact, they live truer to the values and ideals of European American culture than the gatekeepers who have oppressed African Americans and other hyphenated Americans into invisibility. As Asante puts it: "I have the insight that comes from being born black in the United States. That fact puts me in a critical mood within the intellectual and social milieu I share with Eurocentricists. As the critic, I am always seeking to create a new world, to find an escape, to liberate those who see only a part of reality" (1987:5).

Indeed, from such a perspective, those gatekeepers who have no room in their paradigms for Others than themselves, who Other Others who do not replicate what they happen to see in their own mirrors, are actually the deviants in terms of the culture's expressed ideals. In reality, according to R. Radhakrishnan, there are no such things as non-hyphenated Americans. Those who consider themselves gatekeepers of American-ness have forgotten that they themselves are hyphenated. They are working from the premise that their hyphenated form of American-ness is the only perspective which is "American." He argues that they have "violently ideologized" their own "male, white, heterosexual identity" as "normative." From such a "dominant perspective," ethnicity becomes an "absolute form of racial otherness," becomes "dehistoricized." Worse, it then comes to mean "something alien, dangerous, criminal, violent and spontaneously and instinctually terroristic." In "effecting this rhetorical connection," this "mainstream ideology" forgets that it "itself is constituted ethnically." It sees itself now as "nationalized and generalized to the point of absolute ideological dominance." It then "disallows" every other ethnic group "the very same political and representational rights and privileges that in the first place made 'the mainstream' possible." Radhakrishnan also notes that by totalizing the use of the term "ethnic," the mainstream "lumps together" the diversity of ethnicities "each of which has a history of its own." Thus "the dominant ideology" avoids "dealing with a whole range of "minority" groups and discourses (1987:15).

Because of the oppositional stance of African American writers to "American" culture, I will, for the sake of convenience separate European American and African American perspectives. However, as I argued earlier, African American writers are actually African American/European American writers simultaneously, not simply African American writers, just as Japanese American writers are Asian American/European American writers, and so on. Accordingly, the African American women writers I analyze in this text in terms of their responses to European American (male) success myths, in my opinion always do so from an African American/European American *complex* of perspectives and not just an African American perspective.

If the writers under discussion were solely European American writers, I could begin with an analysis of Benjamin Franklin's major contribution to the formulation and creation of (male) American success mythologies, as well as having been their foremost exponent and model. I could then analyze the complex of ways in which the African American women writers reacted to those myths. However, the writers I have selected are African American women writers. Therefore, I consider them to be African American as well as European American culturally. This, in my opinion, makes their response to European American (male) success mythologies more complex than had they been simply European American female writers, like Kate Chopin or Edith Wharton, for example. I provide an overview of African American women writers' attitudes in the third chapter. Chapter Two begins with an analysis of Phillis Wheatley's life in relation to Benjamin Franklin's in terms of European American (male) success mythologies from both an African and colonial perspective. In the final half of this second chapter, I analyze Wheatley's work as an African/English colonial writer, especially in terms of her self-awareness as an African writer and her syncretization of African rhetorical and aesthetic techniques with European ones.

From the glittering pantheon of writers in the 200 years following Wheatley's death, I have narrowed my discussion of responses to American (male) success myths to Harriet Jacobs, Zora Neale Hurston, and Alice Walker. I close with Alice Walker because in my estimation her appropriation in *The Color Purple* of Booker T. Washington's variation of the Franklin model represents a historic development, not only in the literary history of African American women writers, but in African American and European American literary history as well.

The European American perspective has been institutionalized for nearly 400 years, ever since the founding of this country's first universities by English émigrés and their descendants. Millions and millions of immigrants have landed on these shores in all that time. In addition, some hundreds of thousands of indigenous peoples were already here. All these Americans have been expected to melt down the "e pluribus" diversely hypenated parts of their identities through a homogenizing education termed "the melting pot." This process was presumed to make us all come out "unum," and that "unum" the traditional European American culture.

The life trajectories of males followed cultural gender constructions (myths) completely different from those prescribed for females. As sociologist Dorothy Smith sees it, women's training in terms of "the overall division of labor" in "the whole system of ruling relations" was to "produce the conditions of its own ruling and the existence of the ruling class [males]." Women were to make "the concrete, the particular, the bodily thematic of . . . work" so that men could "operate as knowing subjects in the abstracted conceptual mode of ruling" (1987:80–81).

Thus women were required by their menfolk to be responsible for all spousal, domestic, childbearing and child raising services. According to the constructed mythology, they were to obey men without question, without deviation from their primary obligations in private within the family and in public within the culture. These private activities were separated from public activities which were defined as "work" performed by males who received payment for them.

From this perspective, Booker T. Washington's lifelong attempt to expand the concept of American male success mythology in the workplace to include Black men, as well as Ralph Ellison's objection to the European American privatizing of African American males and rendering them "invisible" in American culture, can be interpreted as objections by Black men to being forced into "female" roles: into living like women in relation to European American cultural mythology. In terms of women's public activities, in those activities which the culture defined as "work," women were severely restricted from engaging in any but service occupations conceptualized as extensions of women's work. Here again, Washington's *Up from Slavery*, his life's work, and Ellison's *Invisible Man* were objections to African American males being circumscribed in work opportunities in this culture, exactly as were women.

Black feminist historian Elsa Barkley Brown best explains the precise nature of the dimensionality for Black women which the African American experience and mythology added to European American mythology.

First, *her* ancestors always acted as members of a group. For example, Barkley Brown's research into washerwomen revealed that like her grandmother who had first organized them, "Black women had always played roles as organizers, planners, policy makers, leaders, and developers of the Black community and its institutions" (1989:7), but in a critically different way from European American women. Unlike most women whose female antecedents' isolated, homebound illiteracy conformed entirely to their culture's construct for women, Barkley Brown comes from "a long tradition of African american scholars who understand the limitations of the paradigms and underlying assumptions that pervade Western educational institutions" (1989:6). Accordingly, Barkley Brown's mother, who graduated from college as a mathematics major, decided after marriage, "despite economic hardship," to stay at home and care for her family as in the Washington model. This decision "to be a wife and mother first in a world which defined Africanamerican women in so many other ways, the decision to make her family the most important priority" was, according to Barkley Brown's interpretation, "an act of resistance to a system which would define her place for her in terms of its own economic and racist needs" (1989:7).

In contrast, Ralph Ellison in *Invisible Man* and Booker T. Washington in *Up from Slavery* described male protagonists whose life trajectories did not include all those "womanly duties" which took up the greater part of Barkley Brown's mother's days. The Invisible Man was a bachelor who between his college days and the time he went underground was taken care of by various women, most memorably and stereotypically by his symbolically nurturing landlady, Mary. Washington describes and thanks three wives in succession as performing those nurturing activities for him.

Second, Barkley Brown's "sisters/aunts/mothers" of her "family and community" assisted her in earning her Ph.D. Given her experience, it is no wonder that Barkley Brown, again representative of Black feminist thinking on this issue, concludes that European American culture distinguishes "family" as to "who is nuclear and who is extended, who is blood kin and who is fictive kin." In marked contrast, African American culture in the persons of her "mothers" have passed on to her a transcendence of such notions, relationships, and roles (1989:7).

Third, Barkley Brown perceived a sharp dichotomy between her mother's strong *verbal* adherence to the European American/African American cultural mythology about appropriate behavior for women, while her *actions* opposed them. When Barkley Brown confided in a letter to her mother that she had her own ambitions; that "while she did not mind working while her husband went to school, what she did mind was all the talk in the family/community about his education and future and none about hers." Her mother's response was to insist that "raising a family" should be the sum total of her school and career aspirations, for "a Black woman's responsibility was to maintain her family." The ensuing events are so interesting that they deserve citation at length:

> Enclosed in that same envelope with that letter was a check in the amount of tuition for graduate school—an enormous sum for the mothers/sisters/aunts who had pooled all and sold some to raise it—an act of faith in another generation of Africanamerican women. When this daughter reached the stage of Ph.D. candidacy exams, this mother came and stayed a month to care for the two granddaughters. Every night at dinner she gave her daughter a lecture on the evils of pursuing a career and neglecting her children and begged her to give this up and be a proper Black mother. And every morning she got the children up quietly and tiptoed 'round the house all day so her daughter's studying would not be interrupted. When time came to take the oral exams, the sisters/aunts/mothers sent an appropriate suit for their child to wear. And the mother loudly

proclaimed the evils of such careerism and neglect of family
priorities as she cooked a very special dinner to celebrate.
(1989:6–7)

Instead of perceiving "that contradiction" in her mother as
an individual Black woman's dilemma, Barkley Brown realized
that in actuality her mother had provided her with an invaluable
insight which led to her current theoretical stance, which
empowered her in the Foucauldian sense to better understand
European American cultural constructs. These "defined
womanhood in one way" while on the other hand requiring
women "to live lives that were in reality totally different from
that definition." For example, "true women" did not work
outside the home at a time when the majority of African
American women were employed. For this reason, she
concludes, "Africanamerican women have lived lives filled with
contradictions and have formed a meaning for themselves and
their people out of those contradictions." Further, what Barkley
Brown saw in her mother's contradictory behavior "was the
possible necessity of the simultaneous promotion of two
contradictory sets of values." It is Barkley Brown's conviction
that "*both* were essential to the survival—of me as a person in the
society in which we live, and of the Africanamerican community
as a whole" (1989:7, 8).

In my chapter on Hurston, I illustrate in terms of African
American women's writing these penetrating insights of Barkley
Brown's into Black women's "simultaneous promotion of two
contradictory sets of values," what I call "disjunctive
conjunctions" at work in Hurston's writing and life. Incidentally,
that Barkley Brown's mother supported her daughter's goals
despite violent disagreement with them reveals that our culture
has inscribed "being a good mother" deeper in *all* women than
any other role, even to the point of "dichotomous" gaps. Those
contradictions form "conjunctive disjunctions" between their
perspective and their actions.

Barkley Brown illustrates yet another European American
cultural construct/myth which the African American community
confronted and which sourced Black feminist pedagogy.
According to Barkley Brown, her mother's experiences with and

response to "white society" required her to deal "up front with Eurocentricity" and its influence in terms of her European American training and scholarship, which valorizes its own world view as "objective" and assumes that scholars can "divorce" themselves from their scholarship and from their "community." Barkley Brown observes the connection between her own life, Black Studies, "and to some degree Women's Studies" in that all three derive from an "understanding of the necessity of connecting the people doing the research and the people who were the subject of the inquiry—to have the academy informed by those whose very lives spoke to that about which we intellectualize" (1989:9). Thus it is again from her own experience that Barkley Brown's Black feminist pedagogy is informed by her great respect for "people's abilities to understand their own lives." She has also "learned to listen, not just to what they tell me about the particulars of their lives, but also to the ways in which they define themselves" (1989:9). This is a pedagogical approach common to feminists.

I have singled out Barkley Brown for extensive analysis because in my opinion she best expresses those elements of contemporary African American/feminist perspective on which this work's approach to African American women writers' responses to American success mythology is grounded. This is the case from Wheatley to Harriet Jacobs' *Incidents in the Life of a Slave Girl*, continuing through Hurston's *Their Eyes Were Watching God*, and on to Alice Walker's *The Color Purple*, in their descriptions of their heroines' efforts to live decent lives despite an obstructive culture.

An elitist European American masculine myth can be deconstructed from the Franklin model of success, because Franklin replicated the English model for education when he educated himself. This was the same model which privileged young men were trained into in the existing universities of the time and in which Wheatley also was trained, albeit privately. This elitist model has basically remained intact into our time, but no longer only for upper class white young men. After World War II, representatives of the other gender, other classes, ethnicities, and races, such as academics like myself and Barkley Brown, have gone through the same elitist training (if not always internalized), and as a result have risen into an elitist class and life-style.

Franklin in his life trajectory epitomized the training of proletarian white males and females, like my own Kean College students who go to college to learn a specialization so they can get a job that will enable them to rise into the middle class. This is different from Barkley Brown and myself, for example, who used education not only for economic advancement, but to rise into an intellectually elite aristocracy, the academic institution, and work within it to democratize it even further.

Franklin, of course, had many avocations, but he concentrated on publishing from childhood, and that is where he made his mark. That is also how he shaped the requisite life trajectory intended to be inscribed in white males only, although Others, like Wheatley and her owners, also internalized it. Franklin worked hard at his chosen occupation. He made it big by forty. He then retired and did what he wanted to do for the rest of his life. Such key incidents as these in his life have been abstracted into major elements of American (male) success mythology. As such, they are inscribed as deeply into *all* Americans from his day to ours as are the Declaration of Independence and the Pledge of Allegiance, although they too were originally meant for white males only.

In the chapter on Phillis Wheatley, Benjamin Franklin, and European American male success mythology, I review the major elements which comprise American (male) success mythology, including the accompanying scenarios still familiar to most of us. Alongside each one, I shall provide a counterpoint in Phillis Wheatley's life trajectory. She was Franklin's contemporary and shared his perspective on life in many ways but came to a dramatically different end, whose implications are worth exploring.

Benjamin Franklin has had an enormous influence for hundreds of years on European American culture in manufacturing and disseminating European American (male) success mythology to Americans and to the rest of the world. In this regard, there is no question that African Americans as Americans also imbibed this mythology. However, I contend that it was mediated for them from around 1895 on, even into the

present, by Booker T. Washington. I further contend that William
E.B. DuBois's seemingly broad and unique influence during this
period is a result of historical revisionism; that, in fact, such a
view of DuBois began comparatively recently, only after Martin
Luther King, Jr.'s and Malcolm X's projects could be interpreted
ex post facto as having followed in a natural sequence from
DuBois rather than from the currently discredited Washington.

At this point the question might arise as to why I do not
choose Frederick Douglass as my paradigm for a Black race
leader who served as mediator and/or reinforcer of European
American male success ideology to his people. Actually, there is
a bit of a debate as to whether Douglass's depiction of himself in
his *Narrative* "deteriorated" into the Franklin paradigm of an
individual "who makes it on his own." Or (as in Washington's
model in *Up From Slavery*), whether Douglass remained loyal to
the African/African American construct of the individual
working for and with others within a community: working for
the community's empowerment first and foremost with a
consciousness that what he is doing is simultaneously a
reflection of self as self and as self embedded in the community.[2]

Douglass's concept of citizenship, far more than Washington's, fits the European American mold. Douglass's concept,
according to Kathleen B. Jones's definition, matches the
"traditional [i.e., European American] concept of citizenship" so
dependent on a "combative, oppositional perspective" to
politics, a perspective which unfortunately does not include a
suffusion of "intimacy" such as the maternal relationship offers
(1990:811). It seems to some critics, in fact, that Douglass's
concept of citizenship was European American rather than
African/African American. Let me illustrate with Barbara J.
Haile's and Audreye E. Johnson's nice summary of the latter
view:

> The Black American experience is derived from an African
> world view, which differs significantly from the White
> American experience, which is derived from a European world
> view. The African world view values the group and the
> survival of the group, in contrast to the individual and
> individualism; it values cooperation over competition, power,
> and dominance; psychological interdependence over

independence; the oral tradition over the visual-written language; a holistic conception of the human condition over mind/body dualism ['good me vs. bad me']. In the African world view, everything is interrelated and emotions are not labeled as bad. Therefore, there is no need to repress feelings of love, compassion, job [sic], or sorrow. In the African world-view, the elderly are valued for their wisdom, in contrast to a reverence for youth. This African world view then served as the framework for explaining and understanding the experiences of Black Americans. According to Black psychologist Joseph White, "it is not possible to explain adequately the behavior of Blacks using psychological and conceptual frameworks that have been developed out of the experience base of Euro-Americans." (1989:70)

Charles Johnson, 1990 Pulitzer Prize winner for *Middle Passage*, also prefers to the European American model the ancient one of his African "ancestors" who—"or so I've read—had a hundred concepts for the African community, but none for the 'individual,' who, as we define him today—the lonely Leibnizean monad—is an invention of the Industrial Age, as romantic love is the product of medieval poets" (1987:134).

Johnson, in signifying language dripping with venom, further contrasts African American concern for the community in all activities with the petty, self-centered egotism verging on megalomania of the European American culture's "myths about men who tried, in their own small way, to create lives that could be, if disciplined, the basis of universal law" (1987:102). Faced with such a dichotomy between the two cultures which he contains within him, the African American, according to Johnson, can't help "feeling his twoness, as DuBois so beautifully put it in a brilliant stroke of classic Dualism, 'an American, a Negro; two souls, two thoughts, two warring ideals in one dark body.' The . . . primordial feeling of *thrownness* that every Negro supports, and I am saying, annihilates him, because he can find reflections of himself nowhere in it [shades of Ellison's Invisible Man]— like a falcon exiled, say, to the Lifeworld of fish, always off-balance, but finally embracing the alien in all its otherness, yet never sure if he's got it right" (Johnson 1987:102).

Some might argue at this point that Douglass should still be chosen as a mediator because he was a heroic figure in the Franklin mold, whereas Washington, they contend, was an infamous accommodationist. Such conduct has consequently ruled him out from even being discussed in the same breath with legitimate race men like Douglass or DuBois. Further, Washington should not just be erased from this discussion of African American women writers and American male success mythology, but in any other discussion in relation to African American literary history. Indeed, many contemporary scholars have whited Washington out of their scholarship. Gates's ironic condescension in distinguishing between Washington and Douglass is typical: "For Booker T. Washington, Frederick Douglass was a John the Baptist who roamed the deserts of antebellum and Reconstruction America clearing the way for that great deliverer, Booker T., sanctioning Washington's social program and Washington himself as the true ideals for turn-of-the-century Afro-America" (*Figures in Black* 109).

When not ignored or dismissed in a phrase, few critics (with the notable exceptions of Washington's biographer, Louis B. Harlan, and Houston Baker, Jr.), are positive about Washington's contributions. In Baker's case, what makes for his positive approach might be the influence of his father, Houston Baker, Sr., who "served for seventy-five years as a dedicated disciple of the teachings of Booker T. Washington." Baker's justifiable pride in his father's successful life is matched by the rage he feels at the society which sought to obstruct that success. He notes that after receiving prestigious graduate degrees from Northwestern University (in hospital administration) and the Wharton School, University of Pennsylvania (M.B.A.), his father "was denied even the barest hint of what the white interior of American 'opportunity' might be." Like Washington and unlike DuBois, Baker Sr.'s goal was not "to gain access to such interiors, because he knew very well that *there was no such access*" [Baker's emphasis]. His purpose in mastering "'standard' educational processes in the West" was, again, like Washington's, and "as any black professional who has made his or her way to productive competence in a racist United States knows. It was to mold himself into what he ultimately became—one of the smartest, most effective, and keenly businesslike black administrators in the United States. . . . My father was an *American* [Baker's emphasis] hospital administrator and businessperson par excellence" (1987:xv).

According to Baker, Booker T. Washington's "most influential set of public utterances is contained in *Up from Slavery* (1901)" (1987:xvi). He analyzes Washington and his major work as exemplars of what he calls "mastery of form," i.e., assuming "the *minstrel mask*" [Baker's italics] (1987:17), which he asserts whites designed for all Blacks in Washington's day to wear "to remind white consciousness that black men and women are *mis-speakers* bereft of humanity (1987:21)." It was composed of distortions of "elements from everyday black use, from the vernacular—the commonplace and commonly sensible in Afro-American life." Baker's reading is that "it was in fact the minstrel mask as mnemonic ritual object that constituted the *form* that any Afro-American who desired to be articulate—to speak at all—had to master during the age of Booker T. Washington" (1987:22).

Baker's interpretation of Washington's strategy in relation to whites reinforces Ellison's devastating portrait of Washington in *Invisible Man*. The only difference is that Baker justifies and historically *explains* why Washington and his contemporaries seemed to "Uncle Tom" whites to death. Baker makes clear that in reality this was an exaggeration which ironically subverted the whites' aims. It mocked them with an overly-broad rendition, by signifying on them, to a Black audience who understood exactly the two-dimensionality of what Washington was doing, precisely where his tongue actually was: in his cheek. Washington chose this "mastery of form," this "minstrel mask" as the best possible strategy for "getting over" on the white power structure during a brutally repressive period for African Americans (post-Reconstruction to World War I).

Baker, in fact, sees Washington's strategies and methods for dealing with whites as productive, as actually "liberating." By "playing *behind* a pious mask" and "beneath his clamorous workings of the minstrel tradition" Washington performed, according to Baker "a liberating manipulation of masks and a revolutionary *renaming*" (1987:25–26). This included

Washington's deliberately playing "the role of a judiciously southern, post- Reconstruction racist" while at the same time supplying "a preposterous character direct from minstrelsy to play the darky role" (1987:28); (i.e., signifying on whites). According to Baker's interpretation, Washington's motivation was not egotistic, as Ellison and Gates maintain, but rather designed to convince Blacks to relinquish reliance on the Reconstruction model in favor of "more realistic goals . . . necessary to meet incumbencies of a new *regional* (the New South) era in which blacks will cast down their buckets where they are and seek advice and counsel from southern whites" (1987:29).

Further, Baker contends, Washington could never have accomplished his goals, given the period in which he lived, unless he had been a master signifier, or in Baker's term, a "master of form," skilled in making those "reassuring *sounds*" to whites "from the black quarters" signifying to them that "there can be no worry that the Negro is 'getting out of hand.' For at all the proper turns, there are comforting sounds and figures of a minstrel theater that we know so well—'Look away! Look away! Look away! Dixie Land'" (1987:30–31). This technique is also characteristic of both Wheatley and Chesnutt, also "masters of form," master signifiers.

To sum up, Baker perceives *Up from Slavery* with its "canny rhetorical appropriation" as providing ". . . a *how-to* manual, setting forth strategies of address (ways of talking black and back) designed for Afro-American empowerment." As for Washington, he possessed a "mind . . . undoubtedly always fixed on some intended gain, on a *mastery* of stories and their telling that leads to Afro-American advancement" (1987:31–32), rather than that of a dupe and accommodationist.

Baker also refreshingly reinterprets Washington's "scandalous" Atlanta Exposition Address of 1895, which is uniformly cited by contemporary critics in order to condemn it. Again, Baker bases his claims on the actual historical situation of Washington's day, of which Baker, unlike other critics, never loses sight. That is, whatever Washington did, he "intended for a common black good" in keeping with the African/African American construct of an individual. As such, "rather than going straight at a possibly somnolent white southern audience in Atlanta—and at lovers of minstrelsy throughout the nation—Washington strikes a 'straight lick with a crooked stick.' He turns minstrel nonsense into what he believes is the only available good sense, or, sense intended for the common good" (1987:32).

Baker sees further evidence of the success of *Up from Slavery* and of Washington's efforts in "the changed status of Tuskegee revealed at the close of the work." Like Washington's great biographer, Louis Harlan, Baker points out that Tuskegee began in a stable and a henhouse and becomes by the end of the narrative, due to Washington's (and his wives') epic exertions "a handsomely endowed and architecturally attractive oasis of skills and morality in the midst of southern 'country districts'" (1987:33). Washington's work in his life and at Tuskegee (which became so much a part and symbol of his life) led "to the growth and *survival* of a nation, because he earnestly projected the flourishing of a southern, black eden at Tuskegee—a New World garden to nurture hands, heads, and hearts of a younger generation of agrarian black folk" (1987:37).

Baker again courageously goes counter to contemporary critical opinion by arguing that Washington's ways and means in accomplishing what he did were neither self-serving nor embarrassing to contemporary African Americans. Rather, Washington "projects a model for the mastery of form that serves as type and prefiguration for the Afro-American spokes-person. . . ." Washington, he contends, the "offspring and descendant of slavery's misappropriations" best represented the mass of southern Blacks of his time who were seeking to lead better lives "from emancipation to the dawn of a new century" (1987:33, 36). I differ with Baker's dating of Washington's influence from 1863–1900 (Washington was not born until 1856, and lived past the century to 1915. Thus his actual influence extended from about 1895, beyond his lifetime into the 1950s, and even to the present). I do agree with Baker so wholeheartedly about Washington's monumental significance, however, that I see his influence extending into Hurston's and Walker's work.

Finally, I see Baker's use of Charles Waddell Chesnutt as objective and contemporary commentator as crucial to my argument in preferring Washington over Douglass, or even DuBois, as the mediator of American success mythology to future generations of African Americans and specifically African American women writers. Chesnutt shows a clear preference for Washington over a "querulous" DuBois filled with "resentment" as Baker describes it, because "Mr. Washington lives in the South, while not more than one or two of the signers of the protest [drafted by DuBois] do, unless Washington [DC] be regarded as part of the South" (1987:37–38). Baker contends that the point is well made against DuBois, that "Washington had a regional (some would say *sectional*, or even *peculiar*) authority in matters black and southern. His avowed goal was to train the Afro-American masses in a way that would ensure their inestimable value to a white world—that would, in a word, enable them to survive" (1987:38).

Like Baker, I view Washington as having realistically assessed the situation for his people and then attempting to do what would best enable them to survive during one of the toughest times in African American history. It is my contention that after analyzing the situation, Washington decided that the best means of survival for his people was to emulate the Franklin model of the American male success mythology. Further, that he would be his people's mediator in this regard; that he would concentrate on its economic aspects in his appropriation of the myth for his people. In this respect, Washington's project has provided inspiration for generations during his time and down to our own.

In this work, however, I focus only on Washington's influence on selected African American women writers: how they responded to his programs, to his appropriation of male American success mythologies for his people at large, and how they depicted its ramifications in the lives of the African American women in their texts.

Baker's remarkable revisionary work on Washington, although published in 1985, still remains the only positive one by any contemporary literary critic of African American culture and history. Nor has it provoked revisionary treatment of Washington's *Up From Slavery*, or his life, in the critical and scholarly literature since then. This is unfortunate, for

Washington's part in African American literary history thus continues to erode into obscurity. For example, Charles Johnson's more recent work, although an historically grounded one like Baker's, perpetuates the common viewpoint for which Ellison's *Invisible Man* has remained the prime source and most powerful influence for interpretation of Washington's character for nearly fifty years.

Johnson views Washington as one of several admirable examples of race leaders who worked from within their own groups, from within an African American centered perspective as opposed to the European American one. However, in *The Sorcerer's Apprentice*, in the signifying title "Popper's Disease," Johnson uses Washington to reflect the tragic naivete of his elderly protagonist. An African American M.D., Dr. Popper is an earnest and sincere type educated in and following the Franklin/Bookerite model in what Johnson calls "a paint-by-numbers curriculum, fed by books for Negro uplift—the modern equivalent, you might say, of Plutarch's *Lives of the Noble Grecians* (which I swore by). Not exactly biography, these odd books from the Negro press, and with titles like *Lives That Lift* [here Johnson contemptuously signifies on Washington's title, *Up From Slavery*]—written by blacks to inspire blacks" (1987:102).

Johnson's position is that Washington seduced innocent believers like Popper by "inspiring" them into believing that the European American male success model applied to them too— that they could live life and be accepted in the United States as individual heroes in the *bildungsroman* mode, just as Benjamin Franklin had, only with dark skins. Johnson sees little difference in the results for Black men who adopt Washington's modifications of the Franklin model, as tailored for Blacks, or the European American white male purveyors of Franklin's model, meant exclusively for white males. Johnson sarcastically describes the latter as feeding gullible Black students "the lofty balderdash of . . . balding, crabbed-face teachers about sober Truth and Science," which leads for African/African Americans aware of their culture and proud of it, to the European American dead-beat anti-hero, "the lonely Leibnizean monad" (1987:102).

Johnson's quarrel with the model Washington offered, therefore, is that Washington colluded with the European

American one. This was a decision which resulted disastrously in the betrayal of the hopes and dreams of aspiring Black Americans such as Dr. Popper. Popper has dutifully followed the Washington and DuBois model symbolized in his having gone to "Tuskegee, then Harvard" for his education. Tuskegee is inextricably linked with Washington's name and philosophy, and Harvard is linked with DuBois's.

Johnson thus maintains that naively following the value systems of both camps inevitably leads to tragic results for Black men. This is symbolized by Popper's marriage (giving himself over or to, integrating with) a beautiful white wife, i.e., white ideals. It is no accident that the same complex of emotions as the young Henry Louis Gates, Jr., now recalls with sardonic amusement that he experienced when *he* was accepted to Oxford is experienced by Popper when Mildred accepts his proposal: "My palms began to sweat, the way they perspired in the days when I first dated Mildred, for as a young man in medical school, the only Negro in my class—the one chosen to prove the Race's worth—I so doubted myself it seemed miraculous that a woman as beautiful as Mildred, with her light voice and brilliant eyes would have me" (Johnson 1987:134).

The form of the betrayal, linking up with a white woman identified with European culture, in the case of Mildred with classical music, signifies on the impassioned protests of James Weldon Johnson's "O Black and Unknown Bards," Margaret Walker's "For My People," and James Baldwin's "Stranger in the Village." In these works, European and African American readers were exposed to a more culturally plural awareness and perspective than their European American education had inscribed in them. This education led them to falsely assume that there is only one great music on this earth, and that, of course, is European music as epitomized by Bach, Beethoven, and Brahms. These African American authors dare to propose as comparable examples their own bards, anonymous African and African American composers of spirituals, of "the sorrow songs" as DuBois labeled them.[3]

Johnson's warning to African American males in "Popper's Disease" is to avoid getting "married" to European American culture. This is what he conceives Washington did by

promising success for Black men if they followed a variation of
the Franklin model while maintaining separatism, and what
DuBois promised Black men through his espousal of elitist
education models and ideal of integration with whites.

Popper's white wife, significantly a music teacher, while
supposedly teaching Beethoven's "Für Elise" to the fifteen-year-
old white paper boy, actually has sex with him. During the act,
both make fun of Popper's "outdated" clothing: "I saw Gary
Freeman [sic], his back glistening with perspiration, pull on a
pair of Danger High Voltage slacks, and dry Mildred with one of
my best Hawaiian shirts. Chuckling, he held it up to his face.
'Does Henry really wear this shit?' My stomach tightened. My
throat squeezed as in a fist. On Mildred's walnut bureau, a
crumpled Trojan lay atop a copy of *The Joy of Classical Piano*"
(Johnson 1987:140). This betrayal transpires while Popper is out
making house calls, philosophizing highmindedly on "the
ontogenesis of personality."

Thus for all of Johnson's ambivalence toward
Washington's accomplishments, he does take him into account,
referring to Washington in a way to show that he did indeed
exist historically and have an impact on naive, upwardly
aspiring Black men. Johnson, at least, is not ahistoric in his
criticism. He does not propose erasure on the basis of
Washington's "accommodationism." He does not practice
anachronistic revisionary ostracism, imposing a contemporary
view on the past, without also taking into account conditions of
historic necessity involved in the actions of individuals. By these
means, not only Washington's contributions, but those of the
likes of Marcus Garvey, Malcolm X, Adam Clayton Powell, and
others have been minimized and flung out into the dustbins of
history.

When judged solely by today's situations and standards,
reinterpretations based on backward lenses are dangerous
because they may erase from the historic consciousness of future
generations individuals of great significance in their time who
worked for and improved the lot of their people *at that time*.
Viewed ahistorically, the positions of these leaders can too easily
be construed as too skewed for our tastes. No leaders, not even
Frederick Douglass and Rev. Martin Luther King, Jr., are free of

human error and limitations. Before dismissing any "race leaders" whose strategies or positions seem "outdated and old-fashioned" today, the nature and extent of the contribution they made *at the time they lived* should be taken into account. What was the situation initially, and *what was it after* these race leaders' efforts?

This is the kind of reinterpretation based on actual historic fact which Baker accorded Washington. However, in my statements about Washington, I take a somewhat different approach to the same issue in an attempt to clear the way for a different interpretation of Washington than that which Ralph Ellison made *de rigeur*. I do this partially to counteract, if possible, that interpretation, which has been so influential ever since, despite Baker's and Harlan's pioneering attempts to place Washington in perspective.

In addition to interpreting Washington's behavior and strategy as the cunning appropriation of the minstrel mask, I also see him as molded by his mother into an African/African American male model of conduct like that of an African chief, as well as that of the typical European American founding father model.

Both King Khama and his son, Tshekedi Khama, are credited with having formulated and begun the concept of "self help" in Bamangwato, now Botswane, at the same time Washington did it at Tuskegee. The African model these chiefs provide, of canny "feudal" leadership combined with apparent accommodationism to their European invaders' demands, should perhaps be examined. It might well provide an alternative reading for Washington's otherwise puzzling, anomalous, and disturbing patterns of political behavior when interpreted solely by European American models of male leadership. Even the minstrel mask is European American in concept, a fact that Baker concedes. However, King Khama the Great almost certainly donned an *African* mask for protection when dealing with the Europeans.

Was not Washington born in slavery? Did he not have nine years on the plantation in Virginia to observe and directly experience African-made masks in dealing with Europeans? Did he have to resort to the white-mediated minstrel mask on the white-dictated stage? Did he not also have time enough to observe and internalize indigenous time-honored African male models of rule and domination (nepotism to friends and vengeance toward enemies), such as the Khamas illustrate? Could not these models account for his hitherto puzzling method of dealing with his fellow "chiefs" (other race leaders like DuBois, Trotter, et al.) as subordinates, and "subjects"? Unaccountable by European American models and training, Washington's "confusing" conduct may in fact be a synthesis like that of his past and contemporary African counterparts, the Khamas, for example, and other lesser known African chiefs, and that of our "founding fathers" like Franklin.

Yet the European American construct of a leadership model has been the only one ever applied to Washington. However, I believe that such a reading is severely limited, as I have previously argued, due to the narrow cultural frames of reference supplied by our European American education that only include European and American perspectives. Washington's frame of reference for his conduct and philosophy in all probability included African models as well as Franklin's European American model. To be comprehensible, his motives and actions should be studied from this double perspective, as Baker does, but without, however, tracing the pattern of signifying masking as an African practice continued and perpetuated in the diaspora.

In Washington's case and that of millions of other African American signifiers, this African masking practice and concept of masculine conduct continued into slavery and into the present. Once this is accounted for, a shift occurs in our reading of Washington's strategic fawning on his white patrons (his public character), while revealing (privately, as a race leader), imperious conduct, demands for feudal loyalty from his followers, and ruthless attempts to immobilize and destroy any perceived rivals for power (most notably DuBois, who apparently had no idea of the extent of Washington's machinations and plots against him)—exactly like King Khama, et al.

In this work I do more than attempt to expand on Harlan's and Baker's efforts to get a fairer reading of Washington. I also maintain that Washington's example and model provided a continual source of inspiration for African American women writers from the late nineteenth to the end of the twentieth century. I hope to reveal the clarifying shift of perspective afforded in taking Washington's economic philosophy into account in readings of selected texts by major African American women writers, beginning with Phillis Wheatley (who illustrates an earlier African/American unmediated but parallel model contemporaneous with and simultaneous to Franklin's, if not influenced by him). I contend that Washington's influence culminated in a radical paradigm shift in relation to African American women in Alice Walker's *The Color Purple*. This despite the fact that Walker's father was an ardent follower of DuBois in his younger days, and that Walker herself trod the freedom road with the Kings. I contend that, nevertheless, Washington's contributions, which were primarily economic, contributed to the economic dimensions of Walker's vision.

Like R. Radhakrishnan, I object to the ahistoricism which consigns Washington and his millions of followers to oblivion. It filters past situations and events through our future hindsights without any awareness of the fact that we are thereby taking unfair advantage of our "knowing better," in part thanks to the very leaders whose actions we are critiquing today! We are where we are today, in some measure, due to their actions.

Every account of the post-Reconstruction period which Washington had to contend against describes it as even more repressive and more organized against African Americans than slavery. And this period lasted from approximately 1872 when the Northern armies were pulled out of the South until the Freedom Marches of the 1950s and thereafter. Comparable analogies of conditions for Blacks during this period would be that of prols in Orwell's *1984*, or what was done to Jews in Hitler's Germany. Orwell's world was imaginary, however, and Jews have suffered genocidal attempts over a longer span of time than perhaps any other group in history. Black Africans, however, have experienced several hundred years of dispersion: first kidnapped, then shipped out via the middle passage to generations of slavery, then (in the United States), subjected to a repressive post-Reconstruction period (which still continues). This was when Booker T. Washington emerged on the scene.

In this context, Washington, having assessed the African diaspora conditions, especially in his native South, resolved to devote his life to the advancement of his people, briefly as a preacher, then as an educator. By the time of his death he had accomplished more hard-nosed, practical, political and especially economic advances for African Americans (including Africans overseas and those attending Tuskegee) than any other race leader before him, including Douglass.

During Washington's lifetime, he triumphed over the now revered DuBois, who had the advantage of living on after Washington for forty-five years. In actuality, DuBois's "talented tenth" solution of this period, given the bleak conditions of American reality, seem to some observers to offer elitist and limited solutions in comparison to Washington's. The essential appeal of DuBois to many of us today is that he advocated a political solution—voting rights—to gain a decent life for his people. This solution today seems to presage that of the Rev. Martin Luther King, Jr., in a seeming logical chain of succession. In actuality, until the early 1960s, all the forces did not yet conspire together to make the advocacy of voting rights a realizable possibility. The times were not yet ripe, although Washington helped in his indirect way to the extent he could.

DuBois always spoke prophetically, not as a practical problem solver. He was and is inspiring, if the goal were integration, which Washington's never was. But DuBois's political position at the time he lived was as unrealistic as a demand by a Black of the time to take a seat on a train wherever desired. The fact is that DuBois did not improve the nitty-gritty, day-to-day, economic living conditions of the majority of his people, as Washington undeniably did. Certainly DuBois did inspire some, mainly middle and upper class intellectuals like DuBois himself, who could perhaps afford to ignore economics— unlike the vast majority of Washington's constituents. These people had to worry over such basics as where their next meal was coming from, how the rent would be paid, and the condition of the roofs over their heads. In contrast, DuBois and his followers attempted to prove to European Americans that they were just as European American in culture as European Americans and were just as capable as European Americans of expressing this form of intellectual cultivation if only they were permitted access to it.

Most African Americans simply did not have the luxury to battle on this ground. Even if they did, perhaps many did not care that much what European American standards, values, and culture dictated, or what they had to do to try to enter the culture club. As Baker puts it in defense of Washington's economic position and accomplishments:

> As an Afro-American, a person of African descent in the United States today, I spend a great deal of time reflecting that in the world's largest geographies the question Where will I find water, wood, or food for today? is (and has been for the entirety of this century) the most pressing and urgently posed inquiry. In "diasporic," "developing," "Third World," "emerging" . . . nations or territories there is no need to pose . . . questions such as Are we happy? Are we content? Are we free? Such questions presuppose at least an adequate level of sustenance and a sufficient faith in human behavioral alternatives to enable a self-directed questioning. (1987:7–8)

Perhaps then, millions of poor, formerly enslaved African Americans were in reality, like Washington, separatist by inclination beneath all his (and their) signifying tactics and subterfuges. After having observed for several hundred years European American culture in its ugliest manifestations, it would have been difficult not to be. This is essentially why Booker T. Washington influenced his people in their daily lives more than DuBois, or even Douglass.

Notes

1. It is unfortunate in this regard that African American writers should have to defend themselves so often for their supposed lack of "consciousness," as Ralph Ellison has complained, according to Gates.

Notice that in the act of doing so, Ellison himself signifies. "Why is it so often true that when critics confront the American as Negro they suddenly drop their advanced critical armament and revert with an air of confident superiority to quite primitive modes of analysis?" (Gates, *Figures in Black*, 1987:125)

2. In this respect, see Patricia Hill Collins, "The Social Construction of Black Feminist Thought," *Signs* 14:4 (Summer 1989): 745–773, esp. 767. She cites "parallels" which in her opinion are "noteworthy" between what she terms "Afrocentric expressions of the ethic of caring" and those espoused by "feminist scholars." Also see Elizabeth Fox-Genovese, *Feminism Without Illusions: A Critique of Individualism* (Chapel Hill: University of North Carolina Press, 1991), for a further discussion of the interesting link between feminist and African American concepts of community.

3. It is interesting that Washington's daughter by his first marriage, Portia Washington, a distinguished music professor at Tuskegee for many years, is considered to have played that piece best which she played in her youth at her successful audition for her musical education in Germany. Portia lost her mother, a race leader in her own right, when very young, and it is said that she played the piece frequently thereafter in an incomparably haunting manner. The piece that was so irresistible to the traditional academicians and on which she staked her successful entrance, was, in her case, the doubly signifying spiritual "Sometimes I Feel Like A Motherless Child."

The selection signified both the historic and contemporary situation of African Americans in the United States and her orphaned condition. This is reminiscent of an incident in the contemporary film *Flash Dance* where the aspiring exotic bar dancer, a working class girl who is a welder by day, gains entrance to a traditional elitist ballet school. In doing so, she expands the judges' paradigm for dancing much as Portia Washington expanded her German judges' paradigm for music when she had the quiet courage to play them a "Negro spiritual."

References

Asante, Molefi Kete. *The Afrocentric Idea*. Philadelphia: Temple University Press, 1987.

Baker, Houston, Jr. *Modernism and the Harlem Renaissance*. Chicago: University of Chicago Press, 1987.

Barkley Brown, Elsa. "Mothers of Mind." *Sage* VI.1 (Summer 1989): 4–11.

Childress, Alice. *Like One of the Family: Conversations From a Domestic's Life*. New York: Beacon Press, 1986. Originally printed 1956.

Duley, Margot. "Review of *Changing our Minds. . . ." Signs* 15.3 (Summer 1989): 648–650.

Ellison, Ralph. "An American Dilemma." *Shadow and Act*. New York: Random House, 1967.

———. *Invisible Man*. New York: Signet, 1952.

Foucault, Michel. *Power/Knowledge*. Trans. Colin Gordon. New York: Pantheon, 1980.

Gates, Henry Louis, Jr. *Figures in Black: Words, Signs, and the "Racial" Self*. New York: Oxford University Press, 1987.

———. *The Signifying Monkey: A Theory of Afro-American Literary Criticism*. New York: Oxford University Press, 1988.

Haile, Barbara J., and Audreye E. Johnson. "Teaching and Learning About Black Women: The Anatomy of a Course." *Sage* VI.1 (Summer 1989): 69–73.

Hurston, Zora Neale. *Their Eyes Were Watching God*. Intro. Sherley Anne Williams. Urbana: University of Illinois Press, 1978.

Johnson, Charles. "Popper's Disease." *The Sorcerer's Apprentice: Tales and Conjurations*. New York: Penguin, 1987.

Jones, Kathleen. "Citizenship in a Woman-Friendly Polity." *Signs* 15:4 (Summer 1990): 781–812.

Radhakrishnan, R. "Culture as Common Ground: Ethnicity and Beyond." *MELUS* 14.2 (Summer 1987): 5–18.

Smith, Dorothy. *The Everyday World as Problematic: A Feminist Sociology*. Boston: Northeastern University Press, 1987.

PHILLIS WHEATLEY, BENJAMIN FRANKLIN, AND EUROPEAN AMERICAN MALE SUCCESS MYTHOLOGY

Benjamin Franklin, born in 1706 in Boston, was "fond of reading" to the point where "all the little money that came into my hands was ever laid out in books" (Lauter 1990:829). By the age of eleven, he had read *Pilgrim's Progress* as well as the rest of John Bunyan's works, Richard Burton's *Historical Collections, Plutarch's Lives*, Daniel Defoe's *Essay Upon Projects*, and Cotton Mather's *Essays to do Good*. He also went on to read *The Spectator*, the work that formed the first key element in the European American success myth. In fact, Franklin credits Joseph Addison and Richard Steele with his learning how to write:

> I thought the Writing excellent, and wish'd if possible to imitate it. With that View, I took some of the Papers, and making short Hints of the Sentiment in each Sentence, laid them by a few Days, and then without looking at the Book, try'd to compleat the Papers again, by expressing each hinted Sentiment at length. . . . I took some of the Tales and turn'd them into Verse: And after a time, when I had pretty well forgotten the Prose, turn'd them back again. I also sometimes jumbled my Collections of Hints into Confusion, and after some Weeks, endeavour'd to reduce them into the best Order, before I began to form the full Sentences, and compleat the Paper. This was to teach me Method in the Arrangement of Thoughts. (Lauter 1990:830–831)[1]

When Phillis Wheatley was only nine, her owners realized that they had a child prodigy on their hands. At that time, wrote her master, John Wheatley, "without any Assistance from School Education, and by only what she was taught in the Family . . . in sixteen Months Time from her Arrival [Wheatley had] attained the English Language, to which she was an utter Stranger before,

to such a Degree, as to read any, the most difficult Parts of the
Sacred Writings, to the great Astonishment of all who heard her"
(Wheatley, Collected Works 1988: 7).[2]

Wheatley also studied religious principles, history,
geography, European contemporary poets (primarily Pope, and
through him, Homer), the Latin satirists Horace and Terence, as
well as Virgil and Ovid. According to an editor of hers, Julian D.
Mason, Jr., "She gained as good an education as (and probably a
better one than) most Boston women had, and her learning and
abilities gradually gained the interest of a wider and wider
segment of the community, especially after she began writing
poetry at about the age of twelve, after having been in Boston
only about four years" (Wheatley, Poems 1989:3–4).

Only forty-eight years earlier, at the same age of twelve,
Benjamin Franklin, also a prodigy, had begun to edit his
brother's paper. However, by the age of seventeen, he had run
away from home forever, an action he later attributed to
difficulty with his brother, to whom he was indentured. Thus
was established a second key element of the European American
(male) success mythology: when frustrated with a situation, run
away from it: change circumstances in order to better yourself
for greater upward mobility.

Wheatley writes in her "Ode to the Earl of Dartmouth"
that she was "from a father seized" and "snatch'd from Afric's
fancy'd happy seat" (Collected Works 1988:74). Although she does
not (and never did publicly) finish the story, we know that after
she was kidnapped, Wheatley was taken to the slave ship Phillis
in which she endured the infamous journey called the middle
passage. She arrived in Boston in 1761, where she was bought
and enslaved by the Wheatleys. This "sea voyage" ruined the
little girl's poor health, for she was described as "sickly" when
found and suffered from asthma for the rest of her brief life.
However, the odds are that she was not in this condition before
her forced departure from Africa. At any rate, Wheatley never
really recovered her health after that voyage.

Wheatley generally praises the Boston climate (which
might also be a hitherto unnoticed instance of signifying, since
only a signifier could possibly do this). In her ode "On

Imagination," however, Wheatley does openly complain about the climate, but presumably only for metaphoric purposes:

> *Winter* austere forbids me to aspire,
> And northern tempests damp the rising fire,
> They chill the tides of *Fancy's* flowing sea,
> Cease then, my song, cease the unequal lay.
>
>   (*Collected Works* 1988:68)[3]

Presumably bemoaning her lack of creativity, Wheatley might also be signifying here through code words on her depression as a result of enslavement in the white European American colonial society. Certainly, for Wheatley's readers, what is remembered most about this work is not her meditation on imagination, but that Wheatley the poet is experiencing severe depression while writing it. Perhaps this is so, because the deep(est), the real feeling, comes at the very end after she has presumably dazzled her readers with a display of poetic virtuosity on a subject so characteristic of the period. However, the last line comes as a sudden disruption of tone and mood. It reads as though Wheatley were suddenly choking, or choked off, stopping herself in disgust.

In contrast, Franklin's landing from *his* sea voyage from Boston to Philadelphia is one of the most celebrated in American history:

> I was dirty from my journey; my pockets were stuffed out with shirts and stockings; I knew no Soul, nor where to look for Lodging. I was fatigu'd with Traveling, Rowing and Want of Rest; I was very hungry, and my whole Stock of Cash consisted of a Dutch Dollar and about a Shilling in Copper. . . . Then I walk'd up the Street, gazing about, till near the Market House I met a Boy with Bread. I had made many a Meal on Bread, and inquiring where he got it, I went immediately to the Baker's he directed me to in second Street; . . . I was surpriz'd at the Quantity, but took it, and having no room in my Pockets, walk'd off, with a Roll under each Arm, and eating the other. . . . Then I turn'd and went down Chestnut Street and part of Walnut Street, eating my Roll all the Way, and coming round, found myself again at Market Street Wharff, near the Boat I came in, to which I went for a Draught of the River

Water, and being fill'd with one of my Rolls, gave the other
two to a Woman and her Child that came down the River in
the Boat with us and were waiting to go farther. (Lauter
1990:838)

Wheatley's arrival on these shores and her experiences
afterward provide a remarkable counterpoint to Franklin's. Of
course it comes as no surprise to her readers that Wheatley
would not refer to her experiences while getting here (the middle
passage), nor refer to her landing on the Boston dock, or her
condition at the time, except to transpose them into spiritually
providential manipulations of her life by a benevolent God.
However, William Robinson, one of Wheatley's premier scholars,
tells us the bare facts. One day in February 1761, Susannah
Wheatley decided that she needed a little slave for light
household duties and went down to the docks. The slave ship
Phillis had just docked, and there she found a little African girl
approximately eight years old. Foreshadowing Wheatley's
ultimate fate, the child stood huddled naked in the cold except
for a rag of a carpet. Naming the child after the ship on which
she arrived, Mrs. Wheatley carried the future celebrated author
home to her new life.

Another important part of the Franklin success myth is the
use of time for maximum efficiency. Franklin codified and
popularized the American treatment of spare time in its
association with success, with "getting ahead." Franklin informs
us how he did it: "My Time for these Exercises and for Reading,
was at Night, after Work or before Work began in the Morning;
or on Sundays, when I contrived to be in the Printinghouse
alone" (Lauter 1990:831). And as he repeated in *Poor Richard's
Almanack* for generations of Americans to dutifully memorize:
"Early to bed and early to rise/Makes a man healthy, wealthy,
and wise." Unfortunately, this assumption was not possible for
the slave child Phillis Wheatley, since her time on earth was not
hers (or any slave's) to allocate.

Franklin's formidable oratorical and debating skills began
with "two little sketches of the arts of rhetoric and logic" in
James Greenwood's *Grammar* (1711) in which he studied a
specimen of a dispute in the Socratic method; and soon after
"procured Xenophon's *Memorable Things of Socrates*." In

philosophy, he read Shaftesbury's *Characteristics* and Anthony Collins' *Discourses*. In relation to the art of persuasion, he advises his readers never to "give the Air of Positiveness to an Opinion; but rather say, I conceive or I apprehend a Thing to be so or so, It appears to me, or I should think it so or so for such and such Reasons, or I imagine it to be so, or it is so if I am not mistaken." It is Franklin's firm conviction that "a Positive, assuming Manner that seldom fails to disgust, tends to create Opposition, and to defeat every one of those Purposes for which Speech was given to us, to wit, giving or receiving Information, or Pleasure" (Lauter 1990:832).

It is not that Franklin was not "positive" or "assuming." He was both. What he is advocating is the *appearance* of modesty and humility. Presenting a good front is the pragmatic point of view at the root of everything, even values:

> I grew convinc'd that *Truth, Sincerity* and *Integrity* in Dealings between Man and Man, were of the utmost Importance to the Felicity of Life, and I form'd written Resolutions . . . to practice them ever while I lived. Revelation had indeed no weight with me as such; but I entertain'd an Opinion, that tho' certain Actions might not be bad *because* they were forbidden by it, or good *because* it commanded them; yet probably those Actions might be forbidden *because* they were bad for us, or commanded *because* they were beneficial to us, in their own Natures, all the Circumstances of things considered. (Lauter 1990:859) [Franklin's emphasis]

"Appearance" also plays a major part in Franklin's famous list of virtues that includes temperance, silence, order, resolution, frugality, industry, sincerity, justice, moderation, cleanliness, tranquility, chastity, and humility (Lauter 1990:875–876). In regard to Franklin's pursuit of humility, he admitted that he could not "boast of much Success in acquiring the *Reality* of this Virtue; but I had a good deal with regard to the *Appearance* of it" (Lauter 1990:881), he concludes with apparent satisfaction. [Franklin's emphasis]. He could very probably have said the same of some of the other virtues, such as sincerity, moderation, and chastity.

To Franklin, apparently, the chief element in life was *appearance*, and this element has become part and parcel of the American success formula in advertising, in politics, and in so much of American life:

> In order to secure my Credit and Character as a Tradesman, I took care not only to be in *Reality* Industrious and frugal, but to avoid all *Appearances* of the Contrary. I drest plainly; I was seen at no Places of idle Diversion [the opposite of Japanese business success]; I never went out a-fishing or shooting; a Book, indeed, sometimes debauch'd me from my Work; but that was seldom, snug, and gave no Scandal: and to show that I was not above my Business, I sometimes brought home the Paper I purchas'd at the Stores, thro' the Streets on a Wheelbarrow. Thus being esteem'd an industrious thriving young Man, and paying duly for what I bought, the Merchants who imported Stationary solicited my Custom, others propos'd supplying me with Books, and I went on swimmingly. (Lauter 1990:864) [Franklin's emphasis].

In this regard there is some similarity between Franklin and Wheatley. With Wheatley and other enslaved Africans, their very survival depended on mastering appearances, of appearing humble. The assumption of acquiescent masks to appease their captors was a matter of life and death. In this connection, Houston Baker, Jr., astutely observes that "The surface sentiments of black literary texts can obscure their more substantive meanings for the unwary observer" (1984:88).[4]

Franklin retired in 1748 at the age of forty-two to go into public life. Again, he here provides an archetypal element for American male success mythology: Make it big and retire by forty. Before retiring, however, Franklin became successful as a printer through "frugality," an element in the American success myth that no longer survives. It may seem a quaint and alien element of American mythology today to most readers, but so recent has been its demise that it is still vaguely familiar to our parents and grandparents.

In addition to the now defunct concept of "frugality," the American success myth was formed on a foundation that included two other lost elements: "industry" and "diligence." In fact, contemporary Americans are industrious and diligent primarily in order to pursue leisure time activities. We prefer what Franklin advises us to avoid and avoid what he advises us to do. As for Franklin's pompous boasts about dining with kings, we today can dine at home while watching royalty on television:

> Reading was the only Amusement I allow'd myself. I spent no time in Taverns, Games, or Frolicks of any kind. And my Industry in my Business continu'd as indefatigable as it was necessary.... I had a young family coming on to be educated.... My Circumstances however grew daily easier: my original Habits of Frugality continuing. And my Father having among his Instructions to me when a Boy, frequently repeated a Proverb of Solomon, "*Seest thou a Man diligent in his Calling, he shall stand before Kings, he shall not stand before mean Men.*" I from thence considered Industry as a Means of obtaining Wealth and Distinction, which encourag'd me, tho' I did not think that I should ever literally stand before Kings, which however has since happened——for I have stood before five, and even had the honor of sitting down with one, the King of Denmark, to Dinner. (Lauter 1990:873) [Franklin's emphasis]

During this period in Franklin's life, from approximately 1761 to 1775, which encompassed Wheatley's childhood and youth, the Wheatleys went to great pains on behalf of their sickly little slave. They educated her beyond their own education. They had her tutored first at home by their own daughter Anne and then by clergymen in religion and Latin. Wheatley quickly came "to be treated almost as a member of the family and . . . assigned only very light housekeeping tasks, with permission and encouragement to ignore even these duties when she felt poetically inclined." Even further than that, she was "allowed the unusual privilege of having both heat and light in her own room in the Wheatley home at night" so that she might write (Wheatley, *Poems* 1989:5).

The more she wrote the more strenuous were the Wheatleys' efforts, both financial and physical, on her behalf. Their son took her to England in 1773. There he worked successfully on her behalf to find her a publisher for a collection of her poems. The Countess of Huntingdon even agreed to become Wheatley's patron. Wheatley also met the lord mayor of London (who gifted her with a copy of Pope) and the Earl of Dartmouth. But just as Wheatley was about to climax her visit with a presentation at court, bad news from home forced her to return to Boston.

Mrs. Wheatley had become terminally ill, a tragedy for Phillis Wheatley. It proved a death blow also to Phillis Wheatley's dream of success in colonial America. The young African's fortunes would change shockingly as a result of Susannah Wheatley's death, followed shortly by her husband's, and then by her son's. Without their financial support and their excellent social contacts, Wheatley's plans all came to grief.

Earlier, in 1773, on the occasion of the publication of Wheatley's *Poems on Various Subjects, Religious and Moral* in London, John Wheatley had gone before eighteen of Boston's weightiest white fathers. These pillars of colonial society included such luminaries as John Hancock, future signer of the Declaration of Independence, the Rev. Samuel Mather, a powerful minister, and Thomas Hutchinson and Andrew Oliver, governor and lieutenant governor, respectively, of Massachusetts. In John Wheatley's words, these were "some of the best Judges" in the colony. These founding fathers spent their precious time in carefully examining the nineteen-year-old African slave girl as to whether or not they "thought [her] qualified to write . . ." (Wheatley, *Collected Works* 1988:8) for the Massachusetts colony.

One can imagine what Phillis Wheatley secretly thought about being cross-examined by this formidable group of white male authority figures, all of whom were apparently so insensitive as to be entirely unaware of the indignity and humiliation to which they were subjecting her. At any rate, Wheatley must have possessed persuasive powers and oratorical skills on a par with Franklin's to have impressed these dignitaries as she did. And it must be borne in mind that she was neither reading, nor writing, nor speaking to her audience in her native language. At any rate, these wise racists finally concluded after an intense oral exam that this "young Negro Girl, who was but a few Years since, brought an uncultivated Barbarian from Africa, and has ever since been, and now is, under the

Disadvantage of serving as a Slave in a Family in this Town" was nevertheless truly capable of authoring the poems purported to be hers (Wheatley, *Collected Works* 1988:8).

During this time, immediately prior to the Revolutionary War, Franklin was serving as ambassador to the French court of Louis XV. Aware of the glamorous and exotic myths about Americans current in Europe and among the French aristocracy, Franklin set himself to the task of making them appear real in his own person. Accordingly, in a court where outrageously extravagant and complicated wearing apparel was the rule for both men and women, Franklin covered his long gray hair with a coonskin cap whose tail hung down the back of his neck and donned a simple black suit like a Quaker's. Although in his seventies by this time, Franklin's astuteness at public relations and image-making created a sensation, especially with women. In this regard, it is recorded that Franklin had more than twenty children out of wedlock, many of whom he took home to his wife, Deborah Read Franklin, to raise. It is not recorded what Deborah thought of her diminished conjugal duties (due to Franklin's long absences from home) or the additional homemaking and child rearing obligations necessitated by his bastards. Still, one wonders.

Wheatley in this period would marry and become the mother of three children. Thus she conformed to *the* basic success myth for women universal in all cultures. Even so, she would neither live to retire, nor be presented at court, even though once she very nearly was. Nor would she go on to be immortalized in American history as great public servant, benefactor to humanity, and ingenious inventor as Franklin did in the forty-two years remaining in his life after his retirement.

Apparently Wheatley was tragically unaware of the extent to which her owners were a factor in all of her apparent acclaim. From her point of view, it would logically appear that the high opinion of her clerical tutors and mentors; her gratifying literary and social success in London; her publication of her poems; her passing through many trials relating to her initiation and acceptance into the white world had surely proved to her public's satisfaction that she truly was a poet and not a parrot.

On this score, Gates maintains that Black artists of this period seem to have been considered by Europeans as "birds" of various kinds: "Hume called the Jamaican poet of Latin verse, Francis Williams, 'a parrot who merely speaks a few words plainly': and Phillis Wheatley has for far too long suffered from the spurious attacks of black and white critics alike for being the original *rara avis* ["odd" bird] of a school of so-called mockingbird poets, whose use and imitation of received European and American literary conventions has been regarded, simply put, as a corruption itself of a 'purer' black expression" (Gates, *Figures in Black* 1987:43).[5]

Wheatley's optimistic attitude, much like Alice Walker's long afterward, may have led her to believe that the positive responses to her ambitions had, and would in the future, far outweigh and offset negatives like the dismissive responses she received on account of her race and gender.[6] Here is an example written by a reviewer in 1773: "The poems written by this young negro bear no endemial marks of solar fire or spirit. They are merely imitative: and indeed, most of those people [Africans] have a turn for imitation, though they have little or none for invention" (Wheatley, *Collected Works* 1988:267). Then there was Jefferson's infamous put down, that "the compositions published under her name are below the dignity of criticism" (Smith 1989:196).

Wheatley attempted to continue her writing career until six years before her death. At that time she apparently stopped, perhaps because as Mukhtar Ali Isani puts it, in "struggling for a living . . . she appears to have had little leisure to phrase more protests on behalf of her race" (Isani, "Wheatley in London" 1979:147). For three or four years after Susannah Wheatley's death, however, Wheatley did continue to publish poetry and make proposals for subscribers for future publications. These activities, I believe, are testimony to her sanguine, perhaps prophetic belief in herself (again like Walker), and that her captors and their society would continue to support her efforts and ambitions.

Given that Wheatley was such "a remarkable individual by any standard . . . accorded considerable status in the society of Boston and London from the time . . . when she was sixteen"

(Isani, "Gambia" 1979:64–72, 70), would not certain close friends of hers be encouraged to make future plans based on her past and current successes? Phillis Wheatley's husband, John Peters, certainly was. Both he and his wife, I suspect, may have made the natural mistake of assuming that Wheatley's merits had played some part in her earlier successes; that her mistress's major assistance to her had been in getting her a hearing. Once that had been accomplished, Wheatley would then be accepted and read in the future on her own merits.

Wheatley, unfortunately, was not the only one to rely on success mythology—that since she had succeeded once on her own merits, her career would then unfold grandly before her. How could Wheatley have guessed that society had no use for her poetry unless it was mediated for her by her socially prominent mistress, and then only in terms of her as a slave phenomenon and not as a free Black woman writing as a citizen of English colonial American society?

Unfortunately for Mr. and Mrs. Peters' hopes and dreams, the American success mythology clearly did not include Africans, and certainly not African women, as intellectual and creative contributors to its discourse. Before her death, Mrs. Wheatley freed Phillis Wheatley as she had promised, to Phillis's joy. However, Wheatley's continued success was tied up in Mrs. Wheatley's social and political contacts. Once gone, none of Wheatley's (now Mrs. John Peters) plans ever came to fruition. She sent out proposals for subscribers to another collected work of poetry, but never published a second collection, and scarcely anything else. Her husband's business failed, as well. The couple moved to the country with their growing family. When that didn't work, Peters went looking for job opportunities while Wheatley returned to Boston where she found room and work as a maid in a hotel.

On a bitter winter day in 1784 at the age of about thirty, Wheatley's body was found in a squalid, filthy attic room, either frozen to death, dead from malnutrition, or both. Two of her children had already died of malnutrition. A dead infant was at her breast.

Only six years later, Benjamin Franklin died of old age, honored, acclaimed, even revered. His fame is undiminished, one of our founding fathers featured lovingly in a Broadway musical. In his will, he left his faithful Black man-servant his velvet suit.

Black feminist scholar Mary Helen Washington concurs with John Shields's complaint that critics have in the past viewed Phillis Wheatley unjustly and incorrectly. However, she narrows her complaint down to "male" critics alone. Male critics, she contends, "go to great lengths to explain the political naivete or racial ambivalence of male writers while they harshly criticize women writers for the same kinds of shortcomings." She gives as an example Richard Wright's essay, "Literature of the Negro of the United States," in which Wright easily forgives George Moses Horton, another early Black poet, for being "'a split man,' trapped in a culture of which he was not really a part." Wright, she contends, does not play by the same rules when he dismisses Wheatley as "'so fully at one with white Colonial culture that she developed 'innocently,' free to give utterance to what she felt without the humiliating pressure of the color line.'" Washington defends Wheatley on the grounds that "banished to the 'nigger pews' in the Christian churches of Colonial Boston, deprived of the companionship of other blacks, totally under the control of whites," and thus "torn by contrary instincts," Wheatley could never have become "at one with her culture" (Washington 1988:xix). Indeed, she wasn't. She was signifying on it, at least some of the time.

Why is it that Wheatley's obvious intellectual and literary prowess has been ignored? As Julian Mason complains as late as 1989: "Seldom is any single poem by Wheatley subjected to extensive critical analysis" (Wheatley, *Poems* 1989:224). Clearly the Wheatleys themselves measured her against their own accomplishments and those of their society's. Despite a heavily inscribed racial belief in white superiority, they nevertheless took actions which nurtured and publicized their slave's superior intellect and talents. Such righteous conduct may have emanated from a belief in the Enlightenment and Christian rhetoric shared by many political and spiritual leaders of colonial Boston society such as those who examined their slave girl. From their point of view, Phillis Wheatley personified and symbolized the possibility of individual worth. Indeed, this approach to Black slaves was later emulated by their abolitionist descendants.

Despite her contemporaries' generally positive assessments, however, later critical evaluations have uniformly condemned with faint praise Wheatley's rhyming couplets and her spirituality as mundane and predictable in form and subject matter. Moses Coit Tyler, according to Cynthia Smith, claimed that "the significance of her career belongs rather to the domain of anthropology, or of hagiology, than to that of poetry— whether American or African" and that the only reason Wheatley attracted some attention in her lifetime was "not . . . because the verses were good, but because they were "written by one from whom even bad verses were too good to be expected" (1989:585).[7] Benjamin Brawley defined her work as "abstract, polite, restrained" (1939:26). J. Saunders Redding thought it "bloodless, unracial" (1937:9–11). M.A. Richmond accused her of writing as if she had had "a near surgical, lobotomy-like excision of a human personality with warmth and blood and the self-assertiveness that is grounded in an awareness of one's self and relationship of this self to contemporary society" (Smith 1989:65). Calvin Hernton agrees with Redding that Wheatley "did not write much out of a black consciousness of slavery," but disagrees with Richmond about Wheatley's coldness, deeming her works "imbued with a sensitivity that is specifically female" (1987:52).

In addition to the anonymous English critic of 1773 quoted earlier, there were other critics over the years, over the centuries, in fact, who claimed that Wheatley was guilty of simple, mindless mimicry of European canonical icons and religion. According to Cynthia Smith, James Parton saw Wheatley's verses as marred by "the fatal facility of imitation." William Long was specific about Wheatley's source for imitation. He claimed that her verses were merely "colorless imitations of Pope." Vernon Loggins, who thought her "impersonal and artificial," concurred with Long, although he did point out that most of Wheatley's contemporaries were writing like Pope (Smith 1989:591). However, within the past five years, the work of Shields, Robinson, Mason, and Sondra O'Neale in rebutting these charges and the generally sympathetic attitudes of eminent

critics Baker and Gates have thawed the critical climate around
Wheatley and her work. In May 1990, I presented an openly
revisionary paper (on which part of this chapter is based) to a
largely receptive audience at Douglass College, Rutgers
University.[8] And in June of that year, June Jordan, latest in the
line of Wheatley's daughters, published a praise song to her:
"The Difficult Miracle of Black Poetry in America or Something
Like a Sonnet for Phillis Wheatley," in which she wrote from the
same revisionary perspective: "We will write, published or not,
however we may, like Phillis Wheatley, of the terror and the
hungering and the quandaries of our African lives on this North
American soil" (1990:22).

Why then, given that they were her masters, construe
Phillis Wheatley's relationship to the Wheatleys (whose circle
consisted of powerful and influential English on both sides of the
Atlantic) from a European American perspective and according
to European American definitions? According to Gates's insights
on signifying, instead of considering her naive and submissive,
we might consider Wheatley and her discourse as signifying.
Perhaps her verse might be sophisticated, reflecting an alert
attention on the part of the author to whatever opportunities
presented themselves.

Given the constraints of her repressive situation, perhaps
Wheatley was not passive when the Wheatleys gave her limited
access to intellectual and spiritual nourishment and the time and
space requisite for her needs. As a poet, perhaps Wheatley was
capable of indirect attempts to forward her political and religious
agenda. Perhaps she was capable of using conscious African
literary artifice, as well as a European one. Given the undisputed
fact of her brilliant intellect, it might be fruitful to examine some
of Wheatley's most problematic poems on the possibility that she
might have been capable of using that intellect to blend
European with African modes of discourse.

The fact is that Wheatley was African. She wrote
poignantly "of Gambia on my soul" where she lived for the first
seven or eight years of her scant thirty years on this earth until:

> I, young in life, by seeming cruel fate
> Was snatch d from *Afric's* fancy'd happy seat:

What pangs excruciating must molest,
What sorrows labour in my parent's breast?
Steel'd was that soul and by no misery mov'd
That from a father seiz'd his babe belov'd:
Such, such my case.
And can I then but pray
Others may never feel tyrannic sway?
(*Collected Works* 1988:74)

Who can read these lines addressed "To the Right Honourable William, Earl of Dartmouth, His Majesty's Principal Secretary of State for North America, etc." and fail to be moved? But why does Wheatley confide such "excruciating" personal experiences to this distant aristocratic public figure? Why does she impose on him her bitterness, her enduring grief over the loss of her father, doubled by the knowledge of his suffering the loss of his beloved daughter? Who was this Lord Dartmouth to whom she uncharacteristically lays herself open, to whom she is writing a praise poem? Seemingly, the poem begins that way; however, African signifiers mock as they mimic.

Hail, happy day, when smiling like the morn,
Fair Freedom rose New England to adorn. . . .
(*Collected Works* 1988:74)

Historian Vincent Bakpetu Thompson, who believes that "Wheatley ironically enough dedicated some of her poems to this man" (although perhaps not in the sense he means), reveals the reason for Wheatley's supposedly joyous and ardently admiring, but mistaken apostrophe: "Lord Dartmouth had, on the eve of the American revolutionary war, quite bluntly stated (and in doing so spoke for many of the opponents of abolition), 'We cannot allow the colonies to check or to discourage in any degree a traffic so beneficial to the nation'" (1987:206–207).

Although Wheatley begins as if writing a praise song, she then protests African slavery with the most vivid, forceful technique available to her as a European poet—satiric heroic couplets. She also uses the most powerful rhetorical technique available to her as an African—signifying. She employs (monkey-like) innuendo more closely aimed in the (lion-like) recipient's direction than the Earl of Dartmouth might have cared to be conscious of. That is, if ever he were able to penetrate to her sarcasm, or even believe she could use it:

> Should you, my lord, while you peruse my song,
> Wonder from whence my love of Freedom sprung,
> Whence flow these wishes for the common good,
> By feeling hearts alone best understood. . . .
> *(Collected Works* 1988:74)

This is a display of African doubling. Wheatley seemingly speaks abstractly and calmly when she maintains that only "feeling hearts" could "best" understand why she should love freedom so much. Actually she is subtly insinuating with rapier-like wordplay that Dartmouth is the one she is indicting as "unfeeling"; as having a "steel'd soul." By subordinating the English colonial argument to the African perspective, Wheatley co-opts the supposed thrust of her poem by making her case in actuality for Africans when she was supposedly speaking from a colonial perspective only. What oppressed English colonials want in relation to the English (her supposed subject), turns into what oppressed African slaves want in relation to English colonials and English—to be freed.

The traumas of her childhood, Wheatley reveals in the biographical lines previously quoted, politicized her on behalf of enslaved Africans anywhere. She does not have to go into further detail for her readers to realize what she alludes to—the infamous middle passage. As a result of that trip, Wheatley's health, if not her spirit, was permanently broken.

That Wheatley interrupts her text to call Dartmouth's (and the reader's) attention to herself as an African before appealing for slavery's repeal (a not uncommon practice for her), lays to rest the charge frequently made that she was disloyal to her compatriots. As Isani puts it, "One cannot help but note her fairly frequent references to herself as an 'Ethiop' or 'African,' especially in her earlier poetry. While a certain ritual humility lies behind most, she was also making artful use of her extraordinary condition as poet and slave to attract attention to her work" ("Gambia" 1979:64).

In another praise song, this time to the young African painter, Scipio Moorhead, Wheatley seeks to advance his career as an African by specifically calling attention to his nationality in her title "To S.M., a young *African* Painter, on seeing his Works." In addition, Wheatley kept up a lifelong friendship and correspondence with her African shipmate, Obour Tanner, whom she called her "sister" as well as her "dear friend." In her last letter to Tanner, written in 1779, her constancy to her closest confidante shines through at a time when Wheatley was faced with overwhelming problems emanating from poverty and starvation: "Pray write me soon," she pleads, "For I long to hear from you—you may depend on constant replies—I wish you much happiness . . ." (*Collected Works* 1988:187).

Wheatley's emphasis on the African is her favorite technique for "destabilizing" European discourse. Her biographical interruptions add a complexity of African "oral-traditional" and "written-modern" African rhetorical strategy, according to Josephat B. Kubayanda. When Wheatley refers to her mother's matutinal libations to the sun, for example, she is intercalating African "principles of ancestrality" and African animism with European neo-classical conventions of pantheistic Greek mythology as practiced by Pope. Given Wheatley's original orientation and background, is it any wonder that she took to this format and its characteristic imagery?

Characteristic of African cultural forms, according to Kubayanda, are praise songs, especially of heroes and other significant events, "mortuary or lament rites," and jokes and riddles (1984:5–8). Wheatley wrote several riddles, but the bulk of her work are odes (praise poems/songs) and religious memorial tributes. In Africa, it is a custom for the griot, or community poet, to perform these tasks, as it was for the bard in Greece or the Native American shaman. It is also customary in Africa and in African American and African diaspora funerals to give the honor of making funeral orations to eloquent or important public personages, or as a mark of respect and honor to close friends and relatives. Wheatley's preference for funerary poems, since she wrote so many, might very well be explained, not only by the fact that it was a popular European convention of the time, but also by its cultural connections to customs and rites she had observed in her original community.

Wheatley's depth of sincerity and religious conviction must, for the mourners, have shone through the formulaic convention of the elegy, as it does today, in, for example, her first published poem, a "fiery" elegy to George Whitefield (1714–1770), a "fiery" and "enormously popular" English evangelist and Methodist preacher. Perhaps Wheatley is signifying here on the style and format he employed to galvanize the huge throngs who flocked to hear him on his "preaching tours" or "prayer visits," as in this mock "preacherly" passage:

> Take him, ye wretched, for your only good,
> Take him ye starving sinners, for your food;
> Ye thirsty, come to this live-giving stream,
> Ye preachers, take him for your joyful theme;
> Take him my dear *Americans*, he said,
> Be your complaints on his kind bosom laid:
> Take him, ye *Africans*, he longs for you,
> *Impartial Saviour* is his title due:
> Wash'd in the fountain of redeeming blood,
> You shall be sons, and kings, and priests to God.
>   (*Collected Works* 1988:23)

Wheatley also seemed to delight in "the question-and-answer structure," again according to Kubayanda, "a recurring norm in African and African-related music and in the black sermon" (1984:5), as it was in European poetry of the eighteenth century. Wheatley used this feature in almost all of her poems, sometimes several times in one poem, as in her lines to Scipio Moorhead where she pays tribute to a fellow artist's creativity. In a series of cascading adverbial queries, Wheatley deploys onomatopoeia like an emotional waterfall, both to convey the "rushing" experience of the "prospects" to which the artist had given "new creation," and as rhetorical question and answer:

> When first thy pencil did those beauties give,
> And breathing figures learnt from thee to live,
> How did those prospects give my soul delight,
> A new creation rushing on my sight?

Still, wond'rous youth! each noble path pursue. . . .
(*Collected Works* 1988:114)

In addition to the charge of disloyalty to her people, European American critics who valorize transcendent individualism (a concept alien to the fundamental African world view), have accused Wheatley of being imitative, especially of Alexander Pope. From the European perspective, where independence and originality are so valorized, mimicry is acceptable because its purpose is satirical. However, "imitation" is despised. As Cynthia Smith puts it: "When Wheatley is accused of being imitative, the charge is always pejorative" (1989:588). Yet every discussion of African/African American rhetorical and aesthetic literary techniques has reiterated what Kefi Owusu stresses, namely that "oral and written forms are not, and have never really been, discontinuous—certainly not to the African" (1989:748). Once accepting this cultural difference as given, we can then read Keith D. Miller's excellent defense of the Rev. Martin Luther King, Jr., as equally applicable to the charges leveled against Wheatley: "Why do folk preachers borrow?" he asks rhetorically, going on to cite Walter Ong to the effect that "'the language of oral culture is highly repetitive for two reasons. First, reiteration ensures that knowledge, which cannot be recorded, will be remembered by both speakers and audiences.'" Second, culture bearers in an oral tradition are not proprietary about rights, written or oral. Only with the arrival of print media did "'a sense of the private ownership of words'" emerge. Print "'made the word into a commodity'" (Miller 1987:77).

Furthermore, according to Gates, mimicry and other rhetorical and aesthetic techniques are in actuality part of signifying, which Africans have developed over many centuries. Gates argues persuasively that African/African American diaspora artists have carried signifying with them wherever they have gone. Signifying is a self-conscious skill, very difficult and complex, the mastery of which might be likened to playing classical jazz (also signifying, but in music). The object of the African/African American in mimicry (mimesis) is not merely to imitate, but to mock with subtle exaggeration of tone and hyperbole the language of the oblivious and complacent opponent. In doing so, the signifying mimic aims to "get over" on the unaware and unwary opponent while amusing the audience at the opponent's expense. Accordingly, critics who confine themselves to discussions of Wheatley solely as a foremother and thereby play down her poetry, are, according to Gates, buying into European American prescriptions, their "master's (pre)script"(ion), to pun off Toni Morrison's term for it.

Gates, in addition to Shields and others, has eloquently debated the representation of African/African American artists as mere mimics: "The representation of black structures" has been "provided by the white masters," he complains. He feels that granting any premise that any African/African American artist such as Wheatley is simple-minded, gullible, or an Aunt Tom fool is to play "the opponent's game on the opponent's court" (Gates, "Authority" 1987: 36); i.e., to abide by European American judges' rules, calls, terminology, and definitions. Such elitist, sexist, and racist assumptions should long since have been suspect as too prejudicial to their own side to merit attention, Gates feels.

It is difficult for European Americans to comprehend a tradition where apparent imitation is a step in a ritual, part of a repertoire of rhetorical and aesthetic techniques which Gates defines as signifying. Houston Baker, Jr., has also written at considerable length on the subject in *Blues and the Modern Tradition*, linking the blues with African American vernacular practices. According to Baker and Gates, repetition/imitation is in African/African American rhetorical and aesthetic practice a ritualized form of respect, a bow in the direction of one's opponent or predecessor or authority figure *prior* to commencing with one's own voice, instrument, or brush. It is a tribute to another way of seeing a subject *before* proceeding to make one's own point. In my analysis of Wheatley's problematic poetry later on, this technique, so intrinsic a part of signifying, will be revealed in Wheatley's practice.

But first, although Wheatley did read and admire Pope, how is it that critics have not for the most part given her the credit that they have to European American poets of the period? Namely, that she is also emulating his famed satirical point of view, as well as his technique of couplets? In any case, before she ever studied the Latin and English satirists, Wheatley spent the first seven or eight years of her life imbibing African religious and social rituals and customs, African ways of expressing satire and irony. Among them was signifying with all its rich and complex attributes. Yet Wheatley's discourse has never been examined for evidence of any satiric intent, only for surface imitative expressions of Pope's style, never for his motives.

This was the case until John Shields made a painstaking study of Wheatley's poetry to find evidence to prove the universal allegation of imitativeness against her, but without success. Instead, he found that Wheatley was "guilty" only of writing in a mode which most other poets of the time were using: heroic satiric couplets (Wheatley, *Collected Works* 1988:xxix, 230). If Wheatley were indeed imitative, so then was every other poet of the period, including Pope. Even those European American critics who castigated Wheatley for imitating Pope would not go so far as to make the claim that Pope pioneered the use of satiric couplets.

Cynthia Smith somehow manages to see through to the racism beneath these claims, keep her temper, and explain the situation clearly. She points out that in the eighteenth century "imitation was not only the literary fashion of the day but the very means to excellence." Every satirical poet did imitations of Greek and Latin writers. Pope and Swift, for example, used their takeoffs as "a forum for wide-ranging and often acerbic comments on manners, morals, politics, and the literature and writers of their own time." Since their readers were familiar with the originals, their work gained "in allusive meaning or effect when read in conjunction with" them (Smith 1989:588).

Unlike Pope's, however, Wheatley's satiric discourse reveals the doubleness characteristic of other "minor" writers, to use Deleuze and Guattari's term. ("Minor writers" are simultaneously knowledgeable products of the culture they live in and yet marginal to it.[9]) Living at a tragic time for Africans, Wheatley variously utilized the linguistic and stylistic strategies available to an African woman enslaved and hence doubly silenced. Wheatley observed that colonial Boston had two discourses, one religious and the other political. Powerful, charismatic men of the cloth with their Christian rhetoric and their famous political, patriotic, and military parishioners who espoused the rhetoric of the Enlightenment were the equivalents of today's "stars" and their vehicles of expression. The three groups served the same purpose for the populace that superbowls, soap operas, sitcoms, rap and rock stars on MTV, movies, news media, etc., provide today.

In this context, as an enslaved African in Boston who wished to express her anguish and her anger and other more socially acceptable emotions, Wheatley had to carry on a "subtle war" in Sondra O'Neale's terms (1986:147). For Wheatley, a white Christian was not the same as a Black African Christian slave. Both religious and political positions had different agendas, for the most part. Yet to get any kind of hearing or credibility, Wheatley had to appear to use the acceptable discourses of her society.[10] Writing from within these two discourses (Christian and Enlightenment), Wheatley nevertheless attempted to forward her own agenda, on appropriate occasions. To this end, when she could, she wrote poems to expose and protest the injustice, cruelty, oppression, and religious hypocrisy of the master race in enslaving Africans.

When Wheatley wished to protest slavery, she addressed the oppressor group in their own religious discourse, but cut against the grain, using signifying irony. This technique can not only be as searing and brutal as those she signified on were in enslaving other human beings, but doubles in force by virtue of its mimicry of those slave takers and masters. Wheatley thereby underscores the fact that her master race and its discourse was not politically enlightened, socially civilized, or Christian, as the masters claimed. Thus, two centuries before the Combahee River Collective maintained that the personal was political, "the African muse" (as Wheatley proudly styled herself) made the personal religious and the personal political (202). However, to an African American, Asian American, Native American, and others, "personal" has a different meaning than to a European. "Personal" is simultaneously oneself and one's *group* self—the community. Wheatley never wrote without this conjunction, "these wishes for the common good," as she put it.

The discourse of European American writers is explored by critics for every nuance of meaning. African American writers, however, have never been suspected of using, let alone being masters of, *double entendre,* double voice, ambivalence, irony, satire, parody, etc., all techniques which Gates reveals are common and in common use; which serve as survival mechanisms, release valves for, and chosen modes of expression of marginal and alienated artists.

As a Black female African slave poet in colonial Boston, Wheatley chose to appropriate, to "deterritorialize" the prevailing master discourse for her own agenda. On occasion she also chose to signify in language which could be taken in two ways, inherently the African "double voice." One voice was heard by her master readers and another by her fellow Africans.

On other occasions, the surface blandness wore thin, however, and she expressed herself with Pope-like sting. Shields, not surprisingly, wonders how she got away with it, and concludes that Wheatley couldn't actually have been read by her white audience. Entrenched in their prejudice, they were probably content merely to glance at her lines and take her at face value. "Perhaps," he concludes, "the reviewers . . . were too bedazzled by the 'improbability' that a black woman could produce such a volume to take the content of her poetry seriously" (Wheatley, *Collected Works* 1988:235).

Actually, an opponent's smug self-complacency, thick skin, and obliviousness are the necessary prerequisites for a signifier. Wheatley's way of "getting over" on her Colonial audience was to appropriate seemingly conventional subjects by "imitating" (actually mimicking) the regular couplet style. This combination of familiar content and technique lulled European American readers to sleep intellectually early in the poems so that they missed Wheatley's powerful subversive attack on the original content. In this regard, what Deborah E. McDowell points out about African American women novelists and African American narratives can perhaps also be said of Wheatley, that when there is "a 'dangerous' story to tell. . . . 'safe' themes, plots, and conventions are used as the protective cover underneath which lies more dangerous subplots" (Larsen 1988:xxx). [11]

In Wheatley's world and time, colonial patriotism and Christian discourse were the "'safe' themes, plots, and conventions" that Wheatley sometimes appropriated to express her "dangerous subplots," i.e., injustices against Africans. Can any critic seriously believe that Wheatley always expatiates on the beauties of heaven or on the soul's redemption and salvation merely for the sheer ecstasy of it? From excess of zeal? And when Wheatley apostrophizes English or colonial heroes such as Lord Dartmouth or General Washington, or dissenting divines like George Whitefield and Samuel Cooper, is it only because she is their "groupie"? Would not Alexander Pope or even an Olaudah Equiano be given more motive in this regard than that Wheatley was flattering them and/or infatuated with them?

On close examination of all her extant poems, I have found that Wheatley has a positive attitude and employs defensive language about Africa and African people. All recent scholars concur, except Hernton. Cynthia Smith's position that "Wheatley is concerned about the survival of her work, and she proudly wishes it to survive as the work of an African writer" (1989:590) is typical of current critical reading. However, several phrases scattered throughout Wheatley's work are still generally considered problematic, phrases such as "Egyptian gloom" and "benighted Africa." Such phrases may now be better understood if we read them as written while Wheatley is in the process of signifying, after she has donned her opponent's mask, and is employing imitation/mimicry of her opponent's language and tone prior to expressing her own position.

Only in relation to the difference in religion between herself as a converted Christian and her fellow Africans as pagans can Wheatley be faulted, and that is for using condescending language. This is the result of her fervid conviction that "Afric's blameless race" back home is missing out on a good thing. She sincerely believes that Africans will get their due if they convert, as she has, to Christianity: "Wash'd in the fountains of redeeming blood,/You shall be sons, and kings, and priests to God" (*Collected Works* 1988:23), she promises African men who have not yet converted.

Implicit in the roles Wheatley envisions for African men is her rage that they no longer hold kingships and priesthoods. Overrun and defeated by Europeans, they have been deprived of religious and political control over their own African earth. Yet the Europeans, who profess to be followers of Christ, the son of

God who cherished all human beings alike, are nevertheless enslaving Africans as if the latter were beasts of burden rather than the dignified sons of God(s), kings, and priests that they had always been.

From 1768 on, all of Wheatley's poetry, no matter what the ostensible subject, deals with African enslavement; the endless suffering of slavery; the necessity to free Africans from slavery; how and when they can achieve freedom or, rather, escape their bonds; under what conditions; who will assist them or do this. Despite Wheatley's proud insistence, often publicly reiterated, of her African identity, it has not hitherto been observed that by the time these poems end, Wheatley (like the African signifying monkey) has exposed her real agenda. This is the case no matter how humbly she has spoken about herself as an African, no matter how seemingly complimentary she has been to her opponents. The latter respond exactly like the lion, which could well be English, although in Africa, the lion is monkey's opponent. In the United States, the signifying monkey is Brer Rabbit befuddling Mars' John.[12]

What the fair-minded English, what colonial patriots, what Protestant divines want for themselves, Africans also want, Wheatley points out. She conveys this by signifying on these groups' empty, hypocritical, grandiose discourse about freedom, representation, rights, etc. The incontrovertible fact Wheatley presents is that all of them own slaves. Yet few critics have hitherto considered the possibility of her deploying African rhetorical and literary techniques to achieve liberation. True, one of Wheatley's foremost editors, William Robinson, first defends her from the charge of "denigration of things black" and then claims that "in several poems . . . Phillis variously registered her racial self-consciousness." He also credits her with being "the first black American poet to . . . rhapsodize about Africa" (Lauter 1990:720–721).

John Shields is the first to credit Wheatley with utilizing African rhetorical strategies when he makes the claim that Wheatley "syncretized" her African world view and cosomogony, "the memory of her mother's sun-worship," with Christian and neo-classic poetic discourse. "Because of the pun on sun and Son, the blend is an easy one to have made," he contends (Wheatley, *Collected Works* 1988:242). However, I submit that Wheatley went further. She did not "syncretize." She signified.

Neo-classic and Christian discourse conveniently fit into and were subsumed by her signifying, a basic African rhetorical and aesthetic expression of the African world view which was and is still done in couplets (in rap, for example). As Shields himself points out tartly to European American critics who view Wheatley as having had cultural amnesia (interestingly, only in regard to things African): "I submit that a young girl of seven or eight with Wheatley's intelligence would hardly require information from her captors regarding her homeland" (Wheatley, *Collected Works* 1988:303–304).

Wheatley can also be analyzed for signifying in her letters to Europeans about Africans. In a letter to the Rev. Samuel Hopkins of Feb. 9, 1774, Wheatley again first mimics her opponent's belief in the necessity of converting her fellow Africans to the Christian dispensation *for their own good*. After distracting him by agreeing with and reassuringly stroking him, Wheatley claims to also wish "to promote this laudable design." However, she then proceeds to do the opposite. She excuses herself from joining "two negromen, who are desirous of returning to their native country to preach the gospel" on the grounds that she is "much indisposed by the return of my asthmatic complaint, besides the sickness of my mistress."

She continues, mimicking the Rev. Hopkins' pompous tone and preachy rhetoric. Wheatley does this by by expatiating with grandiose verbosity and pomposity replete with Biblical references, as in European sermons of the period, on the benefits of converting Africans to Christianity (in itself a mockery of his discourse):

> This is the beginning of that happy period foretold by the Prophets, when all shall know the Lord from the least to the greatest, and that without the assistance of the human Art of Eloquence. My heart expands with sympathetic joy to see at a distant time the thick cloud of ignorance dispersing from the face of my benighted country. Europe and America have long been fed with the heavenly provision, and I fear they loath it, while Africa is perishing with a spiritual famine. O that they

would partake of the crumbs, the precious crumbs, which fall
from the table of these distinguished children of the kingdom.
(*Collected Works* 1988:175–176)

Now that the Rev. Hopkins is sufficiently disarmed (or
perhaps asleep at this point), Wheatley concludes by reversing
her supposed previous arguments (all repetitions/mimicries of
the customary discourse), about African "ignorance" and the
"face of my benighted country" by daringly maintaining the
unthinkable opposite. Africans even have minds, she suggests
heretically in all innocence (that is, with a straight face, with the
African mask on). Moreover, those minds are open, unlike the
Europeans'! "Their [African] minds are unprejudiced against the
truth, therefore 'tis to be hoped they would receive it with their
whole heart. I hope that which the divine royal Psalmist says by
inspiration is now on the point of being accomplished, namely,
Ethiopia shall soon stretch forth her hands unto God" (*Collected
Works* 1988:176).[13]

Here Wheatley openly criticizes Europeans and Americans
who have long had all the advantages of Christianity, but "loath
it." On the other hand, she openly favors Africans who have
"minds" of such quality that they "are unprejudiced against the
truth." This compliment applies, it seems, whether they convert
or not, even if they remain "pagan," although Wheatley hopes
that they do convert. Ultimately, it is respect for Africans and
their mentality which Wheatley attempts to convince Hopkins is
a necessary ingredient for any successful forays by European
missionaries.

In 1774, it was considered "pro-African" to work for
African uplift in religious education, as it was in many Black
circles in 1874 and, indeed, into the present time. Robinson,
representing current opinion on the matter, reminds all those
who would invalidate Wheatley on these grounds that "The
notion that pagan Africa was in critical need of Christianity was
repeated by other literate, eighteenth-century blacks, and has
persisted to this day" (Lauter 1990:718). Bishop Desmond Tutu,
the South African Nobel laureate, would undoubtedly agree with
Robinson. However, it seems to me that Wheatley was shrewdly
"getting over" on Hopkins, claiming to agree with him about the

necessity of converting her fellow Africans to Christianity, but successfully getting out of an "honor" she did not want.

In another letter to Sir John Thornton, she does it again. Wheatley here signifies on European assumptions about African barbarism. Again, she contains her annoyance with mimicry and subtle irony in rejecting her opponent's request that she join two African men as a missionary to Africa. She can do this, he suggests, if she mates with whichever one she chooses, like cattle, merely because they would be going a journey together. She begins:

> You propose my returning to Africa with Bristol Yamma and John Quamine if either of them upon strict enquiry is such, as I dare give my heart and hand to. I believe they are either of them good enough if not too good for me, or they would not be fit for Missionaries, but why do you hon'd sir, wish those por men so much trouble as to carry me so long a voyage? Upon my arrival, how like a Barbarian shou'd I look to the Natives; I can promise that my tongue shall be quiet/for a strong reason indeed/being an utter stranger to the language of Anamaboe. Now to be serious, this undertaking appears too hazaredous, and not sufficient Eligible, to go. (*Collected Works* 1988:184)

Notice Wheatley's elegant and devastating rejection when she reverses the white minister's assumption that the African men are animals by showing the religious hypocrisy of the Englishman's religious discourse. The men are, in fact, "too good" for her. "After all," she seems to be saying, "They have been trained by you Europeans as African missionaries. Presumably you considered them on a high enough level, as good enough for that purpose. Yet, unaccountably, you whites can still somehow imagine either of them marrying me for the sake of expediency."

Of even more significance is Wheatley's signifying on the word "Barbarian." Several years earlier, Wheatley's proposals had described her as "an uncultivated Barbarian from Africa" (*Collected Works* 1988:7).[14] On that occasion, Wheatley described herself (or is described by her European printer) as she appears to Thornton, her Christian European correspondent—as "barbaric" because she is an African. On *this* occasion, Wheatley defines herself as "barbaric," not to the English, but to Africans. To *their* eyes, she would be perceived as European(ized) in clothing, manners, language, culture, and religion and therefore barbaric to *them*. Sir Thornton, however, might never project so far as to imagine Africans capable of having views in the matter, or even having the ability to make such distinctions between the two cultures, and disparaging ones, at that.

Europeanized, Wheatley would be looked upon by Africans as another one of a group that Africans deemed "barbaric" on two grounds. How else would anyone except Europeans define invasion, conquest, and enslavement of them? How else would anyone except Christians define their attempts to convert Africans to their religion and away from their own ancient beliefs on the shaky assumption that Christianity was superior? To Africans and the rest of the globe, it is the European Christians who have been and are "barbaric" in these matters, not the Africans. Wheatley's daring to say all this is admirable: in her "doubling"; in appropriating such a commonly used European word as "barbarian" for Africans; above all, in turning this ugly word against her opponent's internalized assumptions about the nature of Africans.

Immediately after, however, Wheatley apparently fears she may have gone too far, or perhaps is just covering herself by disarming Thornton. As is common in signifying, she pretends to her opponent that she had only been joking: "Now to be serious, this undertaking appears too hazaredous . . ." (*Collected Works* 1988:184).

Wheatley is genuinely spiritual and is preoccupied with death. She writes too sincerely on the rewards in heaven for the redeemed soul of eternal life, of peace, happiness, and beauty to be otherwise. Her faith is genuine for two reasons. The first is wish fulfillment. Christianity provides her with immortality in a site (heaven) where she will be reunited with her ancestors and loved ones, especially her father. Thus she can write to a friend of hers, a bereaved widow:

> Thyself prepare to pass the vale of night
> To join for ever on the hills of light;
> To thine embrace his joyful spirit moves
> To thee, the partner of his earthly loves;

He welcomes thee to pleasures more refin'd,
And better suited to th' immortal mind.
                                        (*Collected Works* 1988:30)

In Christianity, she learned that there existed an omnipotent God, a different source of divinity from that of her ancestors. If one believed in this God and was redeemed by him, then one could live *forever*. This God, paradoxically, had displayed mercy to her by causing her uprooting, exile, and slavery. If she had remained in her native land, she argues, she would, tragically, have never known the possibility of redemption and immortality. Thus the Christian dispensation explained all her sufferings to the satisfaction of her bruised and alienated psyche and simultaneously satisfied her deep spiritual yearnings. Certainly this was sufficient inducement to convert to Christianity, which she did at fourteen.

Wheatley had another reason to cling to the concept of an afterlife in a blissful heaven. This was a political motive which became quite common in African American literature and quite commonly signified on therein, as I have shown in the previous chapter and will show again.[15] Again, the use of conventional religious discourse provides Wheatley and other eighteenth (and nineteenth) century African/African slaves with a perfect vehicle for venting their outrage in an outwardly acceptable manner. Thus Wheatley (and many other slaves) in coded language that only they understand, freely warn their captors and their captors' descendants that they will pay for their sins (in slave taking, holding, and mastering) after death. At that time, all former slaves will go to heaven. Europeans are also told where *they* will go—as elegantly and eloquently as possible. It should come as no surprise, therefore, that Wheatley never includes Africans in these warnings.

Two of Wheatley's poems have long been considered problematic. However, if one reads them as if Wheatley were signifying, then the reading changes. The first poem, "To the University of Cambridge in New-England" (now Harvard), was written in 1767 when she was only fourteen. Wheatley starts disarmingly in the African traditional manner: a mimicry mask,

flat in tone, a seemingly accepting repetition of her opponents'
(and audience's) most cherished convictions:

> 'Twas not long since I left my native shore,
> The land of errors, and *Egyptian* gloom:
> Father of mercy, 'twas thy gracious hand
> Brought me in safety from those dark abodes.
>
> (*Collected Works* 1988:15)

She then reminds her audience in the strongest possible
language that Jesus is offering them redemption and salvation,
even immortality: "Life without death, and glory without end."
For Wheatley, this is the key to her sincere and deep conversion
to Christianity, the belief in the immortality of her soul.

Next directing her sermon to her youthful audience, she
warns them to shun sin, to "suppress the deadly serpent in its
egg." She then rounds on this concept by relating it clearly to the
boys. That although they are now "blooming plants of human
race divine" they will become prey to the serpent ready to be
born, *if* they sin.

Suddenly, just before her conclusion, Wheatley disrupts
the audience-centered flow of her warnings. She turns personal,
using herself as an example in a strategic effort to add even more
impact to the loathsomeness of sin:

> An *Ethiop* tells you 'tis your greatest foe;
> Its Transient sweetness turns to endless pain,
> And in immense perdition sinks the soul.
>
> (*Collected Works* 1988:16)

Why does Wheatley here literally and figuratively
underscore the fact that she is an "Ethiop?" Is it to point out to
the boys that even a humble, simple African can be a vehicle for
God's word? Such a reading assumes that for Wheatley and her
audience, the concept and word "Ethiop" conveys inferiority.
Cynthia Smith, in complaining about the interpretation given to
lines 29–30 in Wheatley's "Lines to Maecenas" (the same given to
the lines above), voices justified annoyance and dissatisfaction
with such an ethnocentric interpretation. "These lines are often
produced to describe Wheatley's sense of inadequacy at being

black or to show her presumed ambivalence about her blackness," she complains. However, what is "traditionally seen as self-deprecatory, should be seen, rather, as a statement of frustration at the limits imposed by time and place, by race and status" (1989:586).

Wheatley was well aware of the European/colonial society's assumption of her inferiority. Indeed, how could she not be? By appearing to go along with it, she could then manipulate it to advance her own agenda. From Wheatley's internal perspective, an Ethiopian slave woman who preaches to her white audience about sin and then underlines her message by addressing them as so many experts on sin is signifying on them. Who is better equipped, she reminds them between the lines, to preach to you young white Christians about the "transient sweetness" which will end in "immense perdition" for the sinking soul than an Ethiopian slave woman who is a long-suffering object of such sin?

Wheatley stands before them as one Ethiop eminently possessed of first-hand knowledge and immense expertise on the subject of their fathers' sinful pleasure in obtaining an easier earthly life through the enslavement of Ethiopians. As I have already pointed out, Wheatley's Christian subject matter on occasion and in this instance consists of reminding her white audience of an afterlife when sinful whites will get theirs. Why else does she doubly bring attention to herself at the end of her sermon in a sudden disruption of the pious Christian language system she has been using with the most startling opposition to that discourse imaginable: "An Ethiop tells you?" To her audience, "Ethiop" equals "barbarian." Yet she purposely points this out, emphasizing herself specifically and individually. What overlay, what extra dimension to the Christian message is Wheatley seeking to add in calling special attention to herself as "an Ethiop," as an expert or authority figure in the matter of white sin?

In traditional African signifying, the signifier draws attention to self as the expert. One can see her at this moment suddenly pointing to and poking at herself with such intensity that her auditors would look at her closely, not as a Black woman in colonial clothing talking the King's English to them, but as an

Ethiopian. As such, Wheatley would never be confronting them in the first place unless she had been brutally uprooted from her African home and enslaved in this distant, cold place. As such, an enslaved member of an enslaved race, proud and dignified, Wheatley is an expert on white sin, on the sins of these young men's fathers. This is the sin which these noisy, raucous, privileged adolescents (who would otherwise pay her scant attention) are going to heedlessly perpetuate. Thus she is signifying with her gestures, her voice and her language, on slavery, the subject on which her most impassioned poetry turns.

In 1768, at age fifteen, Wheatley wrote the second poem, "On Being Brought from Africa to America," which also contains lines considered problematic by many readers. Again, the sequence of her strategies accords with that used in signifying: the clever but weak African signifying monkey confronting the powerful but stupid lion. She begins once again with seeming flat repetition/mimicry of a European voice:

> 'Twas mercy brought me from my *Pagan* land,
> Taught my benighted soul to understand
> That there's a God, that there's a *Saviour* too,
> Once I redemption neither sought nor knew.
> > (*Collected Works* 1988:18)

She then continues with trope of chiasmus, a seeming repetition. In reality, however, each word of the language used by the opponent is turned back against the opponent, i.e., "up in his face":

> Some [white Christians] view our sable race with scornful eye,
> "Their colour is a diabolic die."
> Remember, Christians, Negroes, black as *Cain*
> May be refin'd, and join the angelic train.
> > (*Collected Works* 1988:18)

In this second stanza, as in the first, she repeats the Christian discourse. This time, however, Wheatley employs significant punning variations, thereby effectually reversing and doubling meanings. In the process of repetition, she turns Christian discourse against itself by using sibilants to convey that "some" white Christians are hypocrites. While they are scorning her and her race, *she* scorns them. Through these sibilants, she cleverly and indirectly intimates that her opponents are themselves snakes, not Christians; that they are themselves "diabolic"; that their "view" is that of an evil "eye." Even as they are making the claim of diabolism for Africans, it redounds against the "scornful eye[d]" ones who vaunt themselves over "our sable race" and yet call themselves "Christians."

In the course of his historically significant analysis of signifying, Gates places the first usage of this technique in the colonies at around 1785. However, if Wheatley is indeed signifying in these two poems, then its usage can now be traced even further back—to 1767. Wheatley may perhaps be the first African writer to use the concepts and discourse of the Christian religion consciously to subvert or "get over on" her white Christian audience's most cherished religious beliefs in order to appropriate them for her own purposes. Wheatley's "indirection," her use of doubling to imitate and repeat the opponent, includes satire, irony, puns, and tropes of chiasmus. Some are recognizable European strategies, but the patterning, as laid out by Gates and other recent critics, is clearly characteristic of African signifying which continued and still continues in the diaspora.

Notes

1. Franklin was self-taught. However, his system was identical to that used in the English public schools for centuries until about 1960 to teach boys Latin and Greek. They would be set to translating these languages into English and then back again.

2. Phillis Wheatley, *The Collected Works of Phillis Wheatley*, ed. John Shields (New York: Oxford University Press, 1988). All future citations from Wheatley's works will be from this text, which is a photocopy of the original 1773 edition of her poems owned by Dr. Shields.

3. See also *Collected Works*, p. 88, where Wheatley tells a gentleman going to England to recover his health, to "Leave these bleak regions, and inclement skies,/Where chilling winds return the winter

past,/And nature shudders at the furious blast." In Ernest Gaines's contemporary short story, "The Sky is Gray," even the title signifies on the cultural "cold shoulder" or "freezeout" Africans have always experienced in the United States and other parts of the diaspora. The great Jamaican Calypso singer Bob Marley titled his last song "Coming in from the Cold." Feminists also use cold in the same way, as in Bernice Sandler's expression "the chilly climate in the college classroom" in summarizing the varieties of sex discrimination practiced against female students by their professors and others in the academic community.

4. Also on masks see Sidonie Smith, *Where I'm Bound: Patterns of Slavery and Freedom in Black American Autobiography* (Westport, CT: Greenwood Press, 1974), 14, 15, 16.

5. This is not Gates's term, however. According to Isani, a "hopeful publisher advertised her (in the *Boston Evening Post*, October 30, 1779 [n.p.]) as *'a rara avis in terra,'* (a rare bird on earth), one who promised to delight 'those who are *always* in search of some new thing'" (64).

6. In *Living by the Word* (New York: Harcourt Brace Jovanovich, 1987), Walker writes prophetically about the attacks against her: "In the end this simple injustice will be an undeserved burden and worrisome puzzle to our children, our next generation of rebels and poets (Dare they create from the heart? think with their own brain? make decisions that in a treacherous world inevitably involve risk or invite attack?), many of whom write to me frequently about both the film and the book and exhibit a generosity of heart and a tolerance of spirit sadly lacking in some of their parents" (92).

7. Shields, many years later, responds: Why is it, he asks rhetorically of Tyler specifically, as well as other previous critics, that "hardly a one indicated that he or she ever took seriously the content of her words[?]" He answers that "her work is subsumed in some socioanthropoligical argument whose tenets justified or challenged the grievously erroneous notion of racial supremacy. In the case of the other, more recent position, she and her works were (and continue to be) viewed as typical of eighteenth-century blacks who sold their blackness for pottage of white acceptability" (Wheatley, *Collected Works* 1988:267).

8. On this occasion, a well-known scholar-poet, a fellow member of my panel, wondered aloud after my presentation as to whether Wheatley was really "conscious" of what she was doing. This adjective (always accompanied by this question), no matter who the African American female writer happens to be, seems to be the latest euphemism used to express a deep-seated conviction that African/African American intellectual capacities are inferior, incapable

of grasping complex technical skills, even when creating art. When Blacks do art or are artful, it is therefore "unconscious," accidental, unlike the work of European/European American artists. I heard this reiterated at every conference I have attended in the past few years where white and Black scholars come together.

9. In *Kafka: Toward a Minor Literature* (Minneapolis: University of Minnesota Press, 1988), Gilles Deleuze and Felix Guattari present a theory of literature in a late capitalist, post-modern world system which defines as "minor literature" that literature which is involved in "deterritorialization" and "reterritorialization." They expand and thereby transform the meaning of the term "minor" literature to signify literature which is written in the same language as the majority language but from an alienated, dislocated perspective. "Minor" literature thus implies alternate, subversive meanings other than a surface reading would normally convey, thereby doubling linguistic and political possibilities of meaning "to express another potential community, to force the means for another consciousness and another sensibility." "Minority literature" is thus a literature written in opposition to the literature traditionally defined as "major" literature, those "*master*pieces" written by "*master*writers." For DeLeuze and Guattari, "minor no longer designates specific literatures but the revolutionary conditions for every literature within the heart of what is called great or established literature" (17–18). To my way of thinking, "the heart" is an anatomical location in the body of American literature considerably higher than traditional critical opinion has hitherto consigned "minor literature." Despite this "minor" quibble, I feel that the implications of Deleuze's and Guattari's theory are that "minor literature" subverts and destabilizes mainstream traditional concepts and language in many ways. Called into question, therefore, are time-honored literary genres and their underlying presumptions and assumptions. An example is the epic with its individual hero who fetishizes the cultural hegemonic values and abstractions he represents. One still wonders, however, why Wheatley omits the women of Africa from her appeal for conversion.

10. In all due respect, I disagree with Alice Walker when she quips: "Writing or not writing is not dependent on what the market is— whether your work is going to sell or not. If it were, there is not a black woman who would write. And that includes Phillis Wheatley. Think of *her* antagonistic market!" ("Alice Walker," *Black Women Writers at Work*, ed. Claudia Tate [New York: Continuum, 1983], 182). In my opinion, Wheatley made every effort to sell. It was a matter of life and death to her.

11. Another Black feminist critic, Barbara Christian, in *Black Feminist Criticism: Perspectives on Black Women Writers* (New York: Pergamon Press, 1985), reminds critics that to read an author like Wheatley it is necessary first "to establish the historical origins and context of a literature that emerges from groups of people considered to be marginal or despised" as "critical to its understanding and appreciation." She goes on to explain that "such literature is not only the product of the individual writer's desire to express herself or to create beauty (through these significant aspects), but also to affect the historical moment—that is, to help create social change" (165). In my estimation, Wheatley attempted to do this as one of a group of "those peoples" identified by Christian "who are not seen as part of History or Literature and yet struggle to insist upon their own totality, their own significance in their time." As "the nineteenth century Afro-American women writers (terms that were contradictory in that time) *were* seen through historical images, whether they wanted to be or not," according to Christian, so was Wheatley before them. And as "they *had* to respond to the images of their race and sex that challenged their authority to even perceive of themselves as creators of literature," so, I believe, did Wheatley before them.

12. Kefi Owusu in writing of African parody (in the form of a praise song), could be describing Wheatley when he points out that "There is nothing but 'sound and fury' to these praise names; they 'signify nothing,' precisely because the context emphasizes the 'unnaturalness' and, thus, the 'arbitrariness,' of the relationship between signifier and signified, sign and referent. The cultural necessity of a 'natural' bond is hinted at only to be emphatically denied." (749)

13. See also Isani, "Gambia," 68.

14. In "Proposals" to the edition of 1773.

15. In speaking condescendingly of the tone of one of Wheatley's best poems, Mason remarks of "To the University of Cambridge in New-England" that it sounds "as if it might have been issued from the pulpit" (Wheatley, *Poems* 1989:16). One wonders what is wrong with that, even if it were Wheatley's only motive? Only recently, William Andrews in *Sisters of the Spirit: Three Black Women's Autobiographies of the Nineteenth Century* (Bloomington: Indiana University Press, 1986), and Marilyn Richardson in *Maria Stewart, America's First Black Woman Political Writer: Essays and Speeches* (Bloomington: Indiana University Press, 1987), have argued that Black female preachers of the nineteenth century made the political connection. In fact, one wonders why it was not seen as having been present from the beginning.

References

Baker, Houston, Jr. *The Journey Back: Issues in Black Literature*. Chicago: University of Chicago Press, 1984.

Brawley, Benjamin. *The Negro Genius*. New York: Dodd, Mead, 1937.

Combahee River Collective. "A Black Feminist Statement. April 1977." *Feminist Frameworks: Alternative Accounts of the Relations Between Women and Men*. Eds. Allison M. Jaggar and Paula S. Rothenberg. New York: McGraw-Hill, 1984.

Gates, Henry Louis, Jr. "Authority (White) Power and the (Black) Critic." *Cultural Critique* 7 (Fall 1987): 20–36.

———. *Figures in Black: Words, Signs, and the "Racial" Self*. New York: Oxford University Press, 1987.

Hernton, Calvin. *The Sexual Mountain and Black American Women Writers: Adventures in Sex, Literature, and Real Life*. New York: Anchor Books, 1987.

Isani, Mukhtar Ali. "Gambia on my Soul": Africa and the African in the Writing of Phillis Wheatley." *MELUS*. 6.1 (Spring 1979): 64–72.

———. "Phillis Wheatley in London: An Unpublished Letter to David Wooster." *American Literature* 51.2 (May 1979): 255–260.

Jordan, June. "The Difficult Miracle of Black Poetry in America or Something Like a Sonnet for Phillis Wheatley." *Wild Women in the Whirlwind: Afra-American Culture and the Contemporary Literary Renaissance*. Eds. Joanne M. Braxton and Andrea Nicole McLaughlin. New Brunswick, N.J.: Rutgers University Press, 1990.

Kubayanda, Josephat Bekunuru. "Notes on the Impact of African Oral-Traditional Rhetoric on Latin American and Caribbean Writing." *Afro-Hispanic Review* (September 1984): 5–10. See especially 6–8.

Larsen, Nella. *Quicksand and Passing*. Ed. Deborah E. McDowell. New Brunswick, N.J.: Rutgers University Press, 1988.

Lauter, Paul, ed. *The Heath Anthology of American Literature*. Vol. 1. Lexington, MA: Heath, 1990.

Miller, Keith D. "Composing Martin Luther King, Jr." *PMLA* 105 (1987): 70–92.

O'Neale, Sondra. "A Slave's Subtle War: Phillis Wheatley's Use of Biblical Myth." *EAL* 21.2 (Fall 1986): 144–165, esp. 147–149.

Owusu, Kofi. "Interpreting Interpreting: African Roots, Black Fruits, and the Colored Tree [of 'Knowledge']." *Black American Literature Forum* 23.4 (Winter 1989): 739–766.

Redding, J. Saunders. *To Make a Poet Black.* Chapel Hill: University of North Carolina Press, 1939.

Smith, Cynthia. "'To Maecenas'": Phillis Wheatley's Invocation of an Idealized Reader." *Black American Literature Forum* 23.3 (Fall 1989): 579–592.

Thompson, Vincent Bakpetu. *The Making of the African Diaspora in the Americas 1441–1900.* New York: Longman, 1987.

Washington, Mary Helen. *Invented Lives: Narratives of Black Women 1860–1960.* New York: Doubleday, 1988.

Wheatley, Phillis. *The Poems of Phillis Wheatley.* Ed. Julian D. Mason, Jr. Chapel Hill: University of North Carolina Press, 1989.

———. *The Collected Works of Phillis Wheatley.* Ed. John Shields. New York: Oxford University Press, 1988.

WHEATLEY AND HER LITERARY DAUGHTERS: FROM TRAGEDIES TO TRIUMPHS

In this chapter, I raise and attempt to answer questions about significant works by Wheatley and her "literary daughters" primarily in terms of how and in what ways they responded to two American success myths: the male European American success myth, and the Cinderella myth. For example, did they internalize these myths as European Americans did? Did they respond directly? That is, did they describe their heroines as attempting, like Wheatley, to live out a Franklin life trajectory? Did they accept the myths (with reservations) about the nature of the individual and the community, concepts which differed in Africa? If they rejected these myths, did they directly confront and critique them? Or did they subvert them indirectly through subtle rhetorical and aesthetic signifiers? If they did not identify with the success myth so much for themselves as for males, how did they depict their female characters? As primarily dependent on males? As self-sufficient? As support and backups who stood by (and well behind) their men, no matter what—far away from the front lines of action, far away from the outside world?[1] Or did they reject the male success myth out of hand, not relating it to their heroines, but instead depicting these women as Cinderellas, living out the Cinderella variant/version for female success? Or did they combine both myths, or parts of both myths?

I contend that Jacobs, Hurston, and Walker reflect in their works a powerful commitment, as did Wheatley, to the American male success mythology. They depict their heroines as active change agents for the better in their own lives in the various ways Franklin illustrated. This is the case even when the American success mythology is combined with conflicting

African communitarian values or isolated private individual values. I also contend that the influence of the Cinderella myth is equally pervasive; that it tends to valorize passivity and external agency. Literal fairy godmothers source benefits. The heroines, however, continue to uphold the American male success model for themselves. They will still strive and struggle to rise in life, as Franklin did. As Calvin Hernton says of Ann Petry's heroine in *The Street* (1946):

> She is terribly aware that America is bent on denying black people the "better things" in life. Nevertheless, she staunchly believes in the "higher values" of white America, and that she can achieve these values.
>
> Lutie is in pursuit of the American Dream. This is her *quest*. She believes in all the virtues of the Protestant Ethic: the virtue of middle-class respectability, the virtue of hard work leading to getting ahead, the virtue of moral restraint leading to clean living, the virtue of serious personal purpose, and the virtue of thinking, grooming, dressing, and behaving "respectable"—all leading to happiness. She identifies with Ben Franklin as a model. She is determined to better her situation for herself and for her young son. (1987:81)

Ultimately, in the work of Alice Walker, which successfully combines both disparate myths, the American male success myth is used to empower success on one's own without god-like male agency as the Cinderella myth led European and European American women to expect. Nevertheless, success is achieved with the help of a fairy godmother/Prince Charming and a close-knit and supportive community of men and women. In the latter element, Walker adds African/African American and feminist myths to the European American male success myth. Indeed, to have combined all three visions required Walker to practice the containment of paradox and ambiguity that many contemporary African/African American womanist and feminist scholars propose.[2]

Thus it is that Walker can play with both the materialist European American male success myth and the "romantic" Cinderella myth simultaneously, while supported and reinforced by African-sourced concepts of the individual self as community self. Her heroine's trajectory is economic (poverty to wealth); social and political (under class to middle); European/European American to African/African American (slave-drudge to "matriarch"/African queen over a community of extended family and friends).

Most of the time, I contend, Wheatley's successors have followed American male success mythology which valorized two American success myths. The first, "hard economics," was primarily in the form of how-to manuals. These manuals gave tips on how to achieve economic success through educational and vocational work-study programs (such as Booker T. Washington and Frances E. W. Harper advocated), and to a lesser extent, political success myths (identified with the likes of Frederick Douglass, Harriet Jacobs, Ida B. Wells Barnett, and W.E.B. DuBois).

After Wheatley, the elements I traced earlier in her "daughters" can be seen growing ever more complex. Wheatley's belief in hard work leading to individual and group economic liberation and success becomes, in the nineteenth century and beyond, a vision of success for one's self and the uplift of one's people, as I illustrate in the work of Jacobs. From Jacobs on, the dominant European American romantic female mythology in its literature, i.e., the Cinderella myth, which clashes jarringly with other success myths, begins to intrude into African American women's literature. Its elements include a hated oppressor stepmother and/or stepfather, cruel siblings and onlookers, and a fairy godmother catalyst. Last but not least, there is "Prince Charming," or the next best equivalent. Generally, Prince Charming is some recognized symbol of public superiority in relation to everyone around the heroine, something that will raise her in status high above the crowd and "take her away from all this." It can be education, inheritance, material success, even a sudden win. This does not, as in European/European American mythology, signal ultimate transcendence for the heroine, but greater community harmony, peace, and well-being for the heroine and her crowd, in which she remains an active participant.

From the Harlem Renaissance of the twenties and thirties into World War II and beyond, these writers move to an increasing awareness of the "quicksand," in Nella Larsen's term: the inevitability of failure of private, individual solutions in the face of monolithic social, political, and economic forces arrayed against the aspirations of African Americans and particularly African American women. This view is reflected most powerfully in the work of Jesse Redmon Fauset (1882–1961), in *There is Confusion* (1924), and *Plum Bun* (1928); Nella Larsen (1891?–1964), in *Quicksand* (1928), and *Passing* (1929); and Marita Bonner (1899–1971), in her short stories like "Drab Rambles" (1927), and the prize winning "Tin Can" (1933), or her play, *Purple Flower* (1928). But in *Their Eyes Were Watching God* (1937), Zora Neale Hurston (1891–1960), ignores their depression (and the Great one itself), with a romantic Cinderella resolution to her heroines' problems combined with a valorization of African customs and values. However, Ann Petry (1911–), a bit later in *The Street* (1946), confirms Fauset's, Larsen's, and Bonner's naturalistic vision. In her now-classic novel, Petry depicts Lutie Johnson's tragic attempts to achieve success in keeping with the prevailing American white male economic myths, only to be destroyed by an external environment beyond her control.

Paule Marshall (1929–), in *Brown Girl, Brownstones* (1959), combines the two views in her powerful delineation of the psychic and emotional robotizing which can become the price of a single-minded, epic attempt at the gold ring, even when the attempt is successful. Marshall shows the frightening effects of an obsessively materialistic pursuit by an entire community of Bajun (Barbadian) immigrants in Brooklyn in the thirties and forties. This pursuit is best summarized in the Booker T. Washington motto on the banner attached to the walls of their center: "It is not the depths from which we come/But the heights to which we ascend" (1981:220).

Marshall focuses on a couple in that community, Deighton and Silla Boyce. Diametrically opposed in an epic struggle between nostalgic romanticism and hard-nosed materialism, this pair cancels each other out. However, their daughter, Selina, a composite of both world views, will one day distill the best from each and go on with her life. But not before completing what her father had set out to do—return to Barbados first to reconnect with her roots at first hand.

Silla, the matriarch, achieves her goal, defeating her husband, but she does this at the cost of her needs as a woman. In an interview more than thirty years after the book was written, Marshall still has the same view toward Silla, but has mellowed toward Deighton, reflecting her (re)turn to African-sourced Caribbean cultural values:

> The other side of strong black women is so often weak black men, and I want to get away from that thinking, because it divides rather than unites. I don't see, for example, Silla, the mother in *Brown Girl, Brownstones*, as all that strong a woman. I see her as someone who has perhaps foolishly or unquestioningly bought the whole American materialistic ethic. And the price she pays for that is the death of love and the ruin of her family. I don't see that as being all that strong. I see some strength in the father. He insists upon American success on his own terms. ("Holding onto the View" 1991:24)

Selina balances and reconciles in her person both her mother's practical forcefulness (which when carried too far turns into hard-headed materialism) and her beloved father's sensuality and spontaneity (which carried too far becomes self-indulgence, combined with false, macho pride). This is how Marshall depicted him in 1959, regardless of how she would depict him today.

More recently, Marshall has gone beyond a synthesis of the romantic and the materialistic. Much like Walker in this respect, Marshall's work increasingly calls for a repudiation of the obsessively materialistic and technological aspects of the American dream and a return to African values. Three of the many symbols she uses for this purpose sum up Marshall's position. One is the Empire State Building in "To Da-Duh in Memoriam" (1966), where a Barbadian grandmother duels with her American-born granddaughter, each attempting to show that her culture is superior. The granddaughter vaunts the technological wonder of the Empire State Building; the grandmother, a giant royal palm tree. Another is the race car which kills Vere in *The Chosen Place, The Timeless People* (1969), and most recently, the sickening sundae with its ersatz ingredients served on Avey Johnson's cruise ship aptly named

The Bianca Pride in *Praisesong for a Widow* (1983). This dessert brilliantly epitomizes the plastic quality of the American mythology that African American women like Marshall's heroine, Avey, her husband and friends have all *swallowed* for so many years. The more African diaspora people pursue European American definitions of success, the more authenticity of living escapes them, Marshall maintains.

Finally, Alice Walker (1944–), "capping" on Hurston, transforms the latter's ambivalent perspective into an historically significant appropriation of the American male success myth for African American women. She does this in *The Color Purple* (1982), by successfully combining Cinderella and Franklin's American male success mythologies with African/African American value systems related to the community.

In keeping with ancient African traditions, Phillis Wheatley wrote for pragmatic public purposes. However, the form and language of her poetry were European. But once Wheatley lost her patron and owner to death and was finally freed, she failed in her ambitious careerism and also lost her life. Colonial European society would appear, therefore, to have conveyed a message to Wheatley for presuming to conceive of herself as an artist on her own, without patronage; for attempting to ignore the simultaneous barriers of race, gender, class, and condition of servitude.

During Wheatley's lifetime, few women succeeded in what Wheatley attempted: finding patrons and a modicum of financial and critical success for their writing efforts. As Rachel Blau DuPlessis points out: "If lack of leisure did not suffice to keep women writers from developing their skills, the social stigma attached to stepping outside of conventional gender roles would have offered an additional restraining force" (1990:52–53).[3]

To illustrate, Jane Austen (1775–1817), was fortunate to have had male relatives mediate as agents for her anonymous work. However, she published very little in her lifetime, grateful for making stocking and glove money from her efforts. However, Wheatley enjoyed none of Austen's privileges of class and race, nor that of Mercy Otis Warren (1728–1814), a poet and a colonial, like Wheatley, and an historian, but born into one privileged family and married into another. The English essayist, Mary

Wollstonecraft (1759–1797), who died in childbirth, would have shared Wheatley's fate, except that her influential husband, William Godwin, supported her emotionally and financially against the world. As for the likes of Catherine Macaulay, Wollstonecraft's friend and celebrated historian; Hester Thrale Piozzi, Samuel Johnson's friend; and Margaret Fuller (1790–1838), Emerson's friend, none of them would ever have ended up sharing Wheatley's fate. However, they anticipated Janie Crawford of *Their Eyes Were Watching God* and committed societal suicide by marrying considerably younger men.

Lucy Terry (1730–1821), of Vermont authored "Bars Fight" (1746), but it was transmitted orally and not published until 1885. Like Wheatley, Terry was abducted out of Africa and enslaved. Her husband, also like Wheatley's a free Black, was able to buy her freedom. Nothing is known of Terry, otherwise, or of Ann Plato, another African slave whose essays appeared in 1841.

What the Puritan Anne Bradstreet (1612?–1672) wrote in "The Prologue" (1650) prophesied both Wheatley's difficulties and eventual tragedy as an artist, and that she would not be alone in suffering them. Even Bradstreet, another privileged white woman, labored under the indignity of not being taken seriously as a poet solely because of her sex. For that reason alone she could not get a serious hearing, or write on any other but what we would today consider "greeting card" subjects:

> I am obnoxious to each carping tongue
> Who says my hand a needle better fits,
> A poet's pen all scorn I should thus wrong,
> For such despite they cast on female wits:
> If what I do prove well, it won't advance,
> They'll say it's stol'n, or else it was by chance.
> (Ammons 1990: 259)

Closer to Wheatley, at least in terms of almost as many strikes against him, in colonial and European eyes—was Jupiter Hammon (1711–1806), who wrote "An Address to Miss Phillis Wheatley, Ethiopian Poetess, in Boston, who came from Africa at eight years of age, and soon became acquainted with the gospel of Jesus Christ" (1778). William Robinson, a distinguished

Wheatley scholar, likens the two African slaves in two significant ways: that both "seemed to be truly pious" and that both adopted, consciously or unconsciously, a variety of techniques that enabled their works to be published at a time when "whites would not likely have permitted writings blatantly critical of the dominant culture to reach print." Since they found that "religious narratives, poems and sermons [were] acceptable to white readers" (Ammons 1990:678), this is what Wheatley and Hammon gave them, he shrewdly observes.

Hammon, also a slave, was yet free from one of Wheatley's problems, gender bias. In his praise song to her, he prudently limited himself to the same Christian discourse to which Wheatley had limited herself. In doing so, he unobtrusively repeated/mimicked (i.e., signified or "riffed" with slight, but significant variations) some of the lines in Wheatley's poetry, for example from "On Being Brought From Africa to America," lines such as "In bringing thee from distant shore. . . ./God's tender mercy brought thee here,/Tost o'er the raging main. . . ./God's tender mercy set thee free, . . ./While thousands mov'd to distant shore,/And others left behind, . . ./Thou hast left the heathen shore,/Thro' mercy of the Lord,/Among the heathen live no more . . ./When God shall send his summons down,/And number saints together,/Blest angel chant, (triumphant sound)/Come Live with me forever" (Ammons 1990:683–684).

What if Baker's suggestion that Africans were not entirely passive receptacles for the European world view, nor culturally *tabula rasa*, were applied to Wheatley and Hammon? As he puts it, "The African's or the Afro-American's acquisition of English did not subject him or her to the 'world-view' of the European in the automatic, deterministic way. . . . Only on the assumption that Africans were without 'language' when they encountered the West would such a position be remotely tenable. . . . Under this view, adult African speakers could certainly be conceived of as playing manifold variations on the 'themes' laid down by European vocabulary items" (1980:183–184).

What if when Gates describes a "rhetorical naming by indirection . . . when one writer repeats another's structure by one of several means, including a fairly exact repetition of a given narrative or rhetorical structure, filled incongruously with a ludicrous or incongruent content," he is describing what Hammon is doing with Wheatley's language "under the guise of religious expression" (*Figures* 1987:242, 175)? What if Gates's insights on signifying answer "the problem" of "finding the means to assert the worthiness of those for whom [Wheatley and Hammon] stood without flatly contradicting the notions, almost universally held among whites, that people of color were inferior, and thus their writings were not worth reading" (Ammons 1990:678–679)? Would critical opinion then revise about whether Hammon was unconscious or conscious in his ingenuousness? What if the possibility were considered that Hammon was signifying on Wheatley's lines covertly to Wheatley herself and other enslaved Africans; that, in fact, these lines might have been coded? Would these lines then perhaps unfold themselves for fresh, more complex readings, such as Robinson hints at, and which I attempt for Wheatley?

Gates has written voluminously on signifying, in *Figures in Black* (1984), in *The Signifying Monkey* (1989), which won a National Book Award, and elsewhere. Clearly, therefore, signifying is too complex a combination of rhetorical and aesthetic techniques to easily define briefly. However, here is a brief portion of one of Gates's more succinct attempts: "Signifyin(g) is a uniquely black rhetorical concept, entirely textual or linguistic, by which a second statement or figure repeats, or tropes, or reverses the first" (*Figures* 1987:49).[4]

In the previous chapter, in the course of my analysis of several of Wheatley's poems I argued that there is evidence of signifying. We also know that Wheatley had an African confidante, Obour Tanner, a shipmate of hers on the middle passage, with whom she corresponded all her life. Again, what is published is in the form of the conventional Christian discourse of the period. But it strains credibility that these two women when alone would confine themselves to discussions about the state of their souls and their hopes for an afterlife. One can readily imagine quite other topics for discussion in their private conversations, such as their shared experiences on the slave ship *Phillis*, their experiences as slaves afterwards, their mutual friends, and family concerns. Historians Haile and Johnson agree with this premise; however, they believe that only adults are capable of such complex suffering: "When African females were brought to America (some as late as 1850), *illegally*, many were adults, already socialized into the ways and beliefs of their people. The inhuman middle passage to America and oppressive conditions of slavery could not erase these memories, nor stop slaves from thinking of their homeland and families" (1989:71). However, I contend from Wheatley's reference to the trauma she experienced when she was "snatch'd from her parent's arms" at seven or eight years of age, kidnapped out of Gambia, endured the middle passage, and thence enslavement in "cold" Boston, it is clear that this child, at least, remembered.

In fact, she shared experiences of oppression with Obour Tanner, and the unified perspective which emerged as a result is probably what Tanner and another friend, the Native American minister Samson Occom, had in common with Wheatley. One of her best pieces is a letter to him in 1774 in which this concern is eloquently revealed:

> In evry human breast God has implanted a principle, which we call love of freedom; it is impatient of oppression, and pants for deliverance; and by the leave of our modern Egyptians [slaveholders], I will assert, that the same principle lives in us [Africans]. God grant deliverance in his own way and time, and get him honour upon all those whose avarice impels them to countenance and help forward the calamities of their fellow creatures. This I desire not for their hurt, but to convince them of the strange absurdity of their conduct, whose words and actions are so diametrically opposite. How well the cry for liberty, and the reverse disposition for the exercise of oppressive power over others agree—I humbly think it does not require the penetration of a philosopher to determine. (Ammons 1990:727–728)

Moving on to the nineteenth century, Jo March of Louisa May Alcott's *Little Women*, yearned to be a writer. Jo is so universally beloved a character for so many European American women that she takes on mythological dimensions. On the surface, therefore, she would seem to have little in common with an eighteenth century European-trained, African female writer. However, Elizabeth Keyser's perception about Jo reveals a chilling kinship with Wheatley's thwarted desire for a career after her owners' deaths: "The two wishes are [considered] incompatible [by the culture]: to achieve independence [the would-be writer] will have to assert herself in such a way as to incur blame; and to win the praise of those she loves best, she will have to curtail her striving for independence" (1982:450–451).

Jo attempts unsuccessfully to simultaneously be accepted as a woman, to feel comfortable about her gender, and to achieve a career as a writer. These were biographical problems for Jo's creator, as well. Louisa May Alcott (1832–1888), was roughly contemporary with Harriet Jacobs (1813–1897), whom I discuss at length in the following chapter. Alcott grappled with these issues all her life, apparently without achieving any satisfying resolution to them.

In contemporary times, the personal account by the novelist and playwright Tsitsi Dangarembga provides another chilling repetition of the same tragic experience for women creators. In it, she reveals that nothing has changed for African women since Wheatley's lifetime. Dangarembga, a Zimbabwean, went through hell with the African presses, getting very little of her poetry and playwriting accepted, and then only after epic struggles. Finally, she did succeed in having a novel—*Nervous Conditions* (1989), a powerful attack on sexism—published.

Until now, Dangarembga has been reticent about sharing with the public her demoralizing experiences in relation to her efforts to publish her work on the grounds that she would be "divulging a secret." Fortunately, she "ended up thinking twice" about her culturally programmed unwillingness to assert her talent and to fulfill it in careerism. Tellingly, she has internalized the chorus of voices of her own community, her own culture, used to keep her in line: "Not least among the risks I'd be taking was what people at home would say: 'Well, what did you expect?' (uttered with a fair amount of glee). 'First of all, a career like that! Secondly a career like that for a woman. Truly, the very idea of it!'" (1991:43)

Her attempts to get her work published proved fruitless; she experienced only repeated rejection and ostracism from all sides. As a result, she had begun to internalize the arguments callously fed her (and her sisters throughout time) to silence her protest—the cruelest, that she lacked talent. Ultimately, she descended into financial destitution. Dangarembga's report thus uncannily, eerily, exposes a predicament strikingly similar to Wheatley's in her day.

Dangarembga is now able to muster the courage to continue writing and speak out, but she is aware that in doing so she is considered a traitor to the prevailing notion of European and African female conduct, of the ideal of womanhood. Exactly 200 years before Dangarembga published her report, Wheatley came up against the same Catch-22. In Wheatley's case, however, oppression was compounded by European racist assumptions, which fortunately Dangarembga did not experience in Zimbabwe. Sexism was more than enough. But Dangarembga will in the future be up against racism, now that her work is being published internationally, including in the United States.

I include Dangarembga's experience as "a cautionary tale," as Walker calls Hurston's life. Dangarembga's experience makes the conditions of Wheatley's life after Susannah Wheatley's demise more real. However, Wheatley's sufferings were even worse than Dangarembga's because Wheatley experienced European *and* colonial racism all her life. Dangarembga is only just now beginning to experience racism.

In sum, late eighteenth and nineteenth century European and European American society ostracized and starved Wheatley literally and figuratively, and white women, as well. Unfortunately, Wheatley's literary daughters still receive this message from our culture today. It can be aptly summed up as a culture which "has, sooner or later, divested itself of the impact of any woman writing or producing art works within it," with all that signifies of the terrible impact of these ceaseless "environmental assaults on self worth" (DuPlessis 1990:52–53).[5]

These examples of ambitious women writers from Wheatley's time and our own, comprising only a few out of untold others, reveal clearly that Wheatley's tragedy was not unique, only multiplied. In her person intersected all three culturally constructed debilitating factors simultaneously—race, gender, and class. Mary Helen Washington, in summarizing

African American literary tradition, specifically sees its record in regard to women artists as just as dismal as the larger European American culture, and has a significant point to make on how its women writers should be incorporated into this tradition:

> Nearly every Afro-American literary history reads the tradition as primarily a male tradition, beginning with the male slave narrative as the source which generates the essential texts in the canon. With absolute predictability, Frederick Douglass's 1845 *Narrative* is the text that issues the call, and the response comes back loud and clear from W.E.B. DuBois, James Weldon Johnson, Richard Wright, James Baldwin, and Ralph Ellison. So firmly established is this male hegemony that even men's arguments with one another (Wright, Baldwin, Ellison) get written into the tradition as a way of interpreting its development. As most feminist critics have noted, women writers cannot simply be inserted into the gaps, or be used to prefigure male writers, the tradition has to be conceptualized from a feminist standpoint. (1987:xxix–xxx)

Whether she was naive or not about the rules of the European colonial Christian game, Wheatley revealed an ambition to pursue the career of a published poet after Susannah Wheatley's death. She did so after her marriage to John Peters, most probably in consultation with Peters as to what were the best means to sell her works. Wheatley then unsuccessfully published an appeal for subscribers for a forthcoming collection of poems, which never materialized. Apparently, Peters believed in advertising as the best means of achieving results, for he did so himself, later. At any rate, when he went bankrupt shortly after their marriage, he was too much preoccupied with basic survival, with foraging around the area for work during a period desperately hard for the Peters family, to continue his promotional efforts.

That he cared deeply about his wife's poetry and career as a poet, whether for financial or personal reasons, or both, can be deduced from the fact that the only evidence of Peters' existence after her death is his advertising in the newspapers for the return of one of his wife's manuscripts. This can be interpreted as a poignant and moving effort by her loyal widower to keep intact, to preserve for himself and posterity, evidences of Wheatley's existence and contributions to society as a poet. It could also be interpreted as an attempt to make capital off her reputation and talents. In any event, Peters left evidence for future historians of one fact: that he outlived her and was not in hiding at the time of her tragic death.

The latter point is of crucial significance. Peters would not have publicized his existence and certainly not have emphasized his relationship to Wheatley if he had abandoned his wife and children to die of starvation and cold. There would be great criticism of such ignoble conduct. However, if Peters was traveling around the area in a fruitless attempt to provide sustenance for them when she and their children died, then that would be a different matter. In no way would Wheatley's shameful death have then implicated Peters and prevented him from showing his face to the world.

Ann Wheatley, the daughter of Wheatley's mistress, who had once tutored Wheatley, attended Wheatley's funeral. How is it she did not assist Wheatley in her dire need? Was Wheatley too proud to inform her of her suffering; that she was not making a go of it on her own, that she had sunk to becoming a maid in a public house?

In any case, Wheatley's career both before and after her release from bondage reveal her as living out the fantasy of what was then in formation as the American success mythology, then (as now) meant for white Christian European American males. However, whereas Wheatley and Franklin (the major exponent of this mythology) began life possessed of all the necessary intellectual attributes, Franklin succeeded admirably. Wheatley failed miserably.

For two centuries after her death in 1784, Wheatley's literary daughters, whether in their lives and/or letters, followed her lead down this dead end for Black women—pursuit of the male American success mythology. And as Wheatley had used the prevalent public discourse of her period, that is, the continental and colonial (later European American) political and religious discourse, together with its forms in both poetry and prose, so did they use the discourse and its forms most in favor in their own times.

Frances E. Watkins Harper (1825–1911), for example, utilized sentimental abolitionist and feminist discourse in her poetry and oratory and in one interesting novel, *Iola LeRoy; or Shadows Uplifted* (1892). In this novel, Harper uses the personal experiences and vocational aspirations of both light- and dark-skinned, lower- and upper-class women to achieve "racial uplift" for the first time in African American literary history:

> "Doctor," continued Iola, "I do not think life's highest advantages are those that we can see with our eyes or grasp with our hands. To whom today is the world most indebted— to its millionaires or to its martyrs? . . . To be . . . the leader of a race to higher planes of thought and action, to teach men clearer views of life and duty, and to inspire their souls with loftier aims, is a far greater privilege than it is to open the gates of material prosperity and fill every home with sensuous enjoyment." There was a rapt and far-off look in her eye, as if she were looking beyond the present pain to a brighter future for the race with which she was identified, and felt the grandeur of a divine commission to labor for its uplifting. (1987:219)

After losing two salesclerk jobs in a row, Iola concludes that "prejudice pursues us through every avenue of life, and assigns us the lowest places." Still, she is determined "to win for myself a place in the fields of labor." Her Uncle Robert advises her to "say nothing about your color." Indignantly, Iola responds that she "sees no necessity for proclaiming the fact on the house-top. Yet I am resolved that nothing shall tempt me to deny it. The best blood in my veins is African blood, and I am not ashamed of it" (Harper 1987:208). She then finds a job in New England, to which she has to commute a long distance because the YWCA refuses to "receive her, . . . virtually shut the door in her face because of the outcast blood in her veins" (Harper 1987:209).

Finally, Iola finds a job close to home. Her employer gives her a job in his store where on the first morning "he called his employees together, and told them that Miss Iola had colored blood in her veins, but that he was going to employ her and give her a desk. If any one objected to working with her, he or she could step to the cashier's desk and receive what was due. Not a

man remonstrated, not a woman demurred; and Iola at last
found a place in the great army of breadwinners, which the
traditions of her blood could not affect" (Harper 1987:211).

Also of interest in *Iola Leroy* is Harper's depiction of Iola's
uncle, Robert Johnson, who express impatience with and
repudiates in a sincere, direct manner the religious solution to
the ills of slavery. This solution, as expressed by Uncle Dan'l, is
also Harper's opportunity to have her characters hilariously
signify on the slaveholders and, among other things, covertly
favor the African cosmogony:

> "Oh, I don't take much stock in white folks' religion," said
> Robert, laughing carelessly. . . .
> "An' I," said Aunt Linda, "neber did belieb in dem Bible
> preachers. I yered one ob dem sayin' wen he war dyin' it war
> all dark wid him. An' de way he treated his house- girl, pore
> thing, I don't wonder dat it war dark with him. . . ."
> "Well," said Tom Anderson, "I belieb in de good ole-time
> religion. But arter dese white folks is done fussin' and beatin'
> de cullud folks, I don't want em to come talking religion to me.
> We used to hab on our place a real Guinea man, an' once he
> made ole Marse mad, an' he had him whipped. Old Marse war
> trying to break him in, but dat fellow war spunk to de
> backbone, an' when he 'gin talkin' to him 'bout savin' his soul
> an' gittin to hebbin, he tole him ef he went to hebbin an' foun'
> he war dare, he wouldn't go in. He wouldn't stay wid any such
> rascal as he war."
> "What became of him?" asked Robert.
> "Oh, he died. But he had some quare notions 'bout
> religion. He thought dat when he died he would go back to his
> ole country. He allers kep' his ole Guinea name."
> ""What was it?"
> "Potobombra. Do you know what he wanted Marster to
> do 'fore he died?" continued Anderson.
> "No."
> "He wanted him to giv him his free papers."
> "Did he do it?"
> "Ob course he did. As de poor fellow war dying an' he
> couldn't sell him in de oder world, he jis' wrote him de papers
> to yumor him. He didn't want to go back to Africa a slave. He
> thought if he did, his people would look down on him, an' he
> wanted to go back a free man. He war orful wek when Marster

brought him de free papers. He jis' ris up in de bed, clutched
dem in his han's, smiled, an' gasped out, 'Ise free at las' an' he
war gone. Oh, but he war spunky. De oberseers, after dey foun'
out who he war, gin'rally gabe him a wide birth [*sic*]. I specs
his father war some ole Guinea king." (Harper 1987:21, 22, 23)

Yet Robert and the others remain sympathetically
portrayed throughout. Perhaps this is Harper's covert signifying
of her own attitude. During this period, when religious and
emotional discourse was expressed "in the conventions of
sentimentalism," when "the mainstream . . . prized rather than
avoided the indulgence of feeling" (Ammons 1917), Harper was
wise enough not to express direct criticism. However, it is clear
that the religiosity of Harper's characters is political in strategy
and "every manifestation of poetic sensibility was by definition a
political act" (Gates, *Figures* 1987:180). This applied even to
spirituals, Gates informs us, which were used partly as a vehicle
for publicizing white slaveholders' sins and partly as a genuine
expression of their own spiritual needs. Harper lovingly depicts
such uses in her descriptions of their shouts and prayer
meetings. Clearly, in these descriptions, a political aspect is
expressed through signifying:

> We has our own good times. An' I want you to come Sunday
> night an' tell all 'bout the good eggs, fish and butter. Mark my
> words, Bobby, we's all gwine to git free. I seed it all in a vision,
> as plain as de nose on yer face.
>   Well, I hope your vision will come out all right, and that
> the eggs will keep and the butter be fresh till we have our next
> meetin'. (Harper 1987:13)

Harper explains the significance of the slaves' sudden
interest in butter and eggs; it was the source of the term
"grapevine," as in "I heard it on the grapevine":

> There seemed to be an unusual interest manifested by these
> men in the state of the produce market, and a unanimous
> report of its good condition. Surely there was nothing in the
> primeness of the butter or the freshness of the eggs to change
> careless looking faces into such expressions of gratification, or
> to light dull eyes with such gladness. What did it mean?

During the dark days of the Rebellion, when the bondman was turning his eyes to the American flag and learning to hail it as an ensign of deliverance, some of the shrewder slaves, coming in contact with their masters and overhearing their conversations, invented a phraseology to convey in the most unsuspected manner news to each other from the battle-field. . . . In conveying tidings of the war, if they wished to announce a victory of the Union army, they said the butter was fresh, or that the fish and eggs were in good condition. If defeat befell them, then the butter and other produce were rancid or stale. (1987:8–9)

By explaining to her readers the serious signifying that went on during "the Rebellion," and depicting it in its lighter manifestations, Harper is opening up this ancient African technique to the observation of white readers, perhaps for the first time in American literary history. Harper consciously utilizes "the dozens" as a rhetorical and aesthetic device, among other things, to convey an elderly slave couple's intense love for and devotion to one another far better than if the author were to describe it herself. In the course of doing so, she has old John Salters reveal his wife's (Aunt Lindy's) Bookerite economic philosophy:

"Arter de war war ober I had a little money, an' I war gwine ter rent a plantation on sheers an' git out a good stan' ob cotton. Cotton war bringin' orful high prices den, but Lindy said to me, Now, John, you'se got a lot ob money, an' you'd better salt it down. I'd rather lib on a little piece ob lan' ob my own dan a big piece ob somebody else's. Well, I says to Lindy, I dun know nuthin 'bout buyin' lan', an' I'se 'fraid arter I'se don buyed it an put all de marrer ob dese bones in it, dat somebody's far-off cousing will come an' say de title ain't good, an I'll lose it all."

"You're right thar, John," said Uncle Daniel. "White man's so unsartin, black man's nebber safe."

"But somehow," continued Salters, "Lindy warn't satisfied wid rentin', so I buyed a piece ob lan', an' I'se glad now I'se got it. Lindy's got a lot ob gumption; knows most as much as a man. She ain't got dat long head fer nuffin. She's got lots ob sense, but I don't like to tell her so."

"Why not?" asked Iola. "Do you think it would make her feel too happy?"

"Well, it don't do ter tell you women how much we thinks obs you. It sets you up too much." (1987:172–173)

Meanwhile, Harper's readers are painfully aware of the true depths of the relationship; to what lengths Salters went to reconstruct it: "We war married long 'fore de war. But my ole Marster sole me away from her an' our little gal, an' den sole her chile ter somebody else. Arter freedom, I hunted up our little gal, an foun' her. She war a big woman den. Den I com'd right back ter dis place an' foun' Lindy. She hedn't married agin, nuther hed I; so we jis' let de parson marry us out er de book; an' we war mighty glad ter git togedder agin, an' feel hitched togedder fer life" (1987:167). [6]

Like Harper, Wheatley's literary daughters combined private goals and public persona in their work. They viewed and depicted private experiences as individual examples of collective experience. Even in Elizabeth Keckley's autobiography *Behind the Scenes, Or Thirty Years a Slave, and Four Years in the White House* (1868), Keckley (1824?–1907) used the opportunity to write an extensive and detailed apologia for the conduct of her friend, Mary Todd Lincoln.

Characteristic of African American women writers' work from the beginning is the dual voice pattern, the commingled sensibility of self and the *communitas*, until the work of Jessie Redmon Fauset (1882–1961). It was she who first defined her heroines' experiences as private, unique, and individual. Thus for the first time one sees in African American women's writing the reflection of a European American world view in which human beings are "alone in a crowd," separate entities with an isolated ego-driven life-style, regardless of how many relationships swirl around them. In addition to Jessie Fauset, Nella Larsen (1893–1963), and Ann Petry (1911–), also preferred marching to their own drum rather than bearing the standard aloft for their group. In Deborah McDowell's words about Fauset's heroine in *Plum Bun* (1928): "Angela's self-sufficiency is, significantly, uncovered and sustained by work, and her work becomes empowering. While all of her experiences with power have hitherto been formed by the relational, involving a dialectic of dominance and submission, after her affair with Roger power becomes associated in her mind with individual capacity or the power to act independently. . . . She has developed an independence and autonomy that needs ratification neither from men nor marriage" (1989:xxi).

Interestingly, Fauset's novels begin not "like a classic fairy tale," as McDowell claims, but with middle-aged couples who believe they are successful, that they have fulfilled the American dream: couples who seem to have been Bookerites. Their daughters, however, like Angela Murray of *Plum Bun*, prefer the Cinderella myth, the fairy tale, to their parents' "latter-day Iliad":

> To Junius and Mattie Murray, who had known poverty and homelessness, the little house on Opal Street represented the *ne plus ultra* of ambition; to their daughter Angela it seemed the dingiest, drabbest chrysalis that had ever fettered the wings of a brilliant butterfly. The stories which Junius and Mattie told of difficulties overcome, of the arduous learning of trades, of the pitiful scraping together of infinitesimal savings, would have made a latter-day Iliad, but to Angela they were merely a description of a life which she at any cost would avoid living. Somewhere in the world were paths which lead to broad thoroughfares, large, bright houses, delicate niceties of existence. Those paths Angela meant to find and frequent. (McDowell 1989:12)

Fauset is not only following after Wheatley, but after the example of Maria Stewart, who wrote and orated on behalf of and to African American women (and men) fifty years after Wheatley's death. But generally, Wheatley's literary daughters all through the nineteenth and into the twentieth century, into the twenties and the Harlem Renaissance, not only followed her practice of a unified personal and political persona in their work, but also wrote as she did in the forms and language conventionally accepted at the time they wrote. In retrospect, this strategy backfired more often than it succeeded. Many took it as part of "racial uplift" to learn and use "proper English" (by white European American standards, that is), and to abjure Black idiom.

For example, Angelina Weld Grimke, Georgia Douglas Johnson, and Alice Dunbar-Nelson are all described by McDowell as "avoiding racial themes in their poetry. Instead, they wrote 'traditional feminine' lyrics treating 'themes of love, death, sorrow, nature, selfhood and identity'" (1989:949). Given such a cast of mind, we can understand why his wife berated Paul Laurence Dunbar (1872–1906) for "selling out," i.e., writing in dialect, or what he himself contemptuously referred to as his "jingles in a broken tongue" (Emanuel 1968:37). These poems, supposedly about antebellum plantation life, were comic fantasies for white readers like William Dean Howells (the influential editor of *The Atlantic Monthly* and a novelist in his own right). Although Dunbar achieved a modicum of financial success, status, and respect, at least with whites and some Blacks like James Weldon Johnson (1871–1938), his relegation to writing dialect poetry on demand frustrated him, as Johnson records: "You know, of course, that I didn't start as a dialect poet. I simply came to the conclusion that I could write it as well, if not better, than anybody else I knew of, and that by doing so I should gain a hearing. I gained the hearing, and now they don't want me to write anything but dialect" (Johnson 1961:160), Dunbar bitterly complained to his friend.

For his part, Dunbar preferred to write in "standard English," what he called his "deeper notes," in contrast to his enforced "jingles." Because of dialect verse's inferiority, he brooded ceaselessly, his hopes ever diminishing, about acceptance into the European American literary canon of greatness. According to Long and Collier, Dunbar "was haunted by a feeling of failure because the dialect poems, not the standard poems were considered the more important" (1985:218).

Five years later, just before the great poet's death at the age of thirty-three, Johnson records that Dunbar was in a state of great depression, that he suffered the torments of the damned because he believed he had wasted his talent: "I've kept on doing the same things, and doing them no better. I have never gotten to the things I really wanted to do" (Johnson 1961:161), he mourned.

Dunbar was an American by birth and training and an African by ancestry. As such, he was to a large extent the product of the American dream machine, as are we all: the myth that anyone can achieve individual success. At that time, Booker T. Washington's efforts had succeeded in stretching the myth to include a few token Black men, like himself and Dunbar, providing they played along with the myth. If Dunbar wished to publish in white publications, he could pretend to be a color-neutral writer who employed European American genres and aesthetic techniques and whose persona and voice were rational, dignified, universal. In the Gilded Age, African Americans had to write as if they were European American, both professionally and in the material they used. If they did attempt to write as Blacks, their material had to be mutilated according to the white notion of how Blacks would write (dialect in jingles) and what their experiences and personalities were like (antics on the plantation).

In order to achieve one part of the American dream, Dunbar felt that he was trapped and forced into writing "plantation jingles" for the European American audience that did not want his European American material. He felt that his artistic creativity and talent were thereby minimized, since he wanted to publish this "universal" material, as well as his dialect poetry. At the same time that he was geared for financial success by European American standards, he was also geared for aesthetic success by those same standards. He considered himself an American poet, trained and proficient in the standard European American techniques of poetry like the Shakespearean or Petrarchan sonnet, for example. As such, he wished to be successful on aesthetic elitist grounds, as well as on financial ones. However, he was only permitted to write in dialect, to act the stereotypical Black-face minstrel recording the supposed doings of happy-go-lucky slaves on an antebellum plantation. Ironically, according to Gates, "It is not that Dunbar wrought music in dialect [as Dunbar snobbishly imagined]; dialect wrought music in Dunbar's best poetry" (*Figures* 1987:179).

A question arises here; if Dunbar hadn't internalized the all-pervasive American success mythology so well, would he have spared himself suffering because he was born and bred of that society but prevented from contributing to it as a full participant?[7] This was a dilemma, "this double-consciousness" of the African American, as DuBois defined it in his great meditation, *The Souls of Black Folk* (1903). Selwyn Cudjoe terms it, more appropriately in relation to African American women, "double jeopardy" (1984:7).

Both Dunbar-Nelson and Dunbar valorized elitist European/European American discourse and forms over African/African American ones. Like European Americans, they equated the "slave idiom," customs, manners, cuisine, and religion with ignorance and the primitive. Long after Dunbar's death, whenever Dunbar-Nelson went out on speaking engagements, she was begged to perform Dunbar's dialect poems, even though she was deeply involved in and solely interested in her own career and her own ideas. For example, when she lectured on the "Negro's Literary Reaction to American Life," a very important topic (if only because it also reflects in some measure this work's topic), she angrily records of her audience: "Of course, they would want to hear dialect Dunbar at the end. Makes me sick" (1984:303).

Dunbar-Nelson's view has always been common. In fact, Wheatley has long been considered by critics to have held it uncritically. In previous chapters I have sought to dispel that belief, however. Nor was it shared by Zora Neal Hurston, whom I discuss in Chapter Five, who was excoriated by Richard Wright for her use of Black folk material. He found her embarrassing. For her part, she scathingly signified on Blacks who held this point of view as "Niggeratti." Although Hurston seemed to have lost this battle in her lifetime, she ended by winning the war long afterward. The civil rights, Black arts, and feminist movements all paved the way for Alice Walker's enormous success in recuperating Hurston and her unabashed, proud use of "Black dialect" for posterity. In fact, Walker, erudite and well-educated, chose to write an entire work in dialect, *The Color Purple*, which I discuss in Chapter Six. Walker wrote this work at least partially in tribute to Hurston's position, and to make a conscious political statement.

Unlike Hurston and Walker, the majority of Wheatley's literary daughters chose to follow Wheatley's strategy of indirection, employing the most widely used and conventional of public white European surface discourse. Like her, they attempted by these means to avoid unduly disquieting, antagonizing, threatening, or intimidating their white European American, primarily female, readership. However, *seeming* accommodationism and conformity with their audience's tastes in their writing does not necessarily betoken a matching message. It might, though, betoken that the writers are signifying on their readers as I maintain Wheatley did on occasion. Signifying is a means to an end. It was used to manipulate European, and later, European American audiences for a variety of reasons, primarily political, economic, and social.

Hurston again is the spoiler here. She doesn't apologize to her white audiences for the Black content of her work, for her characters, and/or any aspect of their lives, and/or her books, although sometimes she acts as mediator between the two.[8] At any rate, after Wheatley, African American women writers, including even Hurston, were as sanguine as Wheatley had been about her white readership. They all believed that once informed of the truth and aware of it, their readers would realize that their enslavement and oppression of Africans was untenable. Especially since European Americans believed themselves to be and boasted at every opportunity that they were the most rational, civilized, and advanced culture on earth. It would follow then that these readers would act to alleviate the horrendous conditions (which they had created in the first place), rather than continue as conscious wrongdoers and therefore be made to squirm by recognition of their hypocrisy in the matter.

Like Wheatley, her successors chose to vent furious indignation against slavery and racist and sexist oppression indirectly, through the safety valve of the mask, of signifying forms. They did this, Sidonie Smith explains, because they believed that the mask is the "prerequisite for a less onerous existence, even for sheer survival itself." She sees the mask as the aggregate of signifying in all forms: "The slave learned to perfect the game of 'puttin' on ole Massa!' Deceit, cunning, fawning ingratiation, stupidity—these were only some of the many faces of his mask, a subtle psychological device to prevent the master from knowing what was really happening in the mind and heart of the 'darky'. . . . The mask was an oblique means of rebellion within the system as the Black slave became a confidence man par excellence" (1974:14, 15, 16).

Again, like Wheatley's, the tempers of her successors, for example, Harriet Jacobs, would on occasion wear thin. That is, the mask would sometimes hang too heavy and slip. Instead of careful and politic language and tone, a *saevo indignationis* might on occasion reveal itself.[9] In my discussion of Harriet Jacobs in the following chapter, readers will observe such eruptions of passionate anger dissolving the mask of civility, equanimity, gentility, and sentimentality which comprised Jacobs' favored mode of signifying expression. Ordinarily, however, signifying rather than a direct expression of outrage was the favored technique for such a delicate and difficult project as attempting crucial perspective shifts in white readers.

From Wheatley's time onward until the Black Arts movement of the sixties, white Northern middle and upper class readers, primarily female, comprised the African American women writers' audience. Paradoxically, once African American women writers were no longer especially writing for any other audience than their own community, they succeeded in reaching their largest audience in their literary history, as Gates points out. Responsible for this gratifying result was the feminist movement which he claims (generously giving credit where credit is due), created a demand for and a consequent surge in readership:

> What has happened, clearly, is that the feminist movement, in the form of women's studies on campus and the abandonment of quotas for the admission of women to heretofore elite male institutions, has had a direct impact on what we might think of as black women's studies. Indeed, black studies and women's studies have met on the common terrain of black women's studies, ensuring a larger audience for black women authors than ever before. Scholars of women's studies have accepted the work and lives of black women as their subject matter in a manner unprecedented in the American academy. Perhaps only the Anglo-American abolitionist movement was as

cosmopolitan as the women's movement has been in its
concern for the literature of blacks. ("Tell Me, Sir," 1990:13–14)

Nevertheless, signifying continues to be used and has been
and is, more frequently than not, still meant to be invisible to
white European American readers. It is used as an "in-joke," a
"coded language," a kind of password to which only its inner
circle of users, Africans/African Americans and other diaspora
Africans, have access. White readers' education (and consequently their world view, and thus their notion of rhetoric and
aesthetics) is necessarily limited to European and American
tradition and praxis, as pointed out in my introductory chapter.
So it is that signifying continues to remain invisible to such
readers, even most feminists and women's studies scholars.

Like Wheatley, her literary daughters internalized the
American success mythology meant for white men. And like
Wheatley, they all failed in that pursuit. Consequently, their
writing achieves tension and complexity as a result of much of it
being devoted to the gap between the dream they pursue and the
reality they experience. Like Wheatley, whose life and work
paralleled Franklin's, they struggle to "make it," acknowledging
the help of relatives, friends, and their community along the
way. However, their work, as did Wheatley's, shows a
modification of those European and colonial enlightenment
concepts of the individual which Franklin embodied in the
mythology which emerged from his life and works. This
modification was due to African concepts which embedded
individuals within a community. Unlike Franklin or Emerson,
they do not emphasize the primacy of an integer as an integer; of
a single individual's efforts toward unique personal goals.

The ongoing hegemony of the concept of the individual in
the European American world view cannot be emphasized too
strongly. That "the dominant American national trait was self-
reliance," that "the solitary individual [was] . . . the true social
unit," accompanied by "a belief in political individualism"
(Fellman 1990:552, 561) has been inculcated into both African
American and European American males and internalized by
American females from the early seventeenth century onward.
This to the point of seeming natural and instinctive. After so

much practice, translation, substitution, and appropriation become automatic, second nature. For example, note Emerson's famed "generic" *pronunciamento* in "Self Reliance": "Whoso would be a man must be a non-conformist." This keystone of American success mythology deconstructs to resoundingly betray its context: white European American males only. To Emerson and to this chosen group, women are distant objectified Others, one part of a large group of Others who might in some way prevent the male, the norm, the center, the standard, from fulfillment of his potential, his destiny:

> Live no longer to the expectation of these deceived and deceiving people with whom we converse. Say to them, O father, O mother, O wife, O brother, O friend, I have lived with you after appearances hitherto. Henceforward I am the truth's. Be it known unto you that henceforward I obey no law less than the eternal law. I will have no covenants but proximities. I shall endeavor to nourish my parents, to support my family, to be the chaste husband of one wife,—but these relations I must fill after a new and unprecedented way. I appeal from your customs. I must be myself. I cannot break myself any longer for you, or you. If you can love me for what I am, we shall be the happier. . . .(Ammons 1990:152) [10]

This discourse, common to Emerson, Franklin before him, and to almost every other masculine icon of our culture (except Walt Whitman) excludes every category of human being except white European American males. In order to translate this discourse and any and all parts of the American dream to relate to them, all other groups have had to interrupt the flow as they read in order to add gender nouns and pronouns and race and ethnic adjectives at every point where the author uses the "generic" masculine.

On the other hand, from Wheatley onward and even before, emphasis is always placed on the role of the African/African American writer as mediating between one's own smaller community and a larger, hostile society. Most typically, the perspective assumed by the writing persona seems on the surface to actually replicate the society's. This can be seen as late as in Anna Julia Cooper (1859–1964), author of *A Voice from the South* (1892), when she speaks eloquently for and to her race, as well as to her sisters, for example in "The Higher Education of Women":

> Whence came this apotheosis of greed and cruelty? Whence this sneaking admiration we all have for bullies and prize-fighters? Whence the self-congratulation of "dominant" races, as if "dominant" meant "righteous" and carried with it a title to inherit the earth? Whence the scorn of so-called weak or unwarlike races and individuals, and the very comfortable assurance that it is their manifest destiny to be wiped out as vermin before this advancing civilization? As if the possession of the Christian graces of meekness, non-resistance and forgiveness, were incompatible with a civilization professedly based on Christianity, the religion of love! . . . How like Longfellow's Iagoo, we Westerners are, to be sure! In the few hundred years, we have had to strut across our allotted territory and bask in the afternoon sun, we imagine we have exhausted the possibilities of humanities. Verily, we are the people, and after us there is none other. Our God is power; strength, our standard of excellence, inherited from barbarian ancestors through a long line of male progenitors, the Law Salic permitting no feminine modifications. (Shockley 1989:210–211)

However, this strategy can also be seen as early as Wheatley's work, or Lucy Terry's "The Bars Fight" (1746), about a Native American retaliation against European colonial settlers in Vermont. Terry's discourse and perspective is that of the settlers.

Nevertheless, since Wheatley and her descendants perceive themselves as striving first and foremost for freedom, as conscious representatives of a Black African sourced community, perhaps there is some technique they used to bridge the gap between having to please their audience on the one hand (an audience which rigidly censored them) and, on the other hand, convey a different message entirely to their own group, such as I have shown being done in Harper's *Iola Leroy*. In my discussion of Wheatley I suggested that there was indeed such a technique, and that technique was signifying.

By the late nineteenth century, African American women writers demand civil and human rights for their group as one unit synchronous with themselves. Once and/or whether or not achieved for themselves, success in whatever form is to be used to "uplift" or improve the lot of their group. Again, characteristically, the writers of this period see themselves as mediating between a hostile white society and their own group to effect their group's improvement. Generally, like their antecedents, they use the prevailing discourse of the period as a strategy to disarm their audience.

From approximately 1848 to 1895, Frederick Douglass (1817–1895), is generally credited as if he were alone in such efforts. Without diminishing his contribution in any way, his example alone was not sufficient to convey either the literary gamut of the freedom narrative, or the political gamut of his platform. For just one example of many others, Harriet Jacobs (whom I discuss in the following chapter), like Douglass and Harper, saw herself as mediating in her life and work on behalf of African American women to European American women.

In this work I maintain that there existed another success mythology for women. I call it "the Cinderella myth," and argue that it was used in a variety of ways by the writers under discussion: to reinforce the American male success mythology, to run parallel to it, and even to subsume it. The Cinderella myth is an equally powerful, equally influential success myth for women as is the male success myth for both men and women, and as universal in its irresistible qualities.

The American male success mythology's charismatic force on European/European American culture is well documented. At this writing, Eastern European culture appears to be gravitating toward ever greater acceptance of it. The power of this success myth and its apparently unprecedented possibility of fulfillment have drawn millions to our shores. Most human beings on this planet exist in the conditions of the famous poem by Emma Lazarus inscribed on the base of the Statue of Liberty: "Give me your tired, your poor/ Your huddled masses yearning to breathe free/ The wretched refuse of your teeming shore/ I lift my lamp beside the golden door." Gold imagery has always been linked to this myth, from the European immigrants who maintained that "the streets were paved with gold," to the

Chinese immigrants who called this country "the gold mountain."

The Cinderella myth, although it causes no overt immigration, is just as universal in its appeal. It is evident to anyone who watches television, goes to the movies, reads the newspaper, popular magazines, and books that billions of dollars are spent annually on a mind-boggling array of products, all of which promise women fulfillment of the Cinderella myth. This does not include the countless hours spent by girls and women in fantasy. To give just a few examples from the media, note the enormous popularity of Harlequin romances, the recent films *Working Girl* and *Pretty Woman,* and the enduring popularity of works like Jane Austen's *Pride and Prejudice,* and Alice Walker's *The Color Purple.*

This myth surfaces whenever African American women writers reflect something more than the harsh reality of economics, of questions of survival, which have always played a large part in their lives and works. It surfaces whenever African American women writers reflect something more than the need and/or drive for vocation, for material and worldly success.

The question then arises as to whether and to what extent the Cinderella myth influenced Wheatley and her successors' choices in life. What emphases did they place on Cinderella trajectories in their lives and texts? For example, what impact did this myth have on such crucial decisions as to whether or not to write privately and/or publish, whether and whom to marry, what their heroines would do/not do with their lives, etc.?

As long as males have had hero figures to model themselves on, for so long have females had a parallel source of emulation in Cinderella. Her myth has been traced as far back as the ninth century A.D. in China, when it was first written down, and is found all over the globe, according to Bruno Bettelheim.[11]

There are significant differences between the male success myth and the Cinderella myth. From ancient times, the male model for a hero has been a roving, mobile one. Whether Odysseus, sacker of cities, or Benjamin Franklin, founding father, the male model covers a large space in the sweep of his life trajectory. He traverses large distances, and his life is described over a long period of time. The female model is static, homebound. The male is always subject, center stage forward. She is used as background and Other/Object. The male performs tasks, meets difficult challenges—each one different—in order to achieve goals involving physical strength and mental ingenuity. The female's challenges are petty, repetitious, grinding on day after day. She is confined indoors to the women's quarters, the same limited site. Thus the stress on the woman is internal, acute, psychological.

In analyzing the two models, it is clear that the female model replicates those of the authors I discuss in this work and the lives of contemporary women (and many men). In the United States, we live a daily grind. Our problems are generally mundane and repetitious, changing slightly, if at all, over lengthy periods of time. Few of us, male or female, get to travel widely. Certainly not as a matter of course. Few of us have exciting adventures or get to meet new characters at every turn, each more exotic, glamorous, and/or grotesque than the last. Most of us, in fact, work at the same site with the same cast of characters year after year after year.

At this point, it might be useful to review the common cliches which form the major elements of the European American male success myth. This myth can be traced to Franklin's *Poor Richard's Almanack* (1733–1758), especially *The Way to Wealth* (1758), and his *Autobiography* (1771), although Emerson (1803–1882), in his essays, especially in "The Divinity School Address" (1838), and "Self-Reliance" (1841), and Thoreau (1817–1862), in *Civil Disobedience* (1849), and *Walden* (1854) are responsible for a few more elements. Also, since Franklin was the son of Puritans and the others are descendants of that group, it is safe to say that "the Protestant work ethic" can be traced back to the Puritans who landed on Cape Cod on November 11, 1620. Franklin's pithy sayings were for the most part not original, either. He culled them from European almanac writers and anonymous folk sayings.

Regardless of origin, most Americans would agree that the following cliches with which we are all familiar, were meant for certain landed, white, heterosexual, Christian males in a fiercely competitive world. They do not extend to men and women of color, white women, the differently abled, the elderly, and homosexual:

> Idle hands are the devil's workshop. (Puritans)
> Go from rags to riches.
> Pull yourself up by your own bootstraps.
> Good old Yankee ingenuity.
> A rugged individual/self-reliant.
> Make it big by forty.
> Six feet tall, with blue eyes and blond hair.
> A veteran.
> Born in a log cabin. (or equivalent)
> Become something.
> Make something from nothing.
> Burn the midnight oil.
> A stitch in time saves nine.
> The early bird catches the worm.
> Make hay while the sun shines.
> Early to bed/Early to rise/Makes a man/Healthy, wealthy, and wise.
> A penny saved is a penny earned.
> Inconsistency is the hobgoblin of little minds. (Emerson)
> Whoso would be a man must be a non-conformist. (Emerson)
> March to a different drummer. (Thoreau)

Notes

1. bell hooks, "Feminisms and Black Women's Studies," *SAGE* VI.1 (Summer 1989): 54–56, states on this issue: "The prevailing nineteenth century assumption that Black men and women had to work side by side to eradicate racism gave way as the assumption gained prominence that liberatory change was furthered by Black women standing behind Black men" (54). Also see Susan A. Mann, "Slavery, Sharecropping, and Sexual Inequality," *Signs* 14:4 (Summer 1989): 774–798. "Nevertheless, a number of historians (including feminist and Afro-American historians) suggest that it was normative behavior for Black women slaves and sharecroppers to accept male domestic authority" (787). And "There were certain duties considered women's work that

men declined to do. Thus it appears that, although slave women experienced a masculinization of their roles, slave men did not experience a corresponding feminization of their roles, despite all the attention academics have paid to the so-called emasculated Black male and family structures. Indeed, rather than either the equality or matriarchy claimed by some writers, it seems that slave households were in fact characterized by patriarchy" (795).

2. As I argued previously, this position is articulated most eloquently and persuasively by Elsa Barkley Brown. It is her contention that such a development has been sourced by the conditions of African American women's lives. These conditions, Barkley Brown argues, dictated, *a priori*, the necessity of accepting seemingly mutually exclusive paradigms or world views.

3. Marilyn French is even more pessimistic on this issue: "The only winner permitted in American art is the white male rampant." "A Choice We Never Chose," *The Women's Review of Books* VIII. 10–11 (July 1991): 31.

4. He goes on to complete his definition over two pages: "Its source is the African Signifying Monkey—he who dwells at the margins of discourse, ever punning, ever troping, ever embodying the ambiguities of language—is our trope for repetition and revision, indeed our trope of chiasmus itself, repeating and reversing simultaneously as he does in one deft discursive act. If Vico and Burke or Nietzsche, de Man, and Bloom are correct in identifying four and six master tropes, then we might think of these as the master's tropes and of signifying as the slave's trope, the trope of tropes, as Bloom characterizes metalepsis, a trope-reversing trope, a figure of a figure. Signifying is a trope in which are subsumed several other rhetorical tropes, including metaphor, metonymy, synecdoche, and irony (the master tropes), and also hyperbole and litotes, and metalepsis (Bloom's supplement to Burke). To this list we could easily add aporia, chiasmus, and catechesis, all of which are used in the ritual of signifying. . . . Signifying, it is clear, in black discourse means modes of figuration itself. When one signifies, as Kimberly W. Bentson puns, one 'tropes-a-dope.' Indeed, the black tradition itself has its own subdivisions of signifying, which we could readily identify with the typology of figures received from classical and medieval rhetoric, as Bloom has done with his 'map of misprision.' The black rhetorical tropes, subsumed under signifying, would include marking, loud-talking, testifying, calling out (of one's name), sounding, rapping, playing the dozens, and so on" (Gates, *Figures* 1987:236–237). Much of this language is esoteric. Perhaps Gates is himself signifying in these passages on his European/European American critical sources. However, the context of what he has to say is

significant: that signifying is just as complex a structure as the European American rhetorical and aesthetic techniques to which he is referring (or "capping on" in signifying terminology). For a good, clear, concise summary of Gates's definition, see Nathan Grant, "Image and Text in Jacob Lawrence," *Black American Literature Forum* 23.3 (Fall 1988): 523–537; esp. 528–529.

5. On this issue see also Barbara Haile and Audreye E. Johnson, "Teaching and Learning about Black Women: The Anatomy of a Course," *SAGE* VI.1 (Summer 1989): 72.

6. In this instance the couple displays deep love underlying their "insults." See my Introduction for a noticeable difference in purpose for the signifying. In Hurston's *Their Eyes Were Watching God*, the couple uses the dozens to convey animosity toward one another.

7. Haile and Johnson comment on this dilemma: "Coping with the inclusion-exclusion dilemma [for African Americans] is at the very heart of the identity struggle, and may generate powerful feelings of rage and indignation. The dilemma is further confounded by a conflict between Euro-American and African-American value systems. The task, then, is for the Black female to establish some workable balance between the two value systems, this double consciousness that DuBois and others have talked about" (1989:72).

8. Deborah Plant in "Narrative Strategies in Zora Neale Hurston's *Dust Tracks On a Road" SAGE* VI.1 (Summer 1989): 18–23, makes an excellent defense of Hurston against the charge by Nathan Huggins and others that Hurston "compromised her authentic voice" because she catered too much to her white audience.

9. Swift felt so strongly about inhuman humans, in his case, the English oppressors of the Irish, that he recorded it on his tombstone. "Here lies one who died of 'saevo indignationis,'" i.e., "ferocious indignation." He was born in Ireland, of English ancestry, and thus was Anglo-Irish. His doubleness of perspective is similar to that of American signifiers of African ancestry.

10. Further down on the page, Emerson adds other elements to his list besides "father, mother" (although omitting "wife"). These elements include non-human potential barriers to unfettered self-expression in Emerson's list, namely: "cousin, neighbor, town, cat, and dog."

11. See pp. 236–277 for his discussion of the Cinderella myth.

References

Ammons, Elizabeth. *The Heath Anthology of American Literature*. Eds. Paul Lauter et al. Vol. I. New York: Heath, 1990.

Baer, Sylvia. "Holding Onto the Vision: Sylvia Baer Interviews Paule Marshall." *The Women's Review of Books* VIII.10–11 (July 1991): 24–25.

Baker, Houston, Jr. *The Journey Back: Issues in Black Literature and Criticism*. Chicago: University of Chicago Press, 1980.

Bettelheim, Bruno. *The Uses of Enchantment: The Meaning and Importance of Fairy Tales*. New York: Alfred A. Knopf, 1976.

Cudjoe, Selwyn. "Maya Angelou and the Autobiographical Statement." In *Black Women Writers: 1950–1980*. Ed. Mari Evans. New York: Anchor Doubleday, 1984.

Dangarembga, Tsitsi. "This Year, Next Year. . . ." *The Women's Review of Books*. VIII.10–11 (July 1991): 43.

Dunbar-Nelson, Alice. *Give Us Each Day: The Diary of Alice Dunbar-Nelson*. Ed. and Intro. Gloria Hull. New York: Norton, 1984.

DuPlessis, Rachel Blau. *The Pink Guitar: Writing as Feminist Practice*. New York: Routledge, 1990.

Emanuel, James A and Theodore L. Gross, eds. *Dark Symphony: Negro Literature in America*. New York: Macmillan, 1968.

Fauset, Jessie. *Plum Bun*. Ed. Deborah E. McDowell. Boston: Beacon Press, 1990. First printed, 1928.

Fellman, Anita Clair. "Laura Ingalls Wilder and Rose Wilder Lane: The Politics of a Mother-Daughter Relationship." *Signs*. 15.3 (Spring 1990): 532–561.

French, Marilyn. "A Choice We Never Chose." *The Women's Review of Books* VIII.10–11 (July 1991): 31–32.

Gates, Henry Louis, Jr. *Figures in Black: Words, Signs, and the "Racial Self."* New York: Oxford University Press, 1987.

———. "Introduction: 'Tell Me, Sir, . . . What is "Black" Literature?'" *PMLA* 105.1 (January 1990): 11–22.

Haile, Barbara J. and Audreye E. Johnson. "Teaching and Learning About Black Women: The Anatomy of a Course." *SAGE* VI.1 (Summer 1989): 69–73.

Harper, Frances E. W. *Iola LeRoy, Or, Shadows Uplifted*. Intro. Hazel Carby. Boston: Beacon Press, 1987. First printed, 1892.

Hernton, Calvin. *The Sexual Mountain and Black Women Writers: Adventures in Sex, Literature, and Real Life*. New York: Anchor, 1987.

Johnson, James Weldon. *Along this Way: An Autobiography of James Weldon Johnson*. New York: Viking Press, 1961. First printed, 1933.

Keyser, Elizabeth. "Alcott's Portraits of the Artist as Little Women." *International Journal of Women's Studies* 5.5 (November–December 1982): 445–459.

Long, Richard A. and Eugenia Collier, eds. *Afro-American Writing: An Anthology of Prose and Poetry*. University Park: Pennsylvania State University Press, 1985.

Marshall, Paule. *Brown Girl, Brownstones*. New York: The Feminist P, 1981. First printed, 1959.

McDowell, Deborah E. "Review of *Color, Sex, and Poetry: Three Women Writers of the Harlem Renaissance* by Gloria Hull." *Signs* 14.4 (Summer 1989): 948–952.

Shockley, Ann Allen, Ed. *Afro-American Women Writers 1746–1933: An Anthology and Critical Guide*. New York: New American Library, 1989.

Smith, Sidonie. *Where I'm Bound: Patterns of Slavery and Freedom in Black American Autobiography*. Westport, CT: Greenwood Press, 1974.

Washington, Mary Helen. *Invented Lives: Narratives of Black Women 1860–1960*. New York: Anchor Doubleday, 1987.

HARRIET JACOBS'S USE OF SELF-IMAGE
TO REPRESENT COLLECTIVE SELF

Harriet Jacobs had many reasons for choosing to make public a life replete with personal humiliation and losses: to participate to the fullest in the abolitionist and feminist movement to improve the condition of women of her race; to engage in whatever work this effort necessitated to counter negative stereotypes prevalent about Black women (primarily sexual slanders); to reverse negative sexual propaganda about Black women, in particular, and other invalidating stereotypes and beliefs about Blacks in general; to educate middle and upper class Northern white women about the true realities of the situation of Black female slaves through lectures and first-person written accounts; to raise Northern white women's consciousness so they would be sympathetic to and support Black slave women; to get white women to project into Black slave women's experiences, to identify with them, understand them, to have compassion for their predicaments, and in so doing, learn to respect their Black sisters; to make white women aware of the general oppression and injustice against slaves of all sexes and ages; to focus on the injustices, vices, and weaknesses of the group with whom her white female readers were trained to identify, namely, white men; to get white women to realize that any one of them could be related by consanguinity to these white masters and mistresses; and finally, to get white women to actively work to improve conditions for their Black sisters, a group with whom they were trained not to identify.

It is my contention that Jacobs integrated these diverse goals by signifying. In previous chapters I suggested that Wheatley occasionally used this technique. In this chapter, I maintain that Jacobs did so, as well. Both authors intended to give whites what they wanted to hear in the mode of discourse with which they were most comfortable: what was characteristically heard in church, in the theatre and opera, in political orations, and in fiction and poetry. Baker calls this tactic by Blacks "shaping an expression to fit the marketplace" (1984:38). And the consequences for Black autobiographers, given such a hostile marketplace? According to Craig Werner, a super-sensitivity to European American discourse, if nothing else. But of course there was something else:

> Having attracted this internally divided audience, black autobiographers attempted to reshape its priorities, to increase awareness of the sympathy for aspects of Afro-American experience (individual and communal) alien to, and probably incompatible with, the unrecognized premises of Euro-American thought. In this extremely delicate rhetorical situation, the individual autobiographer was forced to maintain constant awareness of how each segment of the white audience was likely to interpret each statement. Any rhetorical gesture which alerted the audience to the underlying project of redefining the discursive structure risked alienating either "sympathetic" or "neutral" audiences, each of which was likely to resist direct assaults on its sense of moral (or intellectual or cultural) superiority. (Werner 1990:205–206)

Both Wheatley and Jacobs chose to present their cases for themselves in this sophisticated manner: as individuals and as representatives/spokespersons for their group publicly, and in as diplomatic and non-threatening a manner as possible. On the surface, that is. They both bent over backwards to safeguard against violating their readers' sensibilities (i.e., deep-seated prejudices). Again, as Werner points out astutely in this regard: "At the outset, the Afro-American writer must be aware that, whatever its ostensible politics—abolitionist or apologist, conservative or liberal—the white audience is likely to have internalized, often on an un- or a semi-conscious level, aspects of the discursive formation that denies or questions black humanity" (1990:205). To this end, Wheatley and Jacobs employed discourse to psychologically facilitate in their readers the most powerful arousal of sympathy possible: discourse which would not arouse extraneous thoughts or emotions to dilute their readers' attention in any way.

For her purposes, Wheatley had used her English/colonial audience's Christian religious and European discourse in rhymed heroic couplets before segueing into the necessity of freeing Africans from their chains. In the same manner, Jacobs, targeting her audience as Northern white females, couched her narrative in the most currently used, most fashionable discourse of the period—sentimental discourse. In this discourse was embedded her audience's most cherished religious, social, and political sentiments. In addition, Jacobs also utilized prevalent American mythologies. In American narrative of the period (and, in fact, of any period), this was the American success myth. It was dear to both sexes, and is even now, if only vicariously for too many of us. As I have previously shown, this myth was embodied in Benjamin Franklin's life and typified by certain incidents in that life which later became mythologized.

In the male freedom (slave) narrative, the male success myth (whose grounding is economic) is expressed in the sentimental mode of discourse. In Jacobs's narrative, however, in addition, and on occasion, sentimental discourse is embedded in major elements of the female (Cinderella) success myth (whose grounding is romantic).

Although Houston Baker, Jr., does not differentiate between male and female freedom ("slave") narratives, he does see them as part of the American success mythology. In fact, he views all these narratives in African American literature as grounded primarily in economic considerations: "It is difficult to see how economic and expressive-artistic considerations can be ignored in treating a narrative that signals its own origination in a commercial deportation," he asserts. "Surely *economics* [his emphasis], conceived in terms of an ideology of narrative form . . . has much to contribute to an understanding of the classic works of an expressive tradition grounded in the economics of slavery" (Baker 1984:39). Gates, reinforcing Baker's economic theorem, adds the missing but necessary sexual equation to it when he lauds Jacobs's work because "she graphically renders the sexual aspect of economic exploitation in a manner unimaginable before" (Gates 1987:12).

To substantiate both critics' insights, let us examine the very last page of her text, when Jacobs is summing up her life's successes and failures. Note that she reveals chagrin at not having achieved the second goal of her life, a shelter of her own. "The dream of my life is not yet realized. I do not sit with my children in a home of my own. I still long for a hearthstone of my own, however humble. I wish it for my children's sake far more than for my own" (1987:201), she grieves.

Jacobs's use of this deeply inscribed success mythology in both plot and discourse, however, accompanies without displacing her use of sentimental language. It incorporates sentimental language in its tone and style. This is because Jacobs's primary goal is to achieve success according to the American male success myth (freedom and material success), and according to the dictates of the Cinderella myth. She bemoans the fact that she has not married, while achieving motherhood: "Reader, my story ends with freedom; not in the usual way, [according to the European American women's Cinderella mythology] with marriage" (1987:201).

Like Wheatley, she uses the prevalent discourse of her targeted audience, white European American females. As Gates reminds us, "She also appeals directly to a female readership including whites, by selecting as one of her epigraphs Isaiah 32:9; 'Rise up, ye women that are at ease! Hear my voice, ye careless daughters!'" Further, he contends, that "this act, what feminists would call gendering, represents a major break from the male traditions she inherited" (1987:12).

Jacobs disarms her reader even further by adding to Wheatley's disarming mask (namely, that of a humble African slave girl, a pious convert to Christianity) that of a devoted mother. What better argument during the period when white European American women were exponents of "the cult of true womanhood," of the "angel of the hearth" mythology? And to further enrich the mix, Jacobs cleverly insinuates into her text another primary purpose of hers: convincing her readers that she and other Black women are really darker replications or mirror images of white women. This in the face of white women's having been otherwise indoctrinated:

O, you happy free women, contrast *your* New Year's day with
that of the poor bond-woman! With you it is a pleasant season,
and the light of the day is blessed. Friendly wishes meet you
every where, and gifts are showered upon you. Even hearts
that have been estranged from you soften at this season, and
lips that have been silent echo back, "I wish you a Happy New
Year." Children bring their little offerings, and raise their rosey
lips for a caress. They are your own, and no hand but that of
death can take them from you.

But to the slave mother New Year's day comes laden with
peculiar sorrows. She sits on her cold cabin floor, watching the
children who may all be torn from her the next morning; and
often does she wish that she and they might die before the day
dawns. She may be an ignorant creature, degraded by the
system that has brutalized her from childhood; but she has a
mother's instincts, and is capable of feeling a mother's agonies.
(1987:16)

Once identification is achieved, Jacobs then believes that
her white sisters will distance themselves intellectually and
emotionally from the institution of slavery which their menfolk
control. These white women will then rise up against their sons,
husbands, and brothers. Hopefully, these women will then
proceed to actively work for the destruction of the entire
economic and political foundations upon which slavery is
grounded, and for their own continued well-being. These same
white women are by law, religion, custom, and training to a
great extent themselves legal slaves of their menfolk against
whom Jacobs hopes these very women will turn. A tall order
indeed!

Jean Fagan Yellin perceptively reveals the complexity of
Jacobs's intentions and efforts, as well as substantial agreement
with my position when she argues that "Instead of dramatizing
the idea that the private sphere is women's appropriate area of
concern . . . *Incidents* embodies a social analysis asserting that the
denial of domestic and familial values by chattel slavery is a
social issue that its female readers should address in the public
arena." Jacobs's intention is not "to inspire her audience to
overcome individual character defects or to engage in reformist
activity within the private sphere." Rather, it is to urge them "to
enter the public sphere and work to end chattel slavery and

white racism." Yellin claims that *Incidents* is an attempt "to move women to political action" and is informed not by "the cult of domesticity" or "domestic feminism," but by political feminism (Jacobs 1987:xxxii).

Indistinguishable from sentimental diction is the highly charged emotive language that Jacobs uses to pay tribute to her community. Jacobs's own earliest reality, her community's solidarity and support for one another, is conveyed by the large amount of tribute material she devotes to them, to their activities on her behalf, and, later, her reciprocal activities on their behalf. These praise songs, prose variants on Wheatley's praise poems, are African in origin. As such, they are characteristic of the earliest African work, such as Olaudah Equiano's, down to their latest manifestations in Booker T. Washington's formal tributes to his white mentors in *Up From Slavery*, for example.

This reality of community is also reflected in Jacobs's characterization of her*self* in her persona of Linda Brent. Jacobs is never an individual in the sense of being an "isolated self." She is solidly embedded in her community. Toni Morrison, among many others, points this out as the premier characteristic of African American consciousness as revealed in the auto-biographical format which she considers "classic in Black American or Afro-American literature because it provided an instance in which a writer could be representative, could say, 'My single solitary and individual life *is* like the lives of the tribe; it differs in these specific ways, but it is a balanced life because it is both solitary and representative'" (1984:339). Deploring "contem-porary [Black] autobiography," in contrast, she complains that it is all about "'how I got over—look at me—alone—let me show you how I did it.' It is inimical, I think, to some of the characteristics of Black artistic expression and influence" (1984:339–340). Implicit in Morrison's critique is its source: European American valorization of the individual.

In Jacobs's autobiography, like those of her contemporaries and successors, some of whom I have just enumerated, her community consists of supportive women, both Black and white, especially her magnificent grandmother, Aunt Martha. Jacobs also pays tribute to her Aunt Nancy, one of her deceased mother's sisters who "was a good, kind aunt to me; and supplied the place of both housekeeper and waiting maid to her mistress [Mrs. Flint]. She was, in fact, at the beginning and end of everything" (1987:12), Jacobs pointedly comments about the Flints' exploitation of her aunt. The name "Flint" in fact, signifies on the saying that something or someone is as "hard as flint."

Throughout the book, white women, both North and South, provide strong contrast to Aunt Nancy's and Linda's mistress, Mrs. Flint. *They* assist Linda and other members of her family through difficult crises. For example, the white woman who buys Aunt Martha in order to free her, and the extraordinary white woman who, a slaveowner herself, yet keeps Linda for a while until she decides to hide in her grandmother's crawl space: "Though she was a slaveholder, to this day my heart blesses her" (1987:111), Jacobs interjects to call such an unusual contradiction (and its concomitant spiritual benefits) to the attention of her white female readership.

Extravagant praise of white decency and goodness is another characteristic of African/African American literature from Wheatley on, as I have previously pointed out. The purpose of this apparently "fulsome praise" is not so much to flatter, but to signify, to underline the rarity of adherence to Christian principles of conduct. Consequently, the example of the "praiseworthy white" serves as a tactful reminder to and model for white readers as to how they should conduct *themselves* in relation to African/African Americans if they would truly consider themselves Christians. The other side of the coin, a warning to sinful whites, is perhaps more common in African American literature until approximately 1900, and is done for the same purpose: to expose the religious hypocrisy of whites, North and South.

Of the Northern white women, Jacobs's female employers are apostrophized and memorialized at great length: "[The first] Mrs. Bruce was a kind and gentle lady, and proved a true and sympathizing friend," Jacobs tell us, and then goes on to give both strong and moving proofs of her claim. Once, when Mrs. Bruce happened to notice that Jacobs had taken off her own flannel skirt and converted it into one for [Ellen] when Jacobs's daughter was enslaved in Brooklyn, "the tears came to her eyes. . . . She soon returned with a nice warm shawl and hood for

Ellen. Truly of such souls as hers are the kingdom of heaven" (1987:168, 181).

Jacobs eulogized the second Mrs. Bruce even more enthusiastically as "a person of excellent principles and a noble heart" and "a true and sympathizing friend. Blessings be with her and hers!" According to Jacobs, this Mrs. Bruce even went so far as to vow that she would "go to the state's prison, rather than have any poor victim torn from *my* house, to be carried back to slavery." It turns out that Jacobs's encomiums on this Mrs. Bruce surpass those bestowed on the first Mrs. Bruce for good reason. It was the second Mrs. Bruce who bought Jacobs's freedom for her: "The noble heart! The brave heart! The tears are in my eyes while I write of her. May the God of the helpless reward her for her sympathy with my persecuted people. . . . Friend! It is a common word, often lightly used. Like other good and beautiful things, it may be tarnished by careless handling; but when I speak of Mrs. Bruce as my friend, the word is sacred" (1987:190, 194, 201).

Jacobs also bestows praise on white abolitionist feminists such as Amy Post, who became Jacobs's friend and wrote the important introduction to *Incidents*. Lydia Maria Child (1802– 1880), became Jacobs's editor, and Jacobs could not have made a better choice in terms of finding a white woman anywhere who more closely shared her perspective. Child had written a unique historical novel about the Puritans and their relationship with the Native Americans, *Hobomok* (1824), and an essay in "Defense of that Class of Americans Called Africans" (1833), in addition to other works on the latter's behalf.

Child, in fact, deserves far greater attention than she has received. For example, her "Appeal" is as eloquent and powerful as Thoreau's "Civil Disobedience," yet is neglected. As for her *Hobomok*, that interesting work of re-creating history in novel form, provides students of American literature with a unique, almost contemporary feminist perspective on the Puritans, English, and Native American relationship matched only by Helen Hunt Jackson's *Ramona*, a much later work. Such a remarkably prophetic point of view as Child evinced on multiethnic issues has hitherto been effectively suppressed through neglect.

Jacobs, astute and sensitive, realized that here was a woman on her wavelength. Rejecting the more celebrated Harriet Beecher Stowe, who had arrogantly informed her that she intended to appropriate Jacobs's material for her *own* work, Jacobs then chose Child, instead, as her editor. Child, as in everything else, did her job with integrity. It would have justifiably upset her to learn that scholars had discounted her description of herself as Jacobs's editor; that until Jean Fagan Yellin discovered Jacobs's manuscript, the white woman had been believed to be its real author. Does one have to explain any further why this was so and has been so in the case of Black autobiographies?

Jacobs, in her own lifetime, seems to have enjoyed a critical enough mass of positive experiences with whites to account for her willingness finally to overcome her deep misgivings about subjecting her early tormented life to public scrutiny. So many encouraging personal contacts, a few of which I have illustrated, must have strengthened her unusually sanguine expectations that a white female audience of readers would respond favorably to her lurid experiences—strengthened them enough to make Jacobs willing to undergo the suffering of recreating traumatic past "incidents," especially the one in which she decides to become Mr. Sands's mistress in order to deprive her master of her body, to "triumph over [her] tyrant even in that small way."

Selwyn Cudjoe here sheds light on still another motive for Jacobs to publish *her* demeaning experiences in her own voice when ordinarily she was dignified, guarded, cautious, self-contained:

> The unique weight of the "personal" and the integrity of the word or speech can better be perceived, in our discussion of the peculiarity of the Afro-American autobiographical statement, as one of the most important means of negotiating our way out of the condition of enslavement and as a means of expressing the intensity with which Afro-American people experience their *violation* and *denigration*. The capacity of speech to convey the intensely lived experience and the closely guarded manner in which the personal is held give to the Afro-American autobiographical statement its special position of authority in Afro-American letters.

As a direct result of this condition, the Afro-American
autobiographical statement as a form tends to be bereft of any
excessive subjectivism and *mindless* egotism. Instead, it presents
the Afro-American as reflecting a much more *impersonal*
condition, the autobiographical subject emerging as an almost
random member of the group, selected to tell his/her tale. As a
consequence, the Afro-American autobiographical statement
emerges as a *public* rather than a *private* gesture, *me-ism* gives
way to *our-ism* and superficial concerns about *individual subject*
usually give way to the *collective subjection* of the group.
(1984:9–10)

Yellin's position, however, is that Jacobs is courageously
straightforward and descriptive about every subject except sex.
"Passages presenting her sexual history . . . are full of omissions
and circumlocutions," Yellin notes. On this basis, she reasons
that Jacobs had difficulty in determining how best to handle the
delicate subject in terms of its presentation to her white female
audience. Ultimately, Jacobs chose the role of "transform[ing]
herself into a penitent supplicant begging forgiveness." Jacobs
was "both determined and reluctant to address her sexual
history; . . . consciously omitt[ing] what [she] thought—'the
world might believe that a Slave Woman was too willing to pour
out'— that she might gain their sympathies." She was "troubled
about" lacking "an appropriate form for her revelations" and
"her story's sensational elements." Accordingly, Jacobs "used the
style of the seduction novel" and "asked Post [her
abolitionist/feminist friend] to write a public endorsement that
would lend it respectability" (Jacobs 1987:xxvi).

I contend, however (expanding on Morrison's and
Cudjoe's insights), that Jacobs chose the same subtle tactic as
Phillis Wheatley. That is, to signify on her targeted white female
audience. She determined to play on them, to disarm them, to
manipulate them; to soften them up, only to melt them down to
acceptance of her. She chose to do this through the conscious use
of white women's *own* characteristic and habitually used
sentimental discourse which white women associated with the
tenderest and "highest" of emotions. Thus Jacobs's text reads like
a "seduction novel," in Yellin's words. But for Gates, Jacobs's
"bold and gripping fusion of two major literary forms"—the

"popular sentimental novel on one hand, and the slave narrative genre on the other," carved out a historic moment in African American literature. "The fact that Jacobs here has remodeled the forms of the black slave narrative and the white female sentimental novel to create a new literary form—a narrative at once black and female—underscores the significance of *Incidents in the Life of a Slave Girl*, both to the Afro-American and the black woman's literary traditions" (1987:12), he asserts.

I disagree with Gates in his assumption that the "sentimental novel" was uniquely "white female." The term "sentimental" is almost always used in relation to female writers. However, when male writers write that way they are defined as "romantic" and their emotions are considered evocations of "raw, brooding power." Consider novelists such as Samuel Richardson, Oliver Goldsmith, Robert Walpole, Charles Dickens, William M. Thackeray, and Stendhal, in Europe; in the United States, William Wells Brown, Washington Irving, and James Fenimore Cooper; poets such as Lord Byron, Percy Shelley, and John Keats, in England; and Edgar Allen Poe, John Greenleaf Whittier, James Wadsworth Longfellow, and Oliver Wendell Holmes in the United States. In other words, both the sentimental and American male success myth modes reflect the prevalent discourse of Jacobs's audience, regardless of gender, just as the heroic rhymed couplet mode reflected the prevalent poetic discourse of Wheatley's time.

Jacobs uses coded language primarily when discussing sexuality and scenes involving sex. These were formidable subjects on which to address white Christian women. Ordinarily such a confession would result in condemnation, ostracism, and book banning, all of which happened to Kate Chopin as late as 1899, when she published *The Awakening*. Not least, it would add fuel to the racist propaganda that Black women were inherently and inordinately strong, sensual, and immoral, whereas white women were inherently weak and frigid. The culture at that time trained Black women to regard anything relating to sex and sexuality as the severest threat to their survival as members in good standing of their group. Darlene Clark Hine, the historian, points out that this necessity, as Black women saw it, led to their "masking," their tendency to secrecy:

To suggest that Black women deliberately developed a culture
of dissemblance implies that they endeavored to create, and
were not simply reacting to, widespread misrepresentations
and negative images of themselves in white minds. Clearly,
Black women did not possess the power to eradicate negative
social and sexual images of their womanhood. Rather, what I
propose is that in the face of the pervasive stereotypes and
negative estimations of the sexuality of Black women, it was
imperative that they collectively create alternative self-images
and shield from scrutiny these private, empowering definitions
of self. . . . Indeed, the concepts of "secrets" and "dissemblance," as I employ them, hint at those issues that Black
women believed better left unknown, unwritten, unspoken
except in whispered tones. Their alarm, their fear, or their
Victorian sense of modesty implies that those who broke the
silence provided grist for detractors' mills and, even more
ominously, tore the protective cloaks from their inner selves.
(1989:915–916)

Jacobs was acutely aware of all this before beginning her
autobiography. I doubt it, but perhaps she was as apprehensive,
humble, and unassuming about her work as she made herself
out to be in her comment to Amy Post about *Incidents*: "Though I
can never make a butterfly, I am satisfied to have it creep meekly
among some of the humbler bugs" (Jacobs 1987:255). Wheatley's
mask was similar, at least where whites were concerned. Like
Wheatley, Jacobs was far too experienced, clear-eyed, and
pragmatic about what was necessary for Black women to "get
over" in her racist world and time to be coming across to her
audience as anything but humble, demure, modest, and retiring.

Certainly Jacobs would be far more experienced
underneath such a mask, playing such a "secret, undisclosed
persona," than Amy Post, Lydia Maria Child, Harriet Beecher
Stowe, or any white feminist/abolitionist with whom she had
contact. After all, *they* had never been forced to depend on the
good graces of white women. Perhaps this is why in writing
Incidents, Jacobs took such care to stroke them; to prepare her
white female readers to accept her and other Black slave women;
to rhetorically persuade them through signifying on their most
vulnerable points—Christianity and motherhood. "God knows I
have tried to do it in a Christian spirit. . . ." She tells Post about

Incidents, " I ask nothing—I have placed myself before you to be judged as a woman whether I deserve your pity or contempt—I have another object in view—it is to come to you just as I am, a poor Slave Mother—not to tell you what I have heard but what I have seen—and what I have suffered—and if there is any sympathy to give—let it be given to the thousands—of Slave Mothers that are still in bondage . . . let it plead for their helpless Children." (Jacobs 1987:xiii).

Few if any female freedom narratives written by or dictated by African American women, including *Incidents*, are objects of critical discussion. It seems to be argued implicitly that Douglass's is so great and so representative that it is not necessary to give more than a passing reference to Jacobs. This makes Gates very angry: "While hundreds of male ex-slaves were encouraged to tell their tales, few women were able to narrate or publish their indictments of the twin brothers of oppression—slavery and sexism. Indeed, William Andrews, an expert on Afro-American slave narratives, concludes that by 1866, only four black women had published their stories. As if racism and slavery had not been harsh enough, intra-racial sexism stifled even the freed black women's voice" (Jacobs 1987:12).

It is not that stories involving Black slave women's sexual harassments, emotional and physical tortures, and sufferings might be any different when described by men, although Gates believes that this might be the case. When compared to Jacobs, he argues, "the black male narrators' accounts of sexual brutality remain suggestive, if gruesome" (Jacobs 1987:12). Male writers of freedom narratives, and William Craft is perhaps the best example, had always recounted horrifying atrocities committed against slave women. But as with the other male narratives, his wife Ellen's personal experience and those of other female relatives are told by William in his own authoritative voice, whether or not his wife described them to him first, and whether or not both had collaborated at every point. Douglass's (and all the other males') perspective is that of masculine as subject and female as object. Silencing the female voice and perspective while privileging the male's is suspect, even though the rationale given by Yellin is that Black females had even less access to education than their menfolk. This is the reason, it is claimed, that female representation is lacking in discussions of freedom narrative genre. Be this as it may, the perspective from which Jacobs writes makes all the difference. It gives her narrative its immediacy and power, her use of sentimental discourse, Christian piety, and devoted motherhood notwithstanding.

And Jacobs's community consists of supportive Black men. Outstanding among her male characters is her friend Peter, "a kind-hearted, noble fellow, who never turned his back upon anybody in distress, white or black" (1987:151). Then there is her wonderful, ever nurturing and supportive Uncle Phillip, Aunt Martha's son. For example, when Peter finally comes up with an idea for smuggling Linda away, Phillip "rejoiced in the plan." Nevertheless, he is at the same time concerned about his mother's feelings in the matter. He shows more consideration, in fact, than Linda, who thought nothing had better be said to her grandmother "till very near the time of departure. But my uncle thought she would feel it more keenly if I left her so suddenly. 'I will reason with her,' said he, 'and convince her how necessary it is, not only for your sake, but for hers also. You cannot be blind to the fact that she is sinking under her burdens.' [Afterwards] my uncle talked with her, and finally succeeded in persuading her that it was absolutely necessary for me to seize the chance so unexpectedly offered" (1987:150).

Phillip shares top billing with Jacobs's grandmother in the final round of praise songs on the last page of the text. "Time passed on, and a paper came to me from the south, containing an obituary notice of my uncle Phillip. It was the only case I ever knew of such an honor conferred upon a colored person" (1987:201), Jacobs informs her readers with justifiable pride. Historically, Phillip may perhaps be the last sympathetically delineated and strong major African American male character in African American women's works for more than a half century—until Jessie Fauset's *There is Confusion* (1924). There is then another long hiatus for more than a half century, until Gloria Naylor's *Mama Day* (1988). Like Phillip, Anthony Cross and George Andrews are both strong in character, resourceful, and at the same time gentle, warm, and nurturing. So is Alice Walker's Grange Copeland of *The Third Life of Grange Copeland* (1970).

Copeland, however, grows into grandeur of soul, grows into his ability to "cope" with the vagaries of this "land" of ours toward Blacks. But only in old age does he grow mellow, much like Mr._____ of *The Color Purple*.

For whatever reasons, Harriet Jacobs, a very private person, determined after much soul searching to go public, to expose key situations in *her* life in order to improve not only her image, but those of her Black sisters. She used the same autobiographical, confessional framework, combined with key incidents as did Franklin and the Black male freedom narrators who followed him in what Raymond Dolle defines as "that Ben Franklin tradition of secular autobiography created by enterprising, self-made men, who achieve success through hard work, frugality and business acumen, serving God by serving society through material accomplishment and moral improvement" (1989:790).

Jacobs, however, sought public and political activism for women without considering financial and material factors in her equation. Jacobs's work was a how-to manual for white female readers, not for economic purposes, but for consciousness-raising. She recollected the most harrowing incidents of her life. She chose them to convey to her white female readers as much immediacy and descriptiveness about these incidents as she could muster. She attempted to make her readers feel that these incidents could have been their realities too, but for the accident of the privileged class and race into which they were born.

Like a general strategizing before and after battles, Jacobs both foregrounded these "incidents" and the moral choices which they demanded. White female readers were thus invited to vicariously experience the evildoing of her slave masters, Dr. Flint and his wife, in precipitating harrowing incidents for Jacobs. Readers were also invited to second-guess her decisions at every point.

Far from depicting herself as the Flints' victim, Jacobs uses a variety of strategies to "get over" on her opponents. Jacobs's shrewdness is evident even as young as fifteen when she depicts herself in Yellin's terms as "an effective moral agent" who always attempted to assert "her autonomy as a human being" to the point where she became another man's mistress rather than succumb to the eternal harassment of her master, Dr. Flint.

Jacobs's strategy was to invite her white female readers to think of better solutions to her problems, *if they could*, given Jacobs's situation at any point. Such a veiled challenge tactfully informed her readers subliminally that in all probability they could not have succeeded in remaining morally superior to the author as they may blithely have assumed at the outset of reading the text. Only at that early point could Jacobs's white women readers indulge themselves in such feelings, could they still complacently luxuriate in the difference between their lives and the slave girl's: how sheltered, how remote theirs was, by contrast.

By no means was this a book written to facilitate its readers snuggling down before the fire with a box of chocolates. As Jacobs's readers progressed into the work, her personal disruptions of the text continually destabilized their comfort zones; relentlessly leading them to question themselves as to whether they would have done as well as the author (and her family) at each crux, or even as well as other slaves. Jacobs even made them ask themselves whether they would be capable of displaying such delicate scruples as her brother William reveals when he escapes from his master, Sands: scruples which her readers were taught never to associate with Blacks, only with "higher orders of beings": "He was scrupulous about taking any money from his master on false pretenses: so he sold his best clothes to pay for his passage to Boston. The slaveholders pronounced him a base, ungrateful wretch, for thus requiting his master's indulgence. What would *they* have done under similar circumstances?" (1987:151) Jacobs ends by fuming at her readers, daring them to do and be any better if they could.

Freedom narratives include many anecdotes about abuse of slaves, slaves running away, etc. Would Jacobs's readers have themselves successfully endured Dr. Flint's unremitting sexual and emotional harassment, for instance, and still remained inviolate? Could they have endured to salvage a life for themselves and their family during and after such experiences? Could they have done all that Jacobs did and still emerge with dignity intact, with self-respect, clarity and strength of mind, fortitude, and greatness of spirit?

Take the most sensational experience, to me more sensational than even the decision Jacobs made to become Sands's mistress in order to evade Flint's addresses. Behind Aunt Martha's house was a shed with a garret crawl space nine feet long, seven feet wide, and three feet high, "never occupied by anything but rats and mice" until Harriet Jacobs hid there for nearly eight years from Dr. Flint. During that time she read, sewed, and used her prison "as a war room from which to spy on her enemy and to wage psychological warfare against him" in Yellin's apt interpretation of Jacobs's true character and attitude. She also engineered her children's sale to their father and negotiated for her daughter to be taken North. Meanwhile, throughout this period, she tricked Dr. Flint into thinking she had long since left the South, and "quite literally direct[ed] a performance in which Dr. Flint play[ed] the fool while she watch[ed] unseen" (Jacobs 1987:xxviii).

Of course, Jacobs had the benefit of an extraordinary female role-model and an extensive support system in the persons of her grandmother, her relatives, and her friends. It is to her ancestor grandmother's honor and memory that Jacobs pours out her verbal libation in the form of the last words of *Incidents*: "It has been painful for me, in many ways, to recall the dreary years I passed in bondage. I would gladly forget them if I could. Yet the retrospection is not altogether without solace, for with those gloomy recollections come tender memories of my good old grandmother, like light, fleecy clouds floating over a dark and troubled sea" (1987:201).

Further, Jacobs pays frequent tribute to Aunt Martha throughout the text, as well as to a large cast of loving and supportive family and friends who form the community chorus around her. All of them, but especially Aunt Martha, provided Jacobs with literal and figurative support through her nearly eight-years trial of endurance:

> My food was passed up to me through the trap-door my uncle had contrived; and my grandmother, my uncle Phillip, and aunt Nancy would seize such opportunities as they could, to mount up there and chat with me at the opening. . . . The good

grandmother gave me herb teas and cooling medicines. . . . The
kind grandmother brought me bed-clothes and warm
drinks. . . . My brother William came and did all he could for
me. Uncle Phillip also watched tenderly over me; and poor
grandmother crept up and down. . . . My children looked up at
me as though they knew I was there, and were conscious of the
joy they imparted. (1987:113,122) [1]

At the same time, Jacobs is astute in depicting herself along
the lines of a Cinderella heroine. She is fully aware that her white
female readers are indoctrinated in the Franklin *cum* Cinderella
myth, as well as in the sacred nature of family ties, motherhood,
etc. That is, to the extent that these are her trials and tribulations,
and that her community of relatives, friends, and enemies have
theirs as well. She depicts her trials as unique to her and yet that
she is not alone while suffering. For example, Jacobs shows the
implications and complexities of her suffering, even on her
persecutors, primarily on Mrs. Flint, a wicked stepmother type if
ever there was one. After all, this book is targeted at her white
(step)sisters, whom she hopes, will be more compassionate than
their archetypes were in the original story, or than her white
mistress, *their* "mother," had been.

It was not until many years later that she became aware of
the suffering of her persecutors, primarily in the form of Mrs.
Flint's vulnerability which provoked her instability, envy, and
jealous, watchful paranoia toward Jacobs. The latter grew to
understand what successfully undermined and countermanded
the white woman's underlying sympathy and understanding for
her; what caused Mrs. Flint to project her suspicions, frustration,
rage, and impotent jealousy against her innocent slave, instead of
against her husband. "In her angry moods, no terms were too
vile for her to bestow upon me. Yet I, whom she detested so
bitterly, had far more pity for her than he had, whose duty it was
to make her life happy. I never wronged her, or wished to wrong
her; and one word of kindness from her would have brought me
to her feet" (1987:32), she explains to her readers.

Jacobs shows Mrs. Flint as succumbing to her culture's
construct for her at every point, a tragic shortcoming which
Jacobs tells her audience about in order to convince them to
respond otherwise than Mrs. Flint, if placed in a similar

situation. To vent against a slave was socially sanctioned. However, to call a husband to account was to become a shrew, a disloyal wife who holds her husband's side of the story and interests lower in her esteem than those of his slaves. It would be to go against the training of white women in the requisite duties, obligations and conduct of a "proper wife" inscribed in girls by their mothers and fathers; by their schoolmasters and mistresses; by their church; by church-sanctioned and connected social groups, as well as by the religious tracts they were given to read, especially biblical passages and pious exempla in the form of moral tales. All these elements acculturated them into dogged loyalty to their masters in terms of "sacred and holy" female duty. Any deviation therefrom was heresy. All reinforced the laws promulgated by courts and disseminated through print media. The latter also employed the prevailing sentimental mode of discourse, heightened by lurid sensationalism of detail in keeping the citizenry in line, not least of all its female portion. In short, all Southern societal and cultural institutional formations were arrayed against Jacobs and her kind.

Ultimately, Jacobs's, as well as those of other slave girls' complaints to their mistresses about their husbands led only to further widening of the rifts between Black and white women:

> As I went on with my account her color changed frequently, she wept, and sometimes groaned. She spoke in tones so sad, that I was touched by her grief. The tears came to my eyes; but I was soon convinced that her emotions rose from anger and wounded pride. She felt that her marriage vows were desecrated, her dignity insulted; but she had no compassion for the poor victim of her husband's perfidy. She pitied herself as a martyr; but she was incapable of feeling for the condition of shame and misery in which her unfortunate, helpless slave was placed. (1987:33)

Consequently, Mrs. Flint's behavior, as that of many others of her kind, seemed from the abused victim's point of view to focus blame on the victims rather than on the victimizers. Amazingly, Jacobs was astute enough and large-hearted enough to realize that very strong social forces were arrayed against Mrs. Flint to prevent her from doing precisely what Jacobs is attempting to get her white female readers to do by writing this book: rally around her cause. "She was not a very refined woman, and had not much control over her passions. I was an object of her jealousy, and, consequently, of her hatred; and I knew I could not expect kindness or confidence from her under the circumstances in which I was placed. I could not blame her. Slaveholders' wives feel as other women would under similar circumstances" (1987:34). In fact, *her* harrowing experiences with her husband, his abuse of her, made Mrs. Flint sadistic and abusive to Jacobs, in turn. She tortures the fifteen-year-old in her sleep by whispering "in her ear, as though it was her husband," then by maintaining in the morning that Jacobs "had been talking in [her] sleep." Naturally enough, Jacobs "began to be fearful for my life. It had often been threatened; and you can imagine, better than I can describe, what an unpleasant sensation it must produce to wake up in the dead of night and find a jealous woman bending over you. Terrible as this experience was, I had fears that it would give place to one more terrible [Dr. Flint possessing her]" (1987:34).

When he lies to his wife, Dr. Flint does so in such a callous way as to implicate Jacobs sexually with him: "It was to show me that I gained nothing by seeking the protection of my mistress; that the power was still all in his own hands. I pitied Mrs. Flint. She was a second wife, many years the junior of her husband; and the hoary-headed miscreant was enough to try the patience of a wiser and better woman. She was completely foiled, and knew not how to proceed. She would have had me flogged for my supposed false oath; but . . . the doctor never allowed any one to whip me. The old sinner was politic" (1987:34–35).

The impact of Jacobs's persecution by the Flints also had its backlash on the members of her family, on her friends and community, in terms of its enormous psychic and physical cost. And this does not take into account their own private persecutions. Her grandmother's health totally failed at one point from the stress that Flint was causing her through his abuse of her granddaughter, and her life was despaired of.

Of course, hard-hearted and cynical readers could still shrug this off as rationalization. After all, Aunt Martha was elderly anyway, they might argue. But most readers could not respond in this manner when Jacobs recounts the effects on her children. Her readers then realized that *their* children did not have to grow old and wise so fast. For example, after Linda learns that Benny, her son, has known of her hiding so close and yet so far from him for so long, she discovers, to her outrage, its toll on her previously open and wonderfully spontaneous child:

> He said he had kept a close lookout for Dr. Flint, and if he saw him speak to a constable, or a patrol, he always told grandmother. I now recollected that I had seen him manifest uneasiness, when people were on that side of the house [where Jacobs lay in concealment], and I had at the time been puzzled to conjecture a motive for his actions. Such prudence may seem extraordinary in a boy of twelve years, *but slaves, being surrounded by mysteries, deceptions, and dangers, early learn to be suspicious and watchful, and prematurely cautious and cunning* [Jacobs's emphasis]. He had never asked a question of grandmother, or uncle Phillip, and I had often heard him chime in with other children, when they spoke of my being at the north. (1987:154–155)

In the case of her daughter, Ellen (Louisa Matilda Jacobs), Jacobs shows the little girl suffering from the repercussions of her mother's sexual plight in yet another way. Ellen grieves, but not as her mother expects, over what makes her mother suffer:

> I had often resolved to tell her something about her father; but I had never been able to muster sufficient courage. I had a shrinking dread of diminishing my child's love. I knew she must have curiosity on the subject, but she had never asked a question [like Benny]. She was always very careful not to say anything to remind me of my troubles. . . . I thought if I should die before she returned, she might hear my story from some one who did not understand the palliating circumstances; and that if she were entirely ignorant on the subject, her sensitive nature might receive a rude shock. (1987:188)

Instead, Jacobs discovers, Ellen is concerned entirely about *her* relationship to her father (Sands), entirely from her point of view as his daughter:

> I am nothing to my father, and he is nothing to me. All my love
> is for you. I was with him five months in Washington, and he
> never cared for me. He never spoke to me as he did to his little
> Fanny [his child by his white wife]. I knew all the time he was
> my father, for Fanny's nurse told me so; but she said I must
> never tell any body, and I never did. I used to wish he would
> take me in his arms and kiss me, as he did Fanny; or that he
> would sometimes smile at me, as he did at her. I thought if he
> was my own father, he ought to love me. I was a little girl then,
> and didn't know any better. But now I never think any thing
> about my father. All my love is for you. (1987:189)

Tragically also, Jacobs discovers the same vulnerability in
Ellen as she had suffered from, as had her grandmother, as had
her mother, as had all her female relatives. This despite Jacobs's
superhuman efforts to prevent it from recurring for Ellen: "She
was always desirous not to add to my troubles, more than she
could help, and I did not discover till years afterwards that Mr.
Thorne's [Sands' cousin-in-law] intemperance [alcoholism] was
not the only annoyance she suffered from him. Though he
professed too much gratitude to my grandmother to injure any
of her descendants, he had poured vile language into the ears of
her innocent great-grandchild" (179).[2]

In connection with this replication of Jacobs's previous
sufferings, Jacobs has already made what to my mind is the most
powerfully moving, psychologically astute appeal to white
women made before the Civil War, excepting perhaps for those
of the Grimke sisters. Although expressed in the sentimental
mode, it nevertheless in no way detracts from Jacobs's ability to
argue her case persuasively:

> And now, reader, I come to a period in my unhappy life, which
> I would gladly forget if I could. The remembrance fills me with
> sorrow and shame. It pains me to tell you of it; but I have
> promised to tell you the truth, and I will do it honestly, let it
> cost me what it may. I will not try to screen myself behind the
> plea of compulsion from a master; for it was not so. Neither can
> I plead ignorance or thoughtlessness. For years, my master had
> done his utmost to pollute my mind with foul images, and to
> destroy the pure principles inculcated by my grandmother, and
> the good mistress of my childhood. The influences of slavery

had had the same effect on me that they had on other young girls; they had made me prematurely knowing, concerning the evil ways of the world. I knew what I did, and I did it with deliberate calculation.... But, O, ye happy women, whose purity has been sheltered from childhood, who have been free to choose the objects of your affection, whose homes are protected by law, do not judge the poor desolate slave girl too severely! If slavery had been abolished, I, also, could have married the man of my choice; I could have had a home shielded by the laws; and I should have been spared the painful task of confessing what I am now about to relate; but all my prospects had been blighted by slavery. I wanted to keep myself pure; and, under the most adverse circumstances, I tried hard to preserve my self-respect; but I was struggling alone in the powerful grasp of the demon Slavery; and the monster proved too strong for me. I felt as if I was forsaken by God and man; as if all my efforts must be frustrated; and I became reckless in my despair. (1987:53–54)

Incidents contains many such psychologically acute and astute descriptions of the by-products of slavery. Such attention to these details, to these factors in human relations, added a dimension of persuasiveness to Jacobs's cause lacking in male freedom narratives such as Douglass's and Washington's. For example, Douglass formally interrupts his text at intervals in order to make particularly impassioned speeches, much like Jacobs, but more like an actor of the period declaiming in public with his hand over his heart. On one page, he orates about his grandmother and her terrible fate at the hands of the masters to whom her life had been devoted:

The hearth is desolate. The children ... who once sang and danced in her presence, are gone. She gropes her way, in the darkness of age, for a drink of water. Instead of the voices of her children, she hears by day the moans of the dove, and by night the screams of the hideous owl. All is gloom. The grave is at the door. And now, when weighed down by the pains and aches of old age, when the head inclines to the feet, when the beginning and ending of human existence meet, and helpless infancy and painful old age combine together—at this time, this most needful time, the time for the exercise of that tenderness and affection which children only can exercise

toward a declining parent—my poor old grandmother, the
devoted mother of twelve children, is left all alone, in yonder
little hut, before a few dim embers. She stands—she sits—she
staggers—she falls—she groans—she dies—and there are none
of her children or grandchildren present, to wipe from her
wrinkled brow the cold sweat of death, or to place beneath the
sod her fallen remains. Will not a righteous God visit [the slave
masters] for these things? (1990:1669)

Douglass's discourse is heightened, even impassioned, his
rhetoric formal, in the sentimental mode. Booker T. Washington,
on the other hand, uses a flat, spare, simple narrative style to tell
the following tale as if it were nothing that unusual:

As soon as freedom was declared, he [Washington's
stepfather], sent for my mother to come to the Kanawha Valley
in West Virginia. At that time a journey from Virginia over the
mountains to West Virginia was rather a tedious and in some
cases a painful undertaking. What little clothing and few
household goods we had were placed in a cart, but the children
walked the greater portion of the distance, which was several
hundred miles. . . . We were several weeks making the trip, and
most of the time we slept in the open air and did our cooking
over a log fire out-of- doors. One night, I recall that we camped
near an abandoned log cabin, and my mother decided to build
a fire in that for cooking, and afterward to make a "pallet" on
the floor for our sleeping. Just as the fire had gotten well
started a large black snake fully a yard and a half long dropped
down the chimney and ran out on the floor. Of course we at
once abandoned that cabin. (1987:25)

Readers are forced to deduce for themselves Jane
Henderson's indomitable spirit. She garners no such praises as
do Washington's white mentors, Gen. Samuel Chapman
Armstrong and his beloved New England female teachers at
Hampton (all ardent Franklin followers). Washington publicized
these three heavily as having been the source of *his* success in
following the white American male success mythology. As the
carefully chosen and vividly depicted key incidents in Franklin's
life came to be taught to succeeding generations of Americans
and thus became mythologized, so the incidents in Washington's

life (in which these three played Franklin's role to *their* Black initiate), became part of African American male success mythology from 1901 until the present.³

Jane Henderson was already in failing health when she was freed and the Civil War ended. Any contemporary reader who is also a parent and has undertaken the daunting task of walking with three small children simultaneously in the local supermarket, as I have, can vouch for the extraordinary accomplishment of Washington's mother in trekking with her three small children over mountainous and difficult terrain, a journey far more difficult than the archetypal Franklin's or the fictional Huck Finn's. Jane Henderson carried herself and three dependent souls safely to a new life, somewhat like Jacobs, who, although she went alone originally, later took great pains to bring her two children out of bondage to live with her. One of Jane Henderson's children, who emulated her in his heroic and unforgettable trek to Hampton Institute, would live to dine, as Franklin had boasted so proudly of doing, not only with kings and queens, but with presidents and other heads of state, and to become the most influential race leader, politician, and educator of his time. Unlike Franklin, however, Washington did not boast about these occasions, nor did he father bastards and bring them home for his wife to raise.

One wonders about Douglass's and Washington's glaring omissions (especially in contrast to Jacobs), their silences, their seeming blindness to family and domestic matters. One wonders, for example, what was Douglass's grandmother's response to being cast out by her masters after a lifetime of service? Couldn't Douglass have given her even one line to speak? Like Franklin, Douglass's (first Black) wife takes up only a few lines of space, and she never speaks. Washington's mother appears in quite a few scenes. Although she does not speak, we do get a sense of her strong and energetic personality, her intense drive and commitment to her family, primarily in the course of anecdotes her son is telling about himself. In describing his ambitions, Washington reveals his mother's undying support for them in the form of zealous devotion, self-sacrifice, and service. He does the same for each of his three wives.

This is characteristic of all the male autobiographies, speaking for and about their womenfolk. To Abena Busia, however, it isn't only that Douglass's or Washington's female relatives do not speak for themselves. Few women speak for themselves in African American male literature (or in European and European American literature, or *any* literature, for that matter): "The African diaspora woman is as much, if not more silenced than any of her European sisters. It [her voice] is not even heard speaking for itself," she notes. It is her contention that the silencing of women stems from "colonial" practice, not biology. Not only were women completely silenced in literature ("phragectomized" is her wonderful term for the process), their bodies were the lowest elements in the economic systems of exchange. Further, what Busia has to say about European women and African women is, it seems to me, true as well about European American women and African American women, certainly for Harriet Jacobs and all the white women in her life: "It is important to note that images of all women in colonial fiction run in tandem, acting as polar opposites of each other: European women voiced, unsexed, and the focus of much power, the native woman silenced, licentious, and powerless" (1989–1990:86).

In another contrast to male writers, Jacobs gives voices to her grandmother, her relatives, her friends, her community, as well as her enemies, throughout her text. She also reveals herself in dialogue with them; as if reporting their authentic opinions and responses, even when different from hers, as in the case with her uncle Phillip and Ellen, which I have already illustrated, as well as with Dr. and Mrs. Flint. This contrast, Gayle Jones points out, is not limited to that between Jacobs and Douglass and Washington: "With many women writers, relationships within family, community, between men and women, and among women—from slave narratives by black women writers on—are treated as complex and significant relationships, whereas with many men the significant relationships are those that involve confrontations—relationships outside the family and community" (1983:92).

Patricia Hill Collins, in analyzing the source of this observable difference between African American men and women, attributes it, although she denies it, to essential gender differences; to Carole Gilligan's assertion of women's "ethic of caring" rather than cultural socialization. She includes white women in her claim (as Jacobs doubtless would): "When African-American women use dialogues in assessing knowledge claims, they might be invoking a particular female way of knowing as well. Feminist scholars contend that males and females are socialized within their families to seek different types of autonomy, the former based on separation, the latter seeking connectedness, and that this variation in types of autonomy parallels the characteristic differences between male and female ways of knowing." But, she hedges, "While these ways of knowing are not gender specific, disproportionate numbers of women rely on connected knowing" (Collins 1989:765, 767).

Franklin, Wheatley (for as long as the Wheatleys lived, at any rate), Douglass, and Washington all traveled extensively. They all gained entree into exclusive halls of power. They wined and dined with gatekeepers of the culture with whom they negotiated to effect political and economic improvement for their beleaguered groups. Wheatley attempted to do this and failed. Yet she displays no consciousness in any of her statements, in letters or in poetry, of what Busia is talking about, and of what Jacobs reveals to her readers: that Wheatley, a gifted, intelligent, affectionate, human being, nevertheless was viewed by her slavemaster and mistress as basically her body. Wheatley's primary exchange value for them was as a commodity, a piece of flesh.

Jacobs, on the other hand, was bent on rejecting such a (de)valuation. Her choices, from the beginning to the end of *Incidents*, were based on her adamant refusal to allow her body to be so used. She appeals directly to her readers, when to avoid Flint she chooses instead to take up with another white man, Sands (in real life, a prominent North Carolina legislator, Samuel Tredwell Sawyer).

The essential difference was that one man owned her, the other did not. Thus her body was an economic commodity only to one, and that made the difference—to Jacobs. She felt that because of this essential difference, there would be space to negotiate with Sands for peripheral benefits which she did not enjoy with her master and mistress.

Certain benefits had been reaped often enough in previous slave history for Jacobs to attempt to obtain them in her situation. She gambled on the possibility that in her no-win sexual plight, she might at least have some chance of deriving from Sands a few of these benefits. He would continue to address her with greater tact, with seeming respect in tone and language. She would have greater freedom of expression with him. Most significant of all, he might possibly purchase their children out of slavery. At the very least, she would have the pleasure of fending off, by "checkmating," the "tyrant" Dr. Flint if she gained the protection of a more powerful piece in this sadistic chess game, a white "knight" as protector over her "pawn," her own body.

Further, Jacobs's key *Incidents* contrast enormously with Franklin's upbeat mythological situations for men, although hers are equally archetypal. In this they are mythological for enslaved women everywhere throughout history. Jacobs's refusal to participate in such a system, where economic success for a female slave is predicated on her body as a condition of exchange, doubtless created (and still creates) for her white female readers scenes as unforgettable as Franklin provided in his *Autobiography*.

For these reasons, women readers (still) find unforgettably vivid such incidents as Flint's unbearable, infernal, and eternal harassments (which are as common in life as they are in sentimental fiction and film "tear-jerkers"); her grandmother's heroic, ultimately frustrated attempts to stop them, to deal with this obsessed and depraved individual; Dr. Flint's stone-hearted rejection of Jacobs's request to marry a preferred suitor, another Black, whom she regarded as her only chance for personal fulfillment; a white Southern, slave-owning woman's assistance in hiding her; her "escape" over a period of eight years, during which time she was, in actuality, incarcerated in a living tomb; her family's unfaltering devotion to her; her harrowing experiences when hiding in the swamp and escaping on the boat; her friendships with and love for her two white women employers; the incidents depicting her sudden, disrupting moves after her escape, in order to evade recapture; the incidents detailing her repeated attempts to reunite with her children; and, finally, the moving scene(s) of her reunions with them.

In almost all of these incidents, as in those of the American male success myth, Jacobs is both actor and agent, as I previously pointed out in another context. In only one scene (her grandmother's fruitless attempts to interview Flint on her behalf and end his harassment) is Jacobs reactive.

At this point, two question arise. First, did Jacobs succeed in her efforts to improve the image of Black women? If not, it was not possibly for want of trying to refute every damaging stereotype possible. In fact, Jacobs handled the stereotypes so well that they rebounded against her captors. For example, some of the stereotypes which she succeeds in refuting in her persona, Linda Brent, were that Black women were oversexed; that they were savage/barbaric/primitive; inarticulate, incoherent; stupid, if young, bossy, if old.

Economically (in terms of writing strategies), Jacobs makes Dr. Flint the primary repository for all these slanders. For example, Dr. Flint attempted at one point after Jacobs has escaped to write to her directly, assuming the persona of his young son. In her outrage, note that Jacobs reacts strongly on behalf not only of herself, but of her insulted people, simultaneously: "I knew by the style, that it was not written by a person of his age, and though the writing was disguised, I had been made too unhappy by it, in former years, not to recognize at once the hand of Dr. Flint. O, the hypocrisy of slaveholders! Did the old fox suppose I was goose enough to go into such a trap! Verily, he relied too much on 'the stupidity of the African race.' I did not return the family of Flints any thanks for their cordial invitation [to come back]—a remissness for which I was, no doubt, charged with base ingratitude," she ends, signifying on the Flint family (1987:172).

Secondly, in what ways does Jacobs's text reflect the Cinderella myth? Initially, long ago, her position in the Flint home had been that of a Cinderella. She recounts that whole period as having taken place in the distant past, as if she is now looking at it from a separate and privileged present perspective. A lengthy period of inertia, a rigid fixity followed by very brief flight out of the picture's frame to closure, also characterizes the Cinderella myth. This parallels Jacobs's life, at least so far as she takes us in the text.

In addition, like Cinderella (which means "Little Cinder"), Linda Brent means "Pretty Burnt" or "Pretty Sunburnt/Dark/ Black." Like Cinderella, Linda is harassed and imperiled by wicked "legal relatives" in the persons of her three selfish stepsisters and cruel stepmother. Substituting for these "legal" father and mother substitutes are Jacobs's "legal" master and mistress. Dr. Flint, by profession, sex, and age, should have been a protector of her health and well-being. Instead, he plays wicked stepfather opposite Mrs. Flint's combined wicked stepmother and wicked stepsisters. Politically and sexually, she is Jacobs's "stepsister" rather than her "sister," as Jacobs learns to her sorrow. "Step" is also used as an equivalent for "legal mother" or "legal father." By law, Southern whites were placed *in loco parentis*, "in a parental relation" (1987:36) to Blacks, as Jacobs puts it.

Cinderella also has a "fairy godmother," a *dea ex machina*, who provides her with the costume, the coachmen, and the carriage with which to go to the ball. In Jacobs's case, her grandmother, assisted by various relatives, fills this role at key points in her life. Aunt Martha provides all these necessary ingredients for the ball: for Jacobs, a single escape to freedom. When Jacobs sets out on her journey north, her grandmother provides her with clothing and food supplies. The pumpkin and coachmen turn into the good captain, his crew, and the boat which carries Jacobs safely away.

The mythological Cinderella, of course, meets Prince Charming at the ball. Ultimately, he seeks her out and removes her from the dank, dark depths of the kitchen in which she has hitherto languished and to which she was banished to slave for the usurping family. He carries her off to his castle where she will live with him in love and peace and harmony forever and ever after. Dr. Flint, is, of course, the exact opposite to Prince Charming. He is the devil incarnate, who successfully *prevents* Jacobs's Prince Charming from carrying her off.

When Flint forced Jacobs to send her Prince Charming away (the free Black man whom she loved and hoped to marry), she moans to her readers about her "love-dream," a dream which "had been my support through many trials. . . . With me the lamp of hope had gone out. The dream of my girlhood was over. I felt lonely and desolate" (1987:40, 42). Jacobs never got over her disappointment and resentment at having to give up this dream "of her girlhood." She reveals this when she informs her readers that she is grateful for having achieved one basic human right, but disappointed at having been deprived of the most basic female status symbol, so that her "story ends with freedom, not in the usual way [for white women] with marriage" (1987:201).

At the point in the myth where Cinderella is taken off to never-never land by Prince Charming, Jacobs switches to the American male success myth, herself shipping out to different cities in search of job opportunities. This entails geographical mobility in a linear sense as well as an upward one. But from this point on in the text, there is a condensed, dreamy, unreal quality to her narrative, uncharacteristic of the earlier scenes before the escape from slavery. Perhaps this is because Jacobs has completed her key task, that of raising the consciousness of her white women readers in relation to Black women still trapped in bondage. Once free from slavery, Jacobs shows herself primarily motivated in two areas (again like Wheatley)—motherhood, and choosing a career to advance her people.

Her continual underlining and pointing out of her piety, like Wheatley, seems also to involve some delayed gratification in terms of slavers. As with Wheatley, the imagery most frequently associated with these whites is reptilian. For example, when Jacobs hides in the swamp, she uses its dangers to form the best contrast she could think of with whites: "I passed a wretched night; for the heat of the swamp, the mosquitos, and the constant terror of snakes, had brought on a burning fever. I had just dropped asleep, when they came and told me it was time to go back to that horrid swamp. I could scarcely summon courage to rise. But even those large, venomous snakes were less dreadful to my imagination than the white men in that community called civilized" (1987:113). And after her escape: "All that winter I lived in a state of anxiety. When I took the children out to breathe the air, I closely observed the countenances of all I met. I dreaded the approach of summer, when snakes and slaveholders make their appearance. I was, in fact a slave in New York, as subject to slave laws as if I had been in a Slave State. Strange incongruity in a State called free!" (1987:193)

Jacobs always conveys to her readers the sense of an individual embedded in the community, a circular sense of a "collective consciousness" in contrast to the sense of a linear progression upward as embodied in the typical *bildungsroman* of the American success story. Nowhere is this more dramatic than the support provided by her family while Jacobs is literally buried alive. This kind of support from their communities is the saving grace for Africans/African Americans in the diaspora.

African American scholars stress this characteristic in all genres, but nowhere more so than in autobiography. They stress, as well, the opposition between European American literature, which valorizes "the apotheosized private self, tragically masked as the alienated rebel . . . and the communal, consciously political self of Black autobiography," as Butterfield claims for Black autobiography, a claim which as a whole is characteristic of Jacobs's work. In his phrase, "The dominant tradition in white personal narratives since the Renaissance . . ." Butterfield seems to be including both European and European American autobiographical practice. He nicely sums up concerns characteristic of both cultural traditions, such as "the individual's forging a career, a reputation, a business, or a family out of the raw material of his neighbors." In contrast, Butterfield sums up Black autobiographies as characterized more by "their political awareness, their empathy for suffering, their ability to break down the division of 'I' and 'you,' their knowledge of oppression and discovery of ways to cope with that experience, and their sense of shared life, shared triumph, and communal responsibility. The self belongs to the people and the people find a voice in the self" (1974:3).

In terms of rhetorical and aesthetic techniques employed by Jacobs to raise the consciousness of her white female audience about their Black sisters, the very symbolic heart's core of the text is that portion in which Jacobs lies entrapped as if in a living tomb. That the Black female slave should be forced to lie supine and silent without movement in a coffin-like enclosure is perhaps the situation with which her white women readers most closely identified and identify with today. It was, as a matter of fact, similar, in essence, to one which they themselves shared and share. "She's Only a Bird in a Gilded Cage" describes homebound and "kept" women trapped by their duties to men.

There are a number of similar phrases which easily come to mind when one thinks of the "true woman" of the period. Many white women's texts when deconstructed also reveal the motif of imprisonment in small spaces, from Emily Dickinson to the protagonist of Charlotte E. Perkins Gilman's, "The Yellow Wallpaper," who is confined to the upstairs nursery. In Russia, there was Anna Karenina, who, when faced with the loss of her children as a result of adultery, throws herself under a railway carriage (obviously a work not written by a woman). And the pathetic Emma Bovary, who hurls herself from a roof rather than endure a boring life with her boring husband (again, obviously a work not written by a woman). Even though Kate Chopin based *The Awakening* on Flaubert's novel, *her* Emma retreats to a pigeon house in her bid for success as an artist. She ends in a suicidal swim out to sea because she really has nothing further to live for; no adequate outlet for her career aspirations or for her passionate sexuality.

Chopin, however, makes Edna Pontellier's suicide more believable for women, as well as more open to diverse interpretations than does Flaubert with Emma Bovary. If Chopin, as it would appear, was trying to make her Emma as self-centered and degenerate and disloyal to her husband and children as Emma Bovary, she doesn't succeed. Too large a part of Chopin's own constricted feelings obviously went into her originally limited character and thereby gave to Edna Pontellier a dimension and a complexity and a motivation lacking in Flaubert. His intention was to condemn Harlequin-type novels. He felt that they gave women unreal Cinderella fantasies and tragically unrealizable expectations.

More like what suppressed women actually did is what Thomas Hardy's wife, Emma Lavinia, chose as a solution. Like Jacobs, but for different reasons, she retreated to the attic. Frustrated with being ignored whenever she made the claim that she had helped her husband write *Tess of the D'Urbervilles,* she turned "peculiar." Since she couldn't go *out,* she went *up* like Emily Dickinson. Rochester also thought of this solution for his mad mulatto wife, Bertha, in *Jane Eyre.* Her mental defectiveness is attributed to her admixture of African blood. Such retreats are immortalized in Gubar and Gilbert's, *The Madwoman in the Attic,* which contains many more examples of women confined, either voluntarily or involuntarily, to attics.

Only Lydia Maria Child's *Hobomok* is an exception, a fact which should be more celebrated and could be one of the reasons for the appropriateness of Jacobs's choice of her as her editor. Child, in the first third of the nineteenth century, allows her heroine to break away and live! And with a Native American husband, to boot. Child does, however, have him nobly yield precedence to the English aristocratic lover, to whom the heroine had originally been engaged. Hobomok masochistically fades away into the forest, once his wife's original lover returns from England alive.

Nevertheless, *Hobomok* still provides an exception to a long-standing rule for unruly women. Recently, someone deploring Kate Millett's lengthy incarceration in an Irish asylum on the flimsiest of grounds aptly quipped on this subject: If a white woman protests, she is labeled "hysterical" and "crazy" and institutionalized. If a Black woman protests, she is labeled a "militant" and promptly thrown into jail. In either event, they are confined.

Finally, for Harriet Jacobs, what then truly constituted "success?" Was it like Franklin's definition, to win fame and fortune through certain formulas which he systematized and taught as "how-to manuals?" Or was hers closer to the African concept of a collective consciousness: an individual writing primarily to project her community's problems to the larger community and to assist in publicizing certain problems relevant to her experiences so that her life could be used as a catalyst for their solution?

Like Phillis Wheatley, Harriet Jacobs's concept of success was a public one. It was important for her to act as a change agent to improve the lot of her kind, especially her Black sisters, in order to set the record straight. She wished to educate her white female readers as to the true reality of the institution of slavery, primarily in relation to sexual matters. This aim was so compelling that she was willing to sacrifice her most important possession—her privacy—the precious right to keep her tragic memories to herself with no one the wiser except those involved. To gain the confidence and good will of her white female readers, however, and to educate them, she was willing to risk losing their respect. She was willing not only to subordinate, but to subsume her personal ego needs to the collective's.

Jacobs made every effort humanly possible to get her white women readers to side with her view of things; to sympathize with her; ultimately to identify with her and project themselves into her being. All that she wrote in *Incidents* was to that end. But Jacobs also chose the most popular, the most widely accepted plot in American literary history—the classic American success story.

Jacobs's education, like Wheatley's *succès d'estime*, was unfortunately cut off by her first mistress's death. At this point, she became Dr. Flint's slave. A great deal of the book then concerns Linda's trials and tribulations. Each one includes parallel examples from the experiences of other Black female slaves. This is characteristic of the freedom narrative tradition, especially the Crafts' narrative, which, of all the works in this genre, is most chock-full of legal precedents, citations from laws, examples, etc. The aim and the result is to lend journalistic, even scholarly, credence to the incidents. Yet it is woven in so masterfully in Jacobs's case, unlike the Crafts', that it does not intrude into the narrative or mar its pace.

At exactly the same point in life (age twelve) that Franklin ran away from home to start a new life, Jacobs was enslaved to the Flints. While Franklin explored a new city (Philadelphia and its environs), and even traveled to France and England, Jacobs stagnated in servitude. She was caught between a lascivious master (endlessly thinking up new torments for her in order to get Jacobs to accede to what he considered were his sexual rights), and a tormented and tormenting mistress. At the time when Mrs. Flint was most cruelly persecuting Jacobs, the latter considered a flight to freedom. But the results for the young

Jacobs would have been far worse if she had been caught and forced to return than for the young Franklin.

For many years, all the time that Franklin was painstakingly building his reputation and his successful business, Jacobs was trapped in a nightmare, constantly veering from thinking up ploys and stratagems to keep Dr. Flint at bay, to hopes and dreams and plans for flight and freedom. For Jacobs, yielding to Flint meant being deprived of options, of choices. As a slave, it seems that Jacobs would have admitted that she was deprived of such a luxury and given up in defeat. But she never did, as illustrated when she and her Black lover respectfully requested permission of Dr. Flint to marry.

By rejecting their request, Dr. Flint made it as clear as any master could that he had no intention of permitting Jacobs to enjoy any of those situations in life which denote prestige and success for free or slave women. Despite this, Jacobs never acted or thought as a slave, at least in terms of her body. Her flesh became the battleground over which the issue of slavery was waged. By denying Flint possession of her flesh, Jacobs was denying Flint ownership over it, over her corporeal essence. On the other hand, in Douglass's *Narrative*, we see the issue of slavery not as one of physical violation, but as bound up with culturally inscribed masculinity values devolving around the nature of manhood. The famous "manhood" passage is a case in point. Douglass declares that he is a man and no longer a slave after he has fought Covey, the slave breaker, to a stand-still: "It was a glorious resurrection, from the tomb of slavery to the heaven of freedom. My long-crushed spirit rose, cowardice departed, bold defiance took its place; and I now resolved that, however long I might remain a slave in form, the day had passed forever when I could be a slave in fact. I did not hesitate to let it be known of me, that the white man who expected to succeed in whipping, must also succeed in killing me" (Douglas 1990:1680–1681).

Flogging a man's body and gaining access to and entry into a woman's body were seen as tantamount humiliations. In either case, neither Douglass nor Jacobs was willing to succumb without superhuman resistance, so deeply did they both internalize this connection, so much resonance and power did it have for them. If Douglass were beaten for reasons that he could justify, he would accept it. If Jacobs were to permit sexual knowledge of her by a male, it would be by her choice. Thus the most significant element in each slave's situation was their need for choice. They would rather be deprived of life than the power to make their own decisions. For them both, the privilege of free choice signified freedom, which, in turn, signified ultimate human success.

Jacobs, however, embeds herself within her African/African American community, even after freedom, far more than Douglass does. Yellin sees the difference mainly in Douglass's emphasis on "physical bravery, an important masculine attribute," whereas Jacobs presents it "in terms of motherhood, the most valued 'feminine' role" (Jacobs 1987:xxvi). Noble as Douglass's efforts are, he gives a strong impression of himself as a heroic individual on a quest for individual success and self-fulfillment at the end of his work. This is in the Western tradition, and specifically, the tradition established by Franklin.

Although Douglass never stresses material success, *per se*, he went to great pains to point out to his former master and to American society how gravely Auld underestimated him and his abilities. Douglass was in truth one of the greatest men of his time of any race anywhere on the globe, and at the very least, a national treasure to the United States. Even during the post-Reconstruction period, that hard time for African Americans, he succeeded in attaining positions with the federal government. Before his death, he served as the United States minister to Haiti, employment only somewhat commensurate with his enormous abilities. He saw himself as and was very much a public figure, as his neglect of his home, his wife, and family underscore.

As for Jacobs, at the end of her text, she pays tribute to her family and friends, both white *and* Black. She further expresses joy at living free, but disappointment at not having achieved a home for herself and her children. With this symbol, "home," her ultimate definition of success, Jacobs reveals a private individual who went public only for compelling cause, her people.

Notes

1. She discovered later that her children did know but took advantage of the fact that they were children and pretended otherwise. For example, her son signified on Dr. Flint when the doctor returned from a fruitless search expedition to New York for Jacobs by calling out: "Dr. Flint, did you bring my mother home? I want to see her" (1987:116).

2. Hine writes in this regard: "Virtually every known nineteenth-century female slave narrative contains a reference to, at some juncture, the ever present threat and reality of rape" (1989:912).

3. See Baker's Introduction to his *Modernism and the Harlem Renaissance* (Chicago: University of Chicago Press, 1987), for his depiction of its enormous influence for two generations on African Americans in terms of paradigms for Black male success.

References

Baker, Houston, Jr. *Blues, Ideology, and Afro-American Literature: A Vernacular Theory*. Evanston, IL: University of Chicago Press, 1984.

Busia, Abena P. A. "Silencing Syncorax: On African Colonial Discourse and the Unvoiced Female." *Cultural Critique* 14 (Winter 1989–1990): 81–104.

Butterfield, Stephen. *Black Autobiography in America*. Amherst: University of Massachusetts Press, 1974.

Collins, Patricia Hill. "The Social Construction of Black Feminist Thought." *Signs* 15.3 (Spring 1989): 745–773.

Cudjoe, Selwyn R. "Maya Angelou and the Autobiographical Statement." *Black Women Writers 1950–1980: A Critical Evaluation*. Ed. Mari Evans. New York: Anchor, Doubleday, 1984.

Dolle, Raymond. "Review of 'Surprizing Narrative': Olaudah Equiano and the Beginnings of Black Autobiography by Angelo Costanzo." *Black American Literature Forum* 23.4 (Winter, 1989): 785–791.

Douglass, Frederick. *Narrative of the Life of Frederick Douglass, an American Slave as Written by Himself*. Ed. Paul Lauter, et al. Vol. I. New York: Heath, 1990.

Gates, Henry Louis, Jr. "To Be Raped, Bred or Abused." *The New York Times Book Review*. November 12, 1987: 12.

Hine, Darlene Clark. "Rape and the Inner Lives of Black Women in the Middle West: Preliminary Thoughts on the Culture of Dissemblance." *Signs* 14.4 (Summer 1989): 912–920.

Jacobs, Harriet A. *Incidents in the Life of a Slave Girl Written by Herself*. Ed. and intro. Jean Fagan Yellin. Cambridge, MA: Harvard University Press, 1987.

Jones, Gayle, ed. *Black Women Writers At Work*. New York: Continuum Press, 1983.

Morrison, Toni. "Rootedness: The Ancestor as Foundation." *Black Women Writers 1950–1980: A Critical Evaluation*. Ed. Mari Evans. New York: Anchor, Doubleday, 1984.

Washington, Booker T. *Up From Slavery*. New York: Penguin, 1987. First printed 1901.

Werner, Craig. "On the Ends of Afro-American 'Modernist' Autobiography." *Black American Literature Forum* 24.2 (Summer, 1990): 203–220.

"DIS AIN'T NO BUSINESS PROPOSITION. DIS IS UH LOVE GAME": ZORA NEALE HURSTON'S DISJUNCTIVE CONJUNCTIONS AND EUROPEAN AMERICAN SUCCESS MYTHS IN *THEIR EYES WERE WATCHING GOD*

In *Their Eyes Were Watching God*, Mrs. Turner, who is depicted as a "turner" against her people, fulminates against Washington for Uncle Tomming whites. This is a most ironic charge on her part, considering this is *her* foible. Janie, in contrast, reveals that her family regarded Washington almost as a god, as "a great big man":

> "You oughta meet my brother," Mrs. Turner suggests to Janie. "He read uh paper on Booker T. Washington and tore him tuh pieces." Janie responds with shock. "Booker T? He wuz a great big man, wusn't he?"
>
> "'Sposed tuh be. All he ever done was cut de monkey for white folks. So dey pomped him up. But you know whut de ole folks say 'de higher de monkey climbs de mo' he show his behind' so dat's de way it wuz wit Booker T. Mah brother hit him every time dey give 'im change tuh speak."
>
> "Ah was raised on de notion dat he wuz uh great big man," was all that Janie knew to say.
>
> "He didn't do nothin' but hold us back—talkin' bout work when de race ain't never done nothin' else. He wuz uh enemy tuh us, dat's whut. He wuz uh white folks' nigger." According to all Janie had been taught this was sacrilege so she sat without speaking at all. (1978:212)

Here Hurston is being autobiographical. Her parents and maternal grandparents were influenced by Washington, whose

155

program was first enunciated and developed in their native state, Alabama, at Tuskegee Institute. From 1895, when he gave his speech at the Atlanta Exposition, Washington's power and influence began to expand throughout the country. On January 1, 1900, it extended to the very shores of Africa itself when nine heroic Tuskegee graduate volunteers (all to perish tragically sooner or later from the rigors of the climate), initiated Washington's "self-help" program there.

In Hurston's works, many of her Black male characters during the post-Reconstruction period in the South are preoccupied, as was her family, with the struggle to achieve this hitherto for-white-men-only goal of economic security. However, the Bookerite mythology, emulating Franklin mythology in terms of white women, conceptualized Black women as only indirectly involved in the struggle upward. If they stood by and well behind their men, went the argument, Black women would thereby benefit.

Beverly Guy-Sheftall believes that this argument emerged out of the European American "cult of True Womanhood" and that Black males, like white males, "were also shaped by their acceptance of the True Womanhood ideal." This despite the fact that Black men knew that "because of their historical circumstances," Black women "could not be expected to conform totally to this ideal." Nevertheless, Black men argued that Black women could somehow "provide a new model of the ideal woman and could be seen as an alternative to the dominant cultural ideal of womanhood." As for Black women "(especially the elite), they were outraged over the persistent attacks on their character and the refusal of the larger society to recognize their womanhood." Even more crucial to my argument is Guy-Sheftall's contention that in "internalizing the values of the cult of domesticity, they also felt that the elevation and protection of women were critical to the survival of the black race" (1990:12).

Hurston's mother lived by this ideal, and Hurston clearly attempts to follow it in her writing, if not in her life. What Diane Sadoff remarks about *Mules and Men* is true of Hurston in general and in *Their Eyes Were Watching God* in particular, in that her stories "articulate sexual politics with race and serve to normalize and regularize conflict between the sexes." (1985:15).

Tea Cake in *Their Eyes* takes the identical position in relation to his wife, Janie, as Hurston recollects her father talking about *his* wife. Here Tea Cake boasts to Janie: "Ah no need no assistance tuh help me feed mah woman. From now on, yuh gointuh eat whutever mah money can buy yuh and wear de same. When Ah ain't got nothin' you don't git nothin'" (1978:191). Similarly, John Pearson, according to his approving daughter, "not only boasted among other men about "his house full of young'uns" but he boasted that he had never allowed his wife to go out and hit a lick of work for anybody a day in her life." Janie's response to Tea Cake's boast was: "Dat's all right wid me" (1978:191). Lucy's is not recorded, but it was probably similar.

Likewise, Janie's previous husband, Joe Starks, had expressed the same attitude toward women: "A pretty doll-baby lak you is made to sit on de front porch and rock and fan yo'self and eat p'taters dat other folks plant just special for you. . . . You ain't never knowed what it was to be treated lak a lady and Ah wants to be de one tuh show you. . . . You come go wid me. Den all de rest of yo' natural life you kin live lak you want" (1978:49).

Joe does not, as Janie and the readers assume, mean that he would treat her "lak a lady" himself, only that his subjects would, once he becomes the "chief" of Eatonville. He treats her like a servant, much as an African chief treats his wives, and even puts Janie to work in his general store. Under his critical, peevish tutelage, Janie serves a bondage which turns out to be "a blessing in the end," according to Houston Baker, Jr. ("Zora Neale Hurston" 1987:37). For after Joe's death, Janie can vaunt her contempt for economics in relation to romance all she wants to without fear, "because she sells Starks's store to finance the relationship [with Tea Cake, her next husband]. It is important to note that the term 'Starks's store' disguises, at least in part, the fact that a share of the store as a commodity is surely a function of the protagonist's labor. Janie works for years in the store without receiving more than subsistence provisions. The 'surplus value' that accrues from her labor as equity is rightfully hers to dispose of as she chooses." This is because "her position derives from the petit bourgeois enterprises she has shared with her deceased husband" ("Zora Neale Hurston" 1987:37).

Thus Janie isn't really dependent on the rise or fall of her next and final husband's fiscal fortunes, although Tea Cake always manages to support both of them adequately. She has inherited a modicum of comfort from Joe Starks, whose ruthless pursuit of property, Baker maintains, is grounded on the "economics of slavery." These economics enable Starks's widow to enjoy "personal freedom." Should she ever need to, she can rely on money in the bank, rentals, and a fine home. Conveniently for Janie, she can also return to all this after Tea Cake's death.

Real life, however, was not so convenient for Janie's creator. After Lucy died, John Hurston's good fortune began to erode, according to their daughter's account. She felt her father's economic problems were in large measure due to the fact that his first wife was no longer around to provide common sense, to anchor him in reality:

> The hard-driving force [Lucy Hurston] was no longer opposed to his easy-going pace. He could put his potentialities to sleep and be happy in the laugh of the day. He could do next year or never, what Mama would have insisted must be done today. Rome, the eternal city, meant two different things to my parents. To Mama, it meant, you must build it today so it could last through eternity. To Papa, it meant that you could plan to lay some bricks today and you have the rest of eternity to finish it. With all time, why hurry? God had made more time than anything else, anyway. Why act so stingy about it? . . . With my mother gone and nobody to guide him, life had not hurt him, but it had turned him loose to hurt himself. . . . Old Maker had left out the steering gear when He gave Papa his talents. (Hurston, *Dust Tracks* 1984:172)

Thus, after her mother's death, Hurston never again enjoyed any such cushions as she fantasizes for her heroine. Nevertheless, Hurston depicts her male characters struggling to provide for their women, usually successfully. In contrast, their womenfolk struggle also (like Lucy Hurston), but entirely for their men and their children, never for personal, direct fulfillment.

James Krasner, in refuting Ann Rayson's claim that Hurston saw "'herself as a kind of black, female Ben Franklin in *Dust Tracks'*" (Krasner 1989:43) comes close to my interpretation of Hurston's point of view when he suggests instead that "Joe Starks is a better candidate for a black Franklin and that Hurston's understanding of the nature of female autobiography precludes the possibility of a Franklinish life story" (1989:117). However, none of these critics, even Baker (whose first chapter of *Modernism and the Harlem Renaissance* is devoted to Booker T. Washington), seems aware that it was Washington's autobiography and life's work to which Hurston was responding, not Franklin's. In fact, Hurston (in addition to the earlier quote in which a sleazy character criticizes Washington), always defends Washington, whose influence on her is strong in many ways. For example, in "My People! My People!" in *Dust Tracks*, Hurston makes a prophetic critique of the same situation as exists today (if for opposite reasons) when she complains that "there was no analysis, no seeking for merits on the part of so-called 'Race Champions' who 'wanted nothing to do with anything frankly Negroid.' This sort simply contented themselves with damning Washington as 'absolutely vile for advocating industrial education'"(1984:233).

Again in the same text, Hurston reveals that she has internalized Washington's sayings to the extent that European Americans have internalized Franklin's. When she returns triumphantly to Eatonville on a scholarship to study folklore there, she uses a saying of Washington's in an attempt to convey her precise emotions: "Booker T. Washington said once that you must not judge a man by the heights to which he has risen, but by the depths from which he came. So to me these honors meant something, insignificant as they might appear to the world. It was a long step for the waif of Eatonville. From the depth of my inner heart I appreciated the fact that the world had not been altogether unkind to Mama's child" (1984:172).

Black women's connection to the European American male success myth is at any rate tenuous: an indirect and secondary one, although some of them, like Janie's grandmother, believe strongly in it as devoted accessories to its achievement. Like Nanny, they accede to their status as subordinates and servants to their men as a given of their lives. But overall, Hurston's response to the "self-help" philosophy is that it is really basically alien and irrelevant to her heroines on some deep inner level of their beings. Essentially, her heroines have different visions, different goals, different desires, different myths from men. Here Hurston links a second myth, the Cinderella love myth for women to the male success myth that Janie is maintaining. Through Janie's romanticism, Hurston reveals that the male success myth is really basically alien and irrelevant to all women, even those who commit themselves to it, like Nanny.

Krasner maintains, however, that "Janie's life story is built on the male model," that in relation to Janie, Hurston, as well as her recent feminist critics, uses a "language of fulfillment, reduction, and possession typical of the success-oriented male autobiography" (1989:117). I contend, despite these arguments, that Hurston is not here working on a male model, but on the Cinderella model. The male success mythology is predicated on action of an external nature. The male is up and doing, goes somewhere, is active out in the world, strives to achieve, attempts upward mobility through exhausting exertions on his own agency. In contrast, the Cinderella model is passive in nature. Fulfillment, etc., comes to the waiting heroine *from* the outside world in the person of Prince Charming. He suddenly erupts into her boring life and sweeps her away to another world far from the prior scene of (in)action. Indeed, in Janie's case this happens twice.

Reflecting these essential differences and Lucy Hurston's example, Hurston postulates women as essentially driven to cleave to their men, once they find them, or, rather, once their men find them, as is generally the case. As Diane Sadoff puts it: "Hurston plays the passive role she deems proper for the woman of color dependent on others for her economic and literary security" (1985:20). True enough, for Hurston's women depend on their men to make the decisions for them. Devoid of interest in financial details because of a blind trust in their men, they fervently believe that what their men decide is best for them.

Hurston's heroines are therefore supportive of their men, no matter what, whether they struggle for material success, like Logan Killicks and Joe Starks, or whether they live spontaneously for the moment, as their whims seize them, like Tea Cake. The *content* of the situation does not much matter to these women. They are willing to compromise with it, even suffer it, so long as the *context* remains a loving relationship with their men. They hand over the reins of power to them. Hurston's female protagonists are depicted as above and beyond material considerations, "business propositions," as Janie puts it. They live in another realm of existence above a mundane world beset by any financial or economic considerations such as Nanny has to deal with all her life.

The heroine's dedication and commitment to her man is total. The love myth, Hurston reveals, is paramount with her, as she writes immediately after her second separation from Arthur Price: "I have the satisfaction of knowing that I have loved and been loved by the perfect man. If I never hear of love again, I have known the real thing" (*Dust Tracks* 1984:43). Her heroine feels the same way: "Of course he wasn't dead. He could never be dead until she herself had finished feeling and thinking. The kiss of his memory made pictures of love and light against the wall. Here was peace. She pulled in her horizon like a great fish net" (*Their Eyes* 1978:286).

The implication left by Hurston for the reader in this passage is that Janie will live on in Eatonville comfortably housebound, in pensive, eternal dedication to her beloved husband's memory. Far from seeing this ending as the romantic resolution it appears to be, Sadoff views it as Hurston's having "motivated her narrative, perhaps unconsciously, to act out her rage against male domination and to free Janie, a figure for herself, from all men," and states that "the novel covers over this subversive material" (1985:22). Whether this is the case or not, Hurston plots it so that once the woman has yielded autonomy to the man she loves, economic sufficiency will somehow accrue to her, according to the tenets of the Bookerite "self help" philosophy.

Hurston applied this Bookerite theorem all over the place—to the fictional Janie of *Their Eyes*, to Lucy of *Jonah's Gourd Vine*, and to the real life Lucy, Hurston's mother, of *Dust Tracks on a Road*, who died before her husband's prosperity and success eroded. But when push came to shove, Lucy's daughter followed her mother's pattern of subordination in her love life. Interestingly, even though Hurston "embalmed" in Tea Cake's and Janie's romance "all the tenderness of her passion" for Price (*Dust Tracks* 1984:268), she would not compromise or sacrifice her writing career for any of her husbands, even her favorite one, Hurston claims in her autobiography.

In *Their Eyes Were Watching God*, Hurston summed up the essence of her marriage to Price: that Janie had been longing for Prince Charming for fourteen years when Tea Cake finally appeared in her life, if only for two years. Here Sadoff sees some further fascinating parallels between Hurston's characteristic conduct and Janie's love relationships:

> Indeed, many incidents between Janie and Jody, and Janie and Tea Cake are clearly transposed from her troubled relationship with Price. Janie's desire, for example, to tell stories and to achieve verbal power in the face of Jody's denial are figures for Hurston's drive to write novels and essays in the face of Price's insecure demand that she give up her career for their relationship. Like many women before and after her, Hurston used work to manipulate her relationship; when things got tough, she left home to do folklore research, to take her Guggenheim fellowship. (1984:20)

Even though she was Lucy's daughter philosophically, even though she believed in the Cinderella myth, when it came to her own career, Prince Charming's attractions could not compete, Hurston informs us:

> If he [her second husband, Arthur Price] could only have realized what a lot he had to offer, he need not have suffered so much through doubting that he could hold me. I was hog-tied and branded, but he didn't realize it. He could make me fetch and carry, but he wouldn't believe it. . . . He begged me to give up my career, marry him and live outside of New York City. I really wanted to do anything he wanted me to, but that one thing I could not do. It was not just my contract with my publishers, it was that I had things clawing inside of me that must be said. I could not see that my work should make any difference in marriage. He was all and everything else to me but that. One did not conflict with the other in my mind. But it

was different with him. He felt that he did not matter to me enough. He was the master kind. All, or nothing, for him. (*Dust Tracks* 1984:40)

It was Hurston who ended up with nothing. She died in such poverty that she was buried in a pauper's grave. Even Alice Walker, her writing daughter, who diligently searched for its location, may or may not have found it.[1]

As long as she is without a man, Janie follows her own inner desires which are attuned to the processes of nature, as symbolized by "the orgasmic pear tree." By herself, she remains true to herself, not to the masculine success myth nor to the hedonistic pursuit of pleasure. Both directions signal for Hurston egotistic individualism. Both ignore the workings of the natural world. But when Janie loves a man, again like Hurston, she cedes autonomy to him, obeys and serves him. Janie even accepts being beaten by Tea Cake, if only for the wonderfully passionate aftermath. Here again, Hurston is recreating her recent experience with Price, who had beaten her (but she had begun it, Hurston says). Moreover, Janie sets her man's judgments and decisions up as law over her, to *his* eventual downfall and her premature widowhood. Here Hurston is no doubt signifying covertly to Price (that is, if he ever set eyes on this work), and perhaps to men as a group. Had he been willing to compromise (in Price's case, to live in New York near her publishers with Hurston), to yield himself to his wife's decision, his life would have been happier.

In Lucy's and John Hurston's relationship; in Janie's and Killicks'; in Janie's and Joe's; in Janie's and Tea Cake's, the husbands' poor judgments and decisions at key points bring them to ruin, destruction, and even death—terrible ones. John Hurston was run over by a car; John Pearson gets crushed by a train; Logan Killicks is deserted by his young wife (and no doubt becomes the butt of community signifying for the rest of his life); Jody Stark dies of a stomach cancer. Tea Cake undergoes transformation into a mad dog and ends up being shot down like one. In the latter situation, especially, one cannot help but wonder if there is any spite aginst Price on Hurston's part. Whether or not this is so, in every instance the wives have superior acumen and common sense, but are never consulted by their husbands.

Nevertheless, economic self-sufficiency automatically and naturally ensues for the heroine, every time. This Bookerite theorem is shown working for the fictional Janie and Lucy, as well as the real life Lucy Hurston. Hurston's attitude toward those who seek fulfillment in life solely in a struggle for material and financial success is reflected in her excellent portrayal of Janie's well-meaning but ultimately wrong and wrong-headed grandmother in *Their Eyes*. That is, wrong and wrong-headed if viewed in the context of the European American mythology about marriage. By African standards, however, Nanny's concept of marriage is the norm. Janie's concept of marriage, however, is European American.

Hurston's superb depiction of the character Nanny is based on several characters. Nanny's materialistic streak comes from Hurston's maternal grandmother, a Bookerite. The tragic aspects of Nanny's past, her repeated rapes and exploitation by her master, are taken from Hurston's paternal grandmother's history. Another important quality of Nanny's, her dogmatic materialism, is taken from Lucy Hurston, as well as her brooding protectiveness and concern for her grandchild's well-being in the face of her own imminent demise.

Hurston's maternal grandparents owned a small farm abundantly stocked with luscious fruit trees which she always remembered as a kind of Eden from which she had been exiled. Once, after Lucy had been disowned for marrying John Hurston, her mother had chased Lucy off the property for attempting to pick some peaches. Obviously an opinionated and domineering individual (traits which her granddaughter evidently inherited), Hurston's maternal grandmother objected to her daughter's choice of John Hurston on the grounds that his family was from "over the creek" (across the tracks) and that he was of illegitimate birth, the result of a master's rape. She refused to attend the wedding and always disapproved of her granddaughter, at least according to Hurston, on the grounds that the child was forward, too sure of herself, and physically resembled her father. Ironically, Hurston did not benefit from this resemblance to her father, as one would expect. He preferred another daughter who favored his wife.

Nanny, a former slave, is a Bookerite. According to Sadoff, she "cooperate[s] to oppress the black woman" by conspiring, due to "her class aspiration," with "male dominance." She does this by working hard for whites while "knowing her place" and keeping it. Meanwhile, she waits for the best financial offer for Janie. Then, she believes, her granddaughter will acquire status through marriage and will not have to work so hard just to survive, as Nanny has had to do.

Work at home for one's husband and children was not considered work, but one's "sacred duty" or mission on the grounds that women were responsible for "the uplift of the race." As Guy-Sheftall puts it in her study of this period: "Black men also internalize at least some of the culture's notions about sex roles. . . . They . . . believe that they should protect their women from the evils of the world and that black women, because of their sex, should assume the major responsibility for the moral stature of the race" (1990:172–173).

Guy-Sheftall agrees with my position that Booker T. Washington's role and influence were paramount in the attitudes of both Black men and women of this period. In terms of women, Washington established at Tuskegee Institute a separate department for them in order to train them in the most efficient and technologically advanced methods (for that time) of household maintenance, food planning and shopping, dressmaking, millinery, horticulture, printing, broom making, mattress making, upholstery, cooking, laundering, basketry, etc.

Margaret Murray Washington herself, Washington's third wife, among her manifold other activities, served as director of Industries for Girls at Tuskegee. A prominent club woman of her time, Mrs. Washington was a member of the National Association of Colored Women and an editor on the board of its house organ, *The Woman's Era*. The publication was founded by Josephine St. Pierre Ruffin, a longtime associate of Elizabeth Cady Stanton and Susan B. Anthony. Other editors on the pro-suffrage publication, which was also strong in its advocacy of the rights of women, especially Black women, included such luminaries as Ida B. Wells-Barnett, Mary Church Terrell, Fannie

Barrier Williams, and Josephine Silone Yates. Guy-Sheftall describes this publication as "the first periodical ever published by black women in this country and perhaps the best vehicle for the articulation of the political aspiration of black women during the period" (1990:107).

In terms of the Hurston family and Hurston herself, Washington can be seen as a powerful influence on John and Lucy Hurston's perception of the role of Black women in the home. Black women, like Lucy Hurston, should work at home. She could involve herself in church organizations related to her role as wife and mother, but never aspire to supplement her husband as a wage earner and family breadwinner. Washington, however, went further than the Hurstons. He saw the making of a home as a full-time occupation, as a profession, as a mission, in fact, for Black women, much as Elsa Barkley Brown's mother saw it (and for the same reasons) a generation later.

Washington took Black women's service in the home seriously, giving it great respect. He nevertheless justified Black women carrying their talents and skills outside the home into public life (always making sure to use the discourse of his audience, in this case, Black men and women). They could do this on one condition however: that their community would be thereby served; if they worked as "teachers, societal workers, freedom fighters . . . evangelists, clubwomen and crusaders for the advancement of black women" [like Margaret Murray Washington and her friends], whom, we are not surprised to learn, he "singles out . . . for special attention" (Guy-Sheftall 1990:150).

Unfortunately, Guy-Sheftall takes Washington at face value. But when signifiers like Washington talk to whites, they *never* express the Black perspective. They always talk as if from deep within the white psyche—with a significant twist, however. Their real purpose is not to empower their white patrons but to disarm and charm them out of whatever it is that the signifier wants: liberty, social and gender equality, money, power, education, etc.

Signifying is a covert technique, neither broadcast nor signaled. This has made it difficult for readers unfamiliar with a "second discourse" to recognize it even when it is crucial that they do so in order to avoid sometimes tragic consequences for a writer's message. This happened to too many signifiers in the past. What Deborah G. Plant points out about Hurston holds equally true for others employing this technique:

> A major irony is that Hurston expects her ideal reader to be able to "interpret the incidents and direction of [her] life" based on what she has said as well as that which she has left unsaid. The parallel strategies at work in the text leave the author open to charges of duplicity, narrative cowardice, and psychological enslavement. And because the author never *clearly* asserts herself or openly contradicts obvious falsehoods, the contradictions which reveal the second discourse are largely implied, and therefore, have, for the most part, gone unexamined. It is left to the reader, the ideal-narratee, to decipher the implications and reconcile the two discourses.
>
> Through the ideal-narratee, Hurston makes an appeal for a sympathetic ear. But most critics have been balked by surface content, focusing only on the discourse directed to whites. Instead of being understood by those from whom she wished it most, *Dust Tracks* is condemned, ridiculed, and understood only partially, at best. If readers/critics will give as much attention to the narrative strategies in *Dust Tracks* as to the narration and audience, they may discover a reading of the text which could give a fuller understanding of Hurston. They may hear her authentic voice. (1989:23)

Guy-Sheftall, in critiquing a speech of Washington's to white theology faculty of Vanderbilt University intended to get them to support "local training schools for domestic servants," unfortunately takes Washington at face value when he argues (to whites) that they should give money to Tuskegee and similar Black schools because white children have always been raised so well by their Mammies that they would be raised even better if their Mammies could have an education which would sharpen their intelligence, help make them cleaner and even more morally fit "to come in contact with that pure and innocent [white] child" (1989:147).

Guy-Sheftall here completely misses Washington's obvious signifying on his audience. This is how she comes to the incorrect conclusion that his discourse was "a clear indication that

Washington's major concern is the welfare of the white family rather than the black home, which distinguishes him from most other blacks during the period"(1989:147). In fact, Washington's "major concern" was keeping a straight face under his "minstrel" mask (as was Hurston's); not laughing too loudly at the expense of his white audience(s) whenever the Black schools for which he raised funds wrote and thanked him for all the millions he was able to extract from whites by beating them at their own game (playing into their deepest prejudices), i.e., signifying.

Throughout this harsh and bleak period in American history for African Americans, Washington served on the board of trustees of most Black colleges, universities, and secondary schools of the time. This was not because he was such a good friend to whites, but because he "got over" on them best. He was a genius at raising money from the rich white "Old Boy" network, at playing off their prejudices to the advantage of Black education.

Most other Blacks of the period knew exactly what Washington was doing—nothing less than "the dozens" on his and his race's smug and unsuspecting white opponents. This is exactly what Wheatley, Jacobs, Harper, Cooper, Chesnutt, and Hurston did and what Africans in Africa and throughout the diaspora have done for centuries to their powerful opponents. As Baker puts it: "He [Washington] demonstrates that he knows that it is a minstrel mask he must master if he wishes to advance a Tuskegee project" (*Modernism* 1987:99).

Baker sees Washington as a brilliant and cynical manipulator of a minstrel mask to "get over." Perhaps Washington (and other signifiers on whites, including Hurston), might better be likened to "double agents." In this sense, Washington comes across as a spy in the enemy camp who successfully convinces a powerful opponent of his unreserved participation in the opponent's ideology. By this definition, Washington might be considered the most successful Black "double agent" of all time.

Washington had an even greater challenge than any spy. His opponents could easily observe that he was not a member of the in-group, whereas other successful double agents have always blended in by speaking the same dialect, going to the same schools, and having the same outward appearance as their enemies. Washington had none of these advantages. As a result, his enormous accomplishment in mediating European American male success mythology economically for his people at perhaps their most difficult period in this country should never be discounted because he did it by signifying rather than head-on confrontation.

Historically, how far would plain talk have gotten the cause of Black education and economic advancement in this country at that time? Charles Waddell Chesnutt, a friend of Washington's and an adept signifier in his own works, described the period accurately when he wrote in *The New York Independent* of April 2, 1891, according to Sally Ann Ferguson:

> All over the country they [the Black race] are the victims of cruel race prejudice, the strength and extent of which none but cultivated, self-respecting colored people can rightly apprehend. It pervades every department of life—politics, the schools, the churches, business, society—everywhere. . . . There is actually no single locality in the United States where a man avowedly connected by blood with the Negro race can hold up his head and feel that he is the recognized equal of other men . . . or where he is not taught to feel every day that he is regarded as something inferior to those who were fortunate enough to be born entirely white. (1988–1989:111–112)

It is ahistoric not to take the circumstances of the time into account in Washington's decision to go the route he chose. He even mediated with success politically for his people, although he claimed publicly that he held no truck with political solutions to race problems. He acted on more occasions and in more acceptable ways than has been recognized by contemporary readers familiar only with the underhanded aspects of his "Tuskegee Machine," especially in contrast to DuBois' courageous directness of approach. Actually, Washington accomplished much more than DuBois politically and in every other arena of his endeavors during his lifetime (1856–1915). He had millions of followers and far more influence than any other African American of his time after Frederick Douglass. His influence reached into the White House and out to Europe and Africa. For example, Washington, not DuBois, was instrumental in the NAACP's successful campaign against lynching. This without the knowledge either of the NAACP or the American public. He got the lawyer, paid the legal fees, etc., all while staunchly maintaining his accommodationist role in public.

Washington had flaws. He was a human being, after all, as were Douglass and DuBois. Yet Washington's covert strategy and indirect techniques in relation to whites are so offensive (because seen only from their surface "accommodationist" appearance today) that other race leaders of the time, particularly DuBois, are iconized at his expense, and he is relegated, instead, to undeserved obscurity.

Hurston's strategy and techniques were identical to Washington's. In fact, her eminent biographer, Robert Hemenway, in his introduction to Hurston's autobiography maintains that "what has not received proper emphasis is the way in which Hurston's pride in region combined with her bicultural perspective to lead to accommodationist politics" (Hurston, *Dust Tracks* 1984:xxiv). Like Washington, Hurston was successfully trashed for being an "accommodationist," for "playing up to whites" among her other "faults," because her discourse in relation to whites was read as transparent and her conduct as problematic, until recently.[2]

Like Washington, Hurston also languished long in obscurity until Hemenway and her writing "daughter" Alice Walker, sparked a reevaluation of her contributions based on a greater understanding of her historical circumstances. What Toni Cade Bambara reminds us not to "continually resist" in regard to Hurston can well apply to Washington in terms of his life as an educator and politician in service to his race:

> Just as Zora wrote against the stereotypes of the day and gave us, particularly those of us who list her among our critical foremothers, new categories of perception (women's images)— and new ways to consider the stuff of our lives (folkways as the basis of "art"), she was also in continual battle against stereotype perceptions of herself as countrified fool, bodacious hussy, etc., many of which she experimented with while doing her numbah, and we/I have to continually resist the various interpretations handed down in the past decades—Zora as

victim, as ritual doll, as hustler, etc., if we are to get to the glory of the work itself. (1984:45)

Although she had the advantage over Washington of being born in an all-Black owned and run town, whereas he was born on a small plantation ("illegitimate" and in the greatest of poverty, like Hurston's father, John), Washington supported the concept of independent and self-sufficient Black towns ideologically and financially and with his own great personal and financial efforts on their behalf wherever they sprang up. This separatism and other planks in Washington's platform attracted Marcus Garvey and the African National Congress. They realized that he was signifying on whites; that the signifying monkey always pretends to fawn on the lion; that Brer Rabbit always flatters Old Master; that underneath all Washington's posturing to whites, he was following an ancient African formula of conduct in the face of a powerful enemy. Washington's "concern" was never, as Guy-Sheftall maintains, for "the welfare of the white," but how to manipulate the white opponent in a life and death battle, in a struggle for survival for his people. Washington specialized in working the southern white power structure (and later the north's, as well); to manipulate them, to work on their prejudices in order to improve the conditions of his own group. Thus he (and Hurston) used discourse these whites both expected and wanted to hear solely in order to disarm them. By seemingly reinforcing their belief systems, he could effectuate his own purposes.

Gates mocks Hurston's mockers. He maintains that Hurston *seemed* to act "the fool who 'cut the monkey' for voyeurs and pandered to the rich white women who were her patrons" (1985:43). It should be evident to any knowledgeable reader that Hurston put on a mask identical to Washington's when it came to forwarding *her* agenda. As Plant informs us:

> "Puttin' on ole Massa" came easy to Hurston; she knew what her white readership wanted and expected to see and hear, and she knew how to satisfy their expectations. Her autobiography wears all the faces of the mask . . . particularly the face of fawning ingratiation. She would play the part of the naive "darky" when talking to her patrons, then . . . she would "wink

when she was through so as to show that she had tricked them
again." (1989:18)

This was the same technique that Wheatley used on
occasion, as I have shown earlier: covert guerilla warfare using
the opponent's own weapon, its discourse. Washington, by
conflating the European American discourse of "True
Womanhood" with their affection for "their Negro Mammy" in
the kitchen and nursery, succeeded in obtaining funding for
Tuskegee for *his* purposes, in accord with *his* agenda. By
dignifying domestic service to whites, Guy-Sheftall informs us,
Washington "provided a means for black women to ease the
financial burden that plagued their families since their husbands
had menial jobs" (1990:148). It also tied in with Mrs.
Washington's efforts to train Black women to serve the Black
community by giving them an education which would improve
Black "home life." Another motive not publicized to whites, but
which both Washingtons, Hurston, and Blacks everywhere
concurred in, was to wrest decent lives for both sexes out of an
intensely hostile and racist society.

So it is that Nanny is motivated to persuade her Janie to
marry another quintessential Bookerite, Logan Killicks, the
successful owner of a sixty-acre farm. It is his economic success
which has decided the elderly grandmother in his favor, aware
that she is soon to die and leave her grandchild without
protection in a brutal world. Nanny is attempting to do the very
best she can for Janie before she leaves her to struggle on alone.
She is by no means insensitive, either, to her granddaughter's
romantic tendency and sexual revulsion for the ugly old Killicks.
However, influenced by Washington's stress on economic
success and by traditional African concepts of marriage (which
are economic and political, not romantic), she believes that
women should suppress such needs when they intrude on
economics:

> "Heah you got uh prop tuh lean on all yo' boawn days,
> and big protection, and everybody got tuh tip dey hat tuh you
> and call you Mis' Killicks, and you come worryin' me 'bout
> love."

"But Nanny, Ah wants to want him sometimes. Ah don't want him to do all de wantin'."

"If you don't want him, you sho oughta. Heah you is wid de onliest organ in town, amongst colored folks, in yo' parlor. Got a house bought and paid for and sixty acres uh land right on de big road and . . . Lawd have mussy! Dat's de very prong all us black women gits hung on. Dis love! Dat's just whut's got us uh pullin' and uh haulin' and sweatin' and doin' from can't see in de mornin' till can't see at night." (Hurston, *Their Eyes* 1978:41)

Nanny's attitude toward sex is not a moral one in terms of Christian values. Rather it is based on her terrible personal experiences, first as a slave abused by her master, then as a mother who lost her only daughter when Janie's mother ran away. After being raped by her teacher, Janie's mother "had gone to the bad," that is, internalized what her society had named her.

For Nanny, sex is dangerous. Succumbing to one's own passion as well as to a man's is a trap. Men use women and then betray them. I believe that Nanny's attitude toward men is also Hurston's. Hurston was bitter about her father's many affairs; about the instantaneous dissolution of the family upon her mother's death; the rapidity with which her father remarried; and her own failures with men, all of which she blamed on sexuality, on making sexual needs paramount.

As I stated earlier in the chapter, Hurston wrote *Their Eyes* in a haze of emotional suffering only weeks after her final separation from her favorite husband, a much younger man. Minimizing his free will in the relationship, Price manipulated society's prejudice against women who marry younger men. He did this by stating that Hurston had only won him through using voodoo (at which she was an adept, having nearly risen to the rank of a mambo or priestess). In summing up what must have been Hurston's most humiliating memories in her final years, Karla Holloway captures this tragedy: "Her artistry scorned, her womanhood mocked, her professionalism sullied . . ." (1987:31), she grieves. For a woman, for Hurston, as Price very well knew, the charge he chose to make is the devastating equivalent of a man being "called out of his name" for impotence. This is exactly what Janie does with Jody, perhaps Hurston's way of paying Price back in kind.

At any rate, Hurston's complex combination of emotions appears to have worked magnificently in *Their Eyes*. For example, in relation to the fate of women who give their all to their men (precisely what Nanny is asking Janie to do, and without love), Nanny speaks the most famous lines in African American women's literature: "Honey, de white man is de ruler of everything as fur as Ah been able tuh find out. Maybe it's some place way off in de ocean where de black man is in power, but we don't know nothin' but what we see. So de white man throw down de load and tell de nigger man tuh pick it up. He pick it up because he have to, but he don't tote it. He hand it to his womenfolks. De nigger woman is de mule uh de world so fur as Ah can see" (1978:29).[3]

While still married to Killicks, Janie is swept off her feet by Joe Starks, another Bookerite. Joe is modelled on the real life character, Joe Clarke, who also appears in Hurston's *Jonah's Gourd Vine*, *Mules and Men*, and *Dust Tracks on a Road*. Clarke and John Hurston together seem to have run Eatonville in their day, both having served as mayor: Hurston three times. Clarke's dream fulfilled, the founding of an all-Black owned and run community, Eatonville, Florida, was also Washington's dream at Tuskegee Institute: farmland with decent housing on each holding; small, entrepreneurial businesses in adjacent hamlets convenient to the farms; and individual homes in a suburban setting surrounding the school. Education was envisioned primarily as utilitarian: training for vocations which served the Black people's most pressing needs at that time. In Washington's opinion, these were industrial skills related to agriculture, teaching, and homemaking, with the humanities and arts secondary but never excluded. Washington's model was based on Hampton Institute and its founder and his mentor, Gen. Armstrong. Armstrong's model, in turn, was based on his missionary father's manual training school for Hawaiians. In turn, all of these models were based on Benjamin Franklin's success model in his *Autobiography*.

Between 1881, when Washington assumed the principalship of Tuskegee, until beyond his death in 1915, his model (which Hurston's characters pursue or oppose) embodies and reflects the historical responses during that period of African Americans to the American success mythology, "the Protestant work ethic." Washington dedicated all of his adult life to spreading the message to his people for their "uplift," for the Negro "lowest down," as he put it, "to cast down your bucket where you stand," and his success in this regard was enormous, if controversial.

In the Franklin/Booker T. Washington paradigm, the founding father, our hero, leaves home and begins an epic journey to fortune, to Walker's "larger freedom," to success, and sometimes to fame. Everything about Washington's auto-biography, *Up From Slavery* parallels and reinforces Franklin's *Autobiography*. Everything about Joe Clarke's/Joe Starks's and Logan Killicks' and John Hurston's biographies does too. They resemble the long line of white male characters from Franklin's time to ours who "make it big by forty," "pull themselves up by their own bootstraps," "go from rags to riches," all by "good old Yankee ingenuity" and Emerson's tenet of "rugged indivi-dualism." Except in Washington's case and that of millions of his followers, it was good old African American ingenuity and rugged individualism.

As a result of Washington's cross-cultural infusion, the latter quality is clearly the one addition among all of the additions to the African/African American world view that created the most clashing combination of elements within the model he proposed for the African American male: a rugged individual who is *simultaneously* community oriented!

To convey some idea of the enormity of Washington's accomplishment in synthesizing these two world views, his "conjunctive disjunction" in this regard, a clear picture of the differing world views is required. To my mind, Barbara J. Haile and Audreye E. Johnson have best summarized the African world view. In addition, they contrast the African and European/European American world views in a clear and concise way (see pp. 21–22 of the Introduction of this book for quotation).

Hurston's description of Joe Starks in *Their Eyes Are Watching God*, is a conflation of her depiction of Joe Clarke and

John Hurston in *Dust Tracks on a Road*. Both Logan Killicks and
Joe Starks of *Their Eyes* are men who pursue the masculine
success myth, who care only about becoming "great, big men":
hollow egomaniacs, incapable of love for anything but outer
manifestations of their power.

John Hurston, self-employed carpenter, at one time
successful enough to employ others, repeatedly mayor of
Eatonville, and a minister as well, appears only in a cameo role
as the Rev. John Pearson in this novel. However, he appears as
the protagonist in *Jonah's Gourd Vine*, his daughter's fictionalized
version of his life. A tormented man who loves his wife, John is
so fatally attractive to women that he is once too often distracted
from her and loses his congregation, his vocation, and finally his
life. (At least in literature, if not in reality, as Hurston seems to
have wished. She never seems to have forgiven him for
disloyalty to her mother.) *Jonah's Gourd Vine* is a fine, underrated
novel with excellent characterizations, especially the complex
relationship between the hero and his wife, Lucy.

When Janie first meets Joe Starks, here is the way Hurston
describes him in what Gates terms "free indirect discourse":[4]

> Been workin' for white folks all his life. Saved up some
> money—round three hundred dollars, yes indeed, right here in
> his pocket. Kept hearin' 'bout them buildin' a new state down
> heah in Floridy and sort of wanted to come. But he was makin'
> money where he was. But when he heard all about 'em makin'
> a town all outa colored folks, he knowed dat was de place he
> wanted to be. He had always wanted to be a big voice, but de
> white folks had all de sayso where he come from and
> everywhere else, exceptin' dis place dat colored folks was
> buildin' theirselves. Dat was right too. De man dat built things
> oughta boss it. Let colored folks build things too if dey wants
> to crow over somethin'. He was glad he had his money all
> saved up. He meant to git dere whilst de town wuz yet a baby.
> He meant to buy in big. It had always been his wish and desire
> to be a big voice and he had to live nearly thirty years to find a
> chance. (*Their Eyes* 1978:47)

In *Dust Tracks on a Road*, here is how Hurston describes
both Joe Clarke and John Hurston:

Joe Clarke had asked himself, why not a Negro town? Few of the Negroes were interested. It was too vaulting for their comprehension. A pure Negro town! If nothing but their own kind was in it, who was going to run it? With no white folks to command them, how would they know what to do? Joe Clarke had plenty of confidence in himself to do the job, but few others could conceive of it. . . . (9–10)

Into this burly, boiling, hard-hitting, rugged-indivi-dualistic setting walked one day a tall, heavy-muscled mulatto who resolved to put down roots. . . . John Hurston, in his late twenties, had left Macon County, Alabama, because the ordeal of share-cropping on a southern Alabama cotton plantation was crushing to his ambition. (12)

There was no rise to the thing. . . . He heard about folks building a town all out of colored people. It seemed like a good place to go. Later on, he was to be elected Mayor of Eatonville for three terms, and to write the local laws. . . . (15–16)

So these two began their new life. . . . Both of them [John and Lucy Hurston] swore that things were going to get better, and it came to pass as they said. They bought land, built a roomy house, planted their acres and reaped. (1984:39)

As all readers of *Mules and Men* and *Their Eyes Were Watching God* know, Joe Clarke also bought and owned the general store which for Hurston "was the heart and spring of the town" (*Dust Tracks*, 1984:61) and which she memorializes in those works: where, as Diane Sadoff sees it, stood the "porch, the public arena for sexual ogling, courting, and joking"; and where the "porch tales" deconstruct to "men's insistence on female submission and inferiority, while they enhance masculine pride and encourage male solidarity" (1985:16).

In *Their Eyes*, not only do Joe Starks's outward success and economic dreams and goals parallel John Hurston's, his private story does also. His relationship with Janie steadily deteriorates because of his rigid masculinist insistence on gender role playing. This tragedy is the by-product of Starks's adherence to his culture's construct of appropriate male and female conduct in terms of masculine success. For example, both husbands use their wives as reflectors of their success, solely as objects to inspire other men's envy. Their women thus become signifiers for what Thorstein Veblen terms "conspicuous consumption" and what Diane Sadoff terms "gender privilege and gender politics." The more Joe Starks manipulates Janie in this manner, the more their relationship deteriorates. According to Sadoff, "when the radiant attraction to 'horizon' and the feeling of possibility wear off between them, the raw power of sexual domination once more appears in Janie's life" (1985:16).

From Joe's point of view, it appeared this way, according to Hurston: "He saw that she was sullen and he resented that. She had no right to be, the way he thought things out. She wasn't even appreciative of his efforts and she had plenty cause to be. Here he was just pouring honor all over her; building a high chair for her to sit in and overlook the world and she here pouting over it! Not that he wanted anybody else, but just too many women would be glad to be in her place. He ought to box her jaws!" (*Their Eyes* 1978:98)

From Janie's point of view, it appeared another way entirely:

> Jody classed me off. Ah didn't. Naw, Pheoby, Tea Cake ain't draggin' me off nowhere Ah don't want tuh go. Ah always did want tuh git round uh whole heap, but Jody wouldn't 'low me tuh. When Ah wasn't in de store he wanted me tuh jes sit wid folded hands and sit dere. And Ah'd sit dere wid de walls creepin' up on me and squeezin' all de life outa me. [Janie's different interpretation of space after Tea Cake's death is telling.] Pheoby, dese educated women got uh heap of things to sit down and consider. Somebody done tole 'em what to set down for. Nobody ain't told poor me, so sittin' still worries me. Ah wants tuh utilize mahself all over. (*Their Eyes* 1978:169)

Unfortunately, over the years, the success myth provides such distractions to the men who pursue it that they lose their sense of humanity and proportion. Joe acquires an "exaggerated sense of "'godliness'" from his success. Hurston broadcasts this to the reader, because every time Joe opens his mouth, he begins with the words "I god." But Janie feels that she has been sold out, not only by Joe, and before him, Logan Killicks, but tragically by her own flesh and blood and sex, her grandmother. Again, note Janie's response to space constraints, so different from the ending:

She hated her grandmother and had hidden it from herself all these years under a cloak of pity. She had been getting ready for her great journey to the horizons in search of *people*; it was important to tell the world that she should find them and they find her. But she had been whipped like a cur dog, and run off down a back road after *things*. . . . Nanny belonged to that other kind that loved to deal in scraps. Here Nanny had taken the biggest thing God ever made, the horizon—for no matter how far a person can go the horizon is still way beyond you—and pinched it in to such a little bit of a thing that she could tie it about her grand-daughter's neck tight enough to choke her. She hated the old woman who had twisted her so in the name of love. . . . But she had been set in the market-place to sell. Been set for still-bait. (*Their Eyes* 1978:127) [5]

Women may temporarily seem to be involved in the men's economic struggle in the market place, but only until Prince Charming arrives, as in the case of Joe Starks and Tea Cake. They sweep their Cinderellas up and away from their constrained lives to high chairs on front porches in Eatonville or to the low muck in the Everglades.

What is not so clear to readers is that Hurston is pitting women's "love game," against the masculine material "success game," and also against the success game's antithesis, the masculine hedonist who lives only at the beck and call of his emotions. The latter attracts women more than the former, whose obsession for power through material wealth desiccates his ability to love. But the hedonistic man is equally guilty of the sin of pride, of setting the self and its drives and whims above all things.

The misfortune for women attached to such men, as those attached to Bookerites, is that they have yielded themselves up to ultimately unbalanced and unnatural men. These women are therefore vulnerable to their men's tendency to make destructive decisions, decisions based on their immediate desires. Hurston is very familiar with this problem, conveying its tragic consequences in the autobiographical, *Dust Tracks on a Road*, and the fictional *Jonah's Gourd Vine*. In only one day, Hurston writes, the day after her mother's death, John Hurston/John Pearson and his children are dissolved as a family. Unfortunately for all of them, once she died, his wife's superior sense of priorities could no longer protect the family from their father's aimless sensualities, despite all his gifts—oratory and charisma as a preacher, carpentering skills, popularity, charm, beauty, and grace of person.

Tea Cake, although not previously recognized as such, fits the John Hurston hedonist mold. For this reason, perhaps, readers for the most part have hitherto failed to note the parallel between Joe Starks and Tea Cake at the end. Each embodies different myths that both pursue to the point of committing the sin of pride. Joe Starks (ego/"I God") and Tea Cake (id) set the individual self, its drives and whims above even natural forces. Whether for the sake of fleeting material success, as in Joe's case, or for fleeting sensual pleasure, as in Tea Cake's, each refuses, with fatal consequences, to yield to reality, to nature. Karla Holloway's contention that "Tea Cake followed the land and its cycles as a migrant worker" is sound; however, it does not necessarily follow that because he enjoys this life-style he therefore lets "nature and its seasons direct him" (1987:54). On the contrary, that he does not do so is his fatal flaw and causes his destruction.

Janie is belittled and invalidated as a woman by Joe Starks publicly and privately, but nurtured and strengthened by Tea Cake when he is not around other men. In fact, Tea Cake is so charming, so devoted to Janie—in private, at home! He croons such magnificent love language to her there (by all odds the best of any male character in all of African American literature) that readers tend to overlook the fact that he has as fatal a flaw as Joe:

> "Moon's too pretty fuh anybody tuh be sleepin' it away," Tea Cake said after they had washed up the plates and glasses. "Less us go fishin'."
> "Fishin'? Dis time uh night?"
> "Unhhunh, fishin'. Ah know where de bream is beddin'. Seen 'em when Ah come round de lake dis evenin'. Where's yo' fishin' poles? Less go set on de lake."
> It was so crazy digging worms by lamp light and setting out for Lake Sabelia after midnight that she felt like a child breaking rules. That's what made Janie like it. They caught two or three and got home just before day. Then she had to

smuggle Tea Cake out by the back gate and that made it seem like some great secret she was keeping from the town. (*Their Eyes* 1978:154)

On another occasion during their early courtship days:

"You crazy thing! Is dat whut you come here for at daybreak?"

"Sho is. You needs tellin' and showin', and dat's whut Ah'm doin'. Ah picked some strawberries too, Ah figgered you might like."

"Tea Cake. Ah 'clare Ah don't know whut tuh make outa you. You'se so crazy. You better lemme fix you some breakfast."

"Ain't got time. Ah got uh job uh work. Gottuh be back in Orlandah at eight o'clock. See yuh later, tell you straighter." (*Their Eyes* 1978:161)

This "child breaking rules," this delightful, irresistible Prince Charming (whom his wife later buries as the African equivalent, an Egyptian pharoah), who turns night into day, ignores time, tide, and societal and nature's systems in favor of his own whims, thus brings his own fate upon himself. When it is a matter of life and death that he do so, from the first to the last caper ("Big jumpin' dance tuhnight right heah . . .") Tea Cake refuses consistently to defer his own pleasures to any higher power, even a hurricane.

No rational being would ignore the Seminoles' departure and warning: "Going to high ground. Saw-grass bloom. Hurricane coming." Tea Cake does. No rational being would ignore animals' flight: "rabbits . . . going east. Some possums slunk by and their route was definite. One or two at a time, then more. . . . Snakes, rattlesnakes began to cross the quarters . . . big animals like deer . . . the muted voice of a panther. Going east and east. . . . A thousand buzzards held a flying meet and then went above the clouds and stayed." No one would ignore the "Bahaman" boys (who, like Tea Cake, are usually loath to give up the possibility of a good time), when even they leave after observing that "De crow gahn up, man" (*Their Eyes* 1978:228, 229, 230). Tea Cake does.

Krasner's interpretation of the hurricane in *Their Eyes* is that "the natural disaster bodies forth the frailty of human control over, as well as comprehension of, the natural world . . . the futility of the human attempt to bind nature within structures of symbolic meaning. . . ."

Unlike Krasner, I believe first that Janie's connectedness with nature reflects both African American cosmology and its connection with voodoo, in which Hurston was an adept. Human beings were basically "part of, not alien to, the Natural Order of things, attached to the Oneness that bound together all matter, animate and inanimate, all spirits, visible or not" (*Their Eyes* 1978:124).

Here I read Hurston as attributing "frailty" and "futility" to Tea Cake and to Joe Starks before him, but not to percipient "humans" such as Janie, the Seminoles, the "Bahamans," or the other "natural" entities purposefully described by Hurston. Janie, like these entities, is attuned to nature. If she had been on her own, she too would have heeded and obeyed the warning signs.

Joe Starks and Tea Cake have, however, alienated themselves from "the Natural Order of things." Alas, Janie relates to life as having purpose and meaning only in terms of being with and doing for the man she loves, whatever it takes, as Janie's highly romantic conduct when in love illustrates. But because of her loyalty to Tea Cake, Janie abdicates judgment:

> "Ah reckon you wish now you had of stayed in yo' big house 'way from such as dis, don't yuh?"
>
> "Naw."
>
> "Naw?"
>
> "Yeah, naw. People don't die till dey time come nohow, don't keer where you at. Ah'm wid mah husband in uh storm, dat's all."
>
> "Thanky, Ma'am. But 'sposing you wuz tuh die, now. You wouldn't git mad at me for draggin' yuh heah?"
>
> "Naw. We been tuhgether round two years. If you kin see de light at daybreak, you don't keer if you die at dusk. It's so many people never seen de light at all. Ah wuz fumblin' round and God opened de door."

He dropped to the floor and put his head in her lap. "Well, then, Janie, you meant whut you didn't say, 'cause Ah never *knowed* you wuz so satisfied wid me lak dat. Ah kinda thought—"

The wind came back with triple fury, and put out the light for the last time. They sat in company with the others in other shanties, their eyes straining against crude walls and their souls asking if He meant to measure their puny might against His. They seemed to be staring at the dark, but their eyes were watching God. (*Their Eyes* 19782:36)

This myth did not work out in Hurston's life, as I have shown, nor in her heroines' lives. In the following quote the Franklin/Washington "self-help" system which Janie sums up contemptuously as "a business proposition" is incongruously combined with Hurston's and her mother's romantic formula for womanly success. This formula entails a seemingly disjunctive Bookerite-influenced but double-pronged approach to love: a strong, independent woman who simultaneously lives entirely to satisfy and please her man in what Janie defines as "uh love game":

"Dis ain't no business proposition, and no race after property and titles. Dis is uh love game. Ah done lived Grandma's way, now Ah means tuh live mine."

"What you mean by dat, Janie?"

"She was borned in slavery time when folks, dat is black folks, didn't sit down anytime dey felt lak it. So sittin' on porches lak de white madam looked lak uh mighty fine thing tuh her. Dat's whut she wanted for me—don't keer whut it cost. Git up on uh high chair and sit dere. She didn't have time tuh think whut tuh do after you got up on de stool uh do nothin'. De object wuz tuh git dere. So Ah got up on de high stool lak she told me, but Pheoby, Ah done nearly languished tuh death up dere. Ah felt like de world wuz cryin' extry and Ah ain't read de common news yet." (*Their Eyes* 1978:171–172)

What Hurston has done with the masculine myths, whether of success or failure, is what white nineteenth-century women did with theirs: wrap them in ambiguity. Some critics view such a strategy, a conflicting and double message, as problematic. James Krasner, for example, believes that "Janie's story is, unmistakably, a tribute to someone she has loved well, if not too wisely. It is an emotional necessity for her to see Tea Cake as the fulfillment of her life's quest, for her understanding of happiness is built on the male model"(1989:118). Diane Sadoff also labels Hurston's view disparagingly as "a double bind" on the ground that "Hurston profoundly distrusts heterosexual relationships because she thinks them based on male dominance and willing female submission; yet such inequality appears [to Hurston] necessary to the institution of marriage" (1985:21).

On the other hand, Elsa Barkley Brown sees continuity, even identity, between contemporary African American women's "disjunctive conjunctions" and Hurston's. She forcefully argues that the simultaneous holding of seemingly oppositional value systems is characteristic of African American women:

> It is not just that African-American women did different, seemingly contradictory things at different times, which they did, but that they did different, seemingly contradictory things, simultaneously. It is the simultaneity of their seemingly contradictory actions and beings for which we must account in our historical analyses. . . . The simultaneous promotion of two seemingly contradictory sets of values . . . is essential to the survival of individual African-Americans and of the African-American community as a whole. (1989:929)

As I previously pointed out, this duality can be seen in African American male writers of the period in their attempts to combine traditional perspectives of the individual as part of a community and European American perspectives of the individual as separate and isolated from the community. With Hurston and other women writers of the period, the duality is based on their continued adherence to a romantic Cinderella love mythology that is at odds with such material concerns as economic and political conditions. However, Booker T. Washington's enormous influence in emphasizing economic success for Black men tended to reinforce in African American women those conventional romantic and religious mythologies and prescriptions which trained them to subordinate themselves to their menfolk.

Sociologist Susan A. Mann, in her important study on this issue during the period in question, bears out historian Guy-Sheftall's, and my own conclusions from reading Hurston's life works. In comparing and contrasting Black households during slavery and the post-Reconstruction periods (following her citation of a passage from *Jonah's Gourd Vine* as illustration of her point), Mann responds to the argument that after slavery adult women's decision to remain in the home doing housekeeping tasks led to advantages for Black families. More time was spent in preparing food, tending gardens, caring for young children, providing varied and balanced diets, and contributing in various ways to the well-being of their families. However, she argues:

> While entire families benefited from the time women devoted to domestic activities, it is still not clear whether or not women benefited relative to men. . . . Legislation allowed Black men to gain control over their wives' property and earnings, to assume custody of children, and to discipline their wives forcefully. Moreover, rights to divorce were limited even in cases of abandonment or domestic violence. . . . Thus it appears that although slave women experienced a masculinization of their roles, slave men did not experience a corresponding feminization of their roles, despite all the attention academics have paid to the so-called emasculated Black male and the corresponding myth of Black matriarchy in discussing Black family structure. Indeed, rather than either the equality or matriarchy claimed by some writers, it seems that slave households were in fact characterized by patriarchy. . . . Even when Black women sharecroppers engaged in a significant amount of production for exchange, control over income generated from agricultural production was in the hands of men—even if this income was produced by the labor of the entire family. Male control over this income, coupled with the domestic decision-making power this entailed, meant that Black women could only have been in an inherently unequal relation to Black men. This situation is not unique to sharecropping but, rather, is characteristic of many family labor enterprises—both rural and urban. (1989:785, 788, 795, 798)[6]

Moreover, Black as well as white women internalized and/or subscribed to the not-so-subliminal messages inherent in the Black and white male success myth. In either event, this myth shaped their behavior, as we have already seen in Wheatley and Jacobs. It dictated absolute loyalty and subservience to men in support of men's aims in life. These were, in Hurston's Bookerite-influenced world view, primarily "business propositions." Thus, indirectly, Black women supported and reinforced the European American male success myths, not for themselves, but for their menfolk. They based their support on the premise that if their men benefited, then *they* automatically would, as Hurston assumes in her works. As bell hooks points out: "The prevailing nineteenth-century assumption that Black men and women had to work side by side to eradicate racism gave way as the assumption gained prominence that liberatory change was furthered by Black women standing behind Black men. Given such thinking, it is not surprising that the voices of Black female intellectuals were no longer accorded full respect and recognition" (1989:55). Were they ever?

In emulation of her foremothers' ideals, Hurston attempted to subordinate herself to the men she loved and admired. All her work validates this side of the mythology, "the blues" side. But she would not subordinate her artistic drive, her ambition for fame as a writer, her need for success in her chosen field, to *any* man, even a husband. Clearly, Hurston's psyche is divided. To the extent that it is, to that extent does her work look forward to and prophesy the perspective of her literary successors, most prominently, Alice Walker.

There are critics, however, who do not perceive Hurston's "disjunctive conjunction" as a limitation or problematic. They posit a future whereby such ability as Hurston's to contain paradoxes and diversity, to juxtapose male myths with female myths, will destabilize the male myths. The veritable flood of recent Black and white feminist scholarship on Hurston generally lauds her ability to reflect such paradoxes and diversity in her life and her texts. This is evident in her heroines and in her male characters as well. Hurston ultimately used the enormous pull of the Cinderella myth for women to subordinate it in support and aggrandizement of the male success myth.

It seems to me that this is still the case in our current society. We live in a world, as did Hurston, in which essentially male models prevail everywhere. If these were destabilized, if what is now perceived of as "reality" were to be conflated with what is perceived of as "insignificant and petty female interests and concerns"; if a "disjunctive conjunction" of these two mythic visions were formed, then what would happen? The reality now is that European American males are perceived mythically as the model for everyone. Both European and African American males are perceived as the model for Black women, as in Hurston's day. Thus Hurston's depiction in her works of an ideal situation for Black women is conventional. Hurston and her heroines are even more bound to such a myth than are Wheatley and Jacobs. The latter apparently did not have to deal with Bookerite men who saw women as "helpmates," i.e., servants and subordinates to men in the sacred task of "racial uplift."

Hurston, therefore, appropriates the masculine success myth for women in her work, although not to the extent she herself did in real life, a fact she would not admit even to herself. As Holloway puts it: "Many of Hurston's personal and professional difficulties were indirectly a result of this duality of her professional desires and individual needs. Her failure at reconciliation is the failure of a woman who was at once in control of her talent as well as victim of a system that meted out rewards to those who maintained and supported the male-dictated norms"(1987:19).

This is evident in and signaled by Hurston's depiction of independent, hardworking, outspoken young women. However, the Cinderella myth and the cult of true womanhood (so deeply inscribed in European and European American women and to which we have seen Wheatley, Jacobs, and now Hurston, subscribing) is superimposed by Hurston over these other qualities until it covers them up and blots them out. Once these women become involved with a Prince Charming, they all turn into Cinderellas. Their Prince Charmings ride off with them sitting behind while they hold on for dear life with one hand and onto their mops with the other.

Notes

1. Walker, after a trek through a snake-infested cemetery, apparently found Hurston's gravesite and erected a marker over it. See "Looking for Zora," in *In Search of Our Mother's Gardens* (San Diego: Harcourt Brace Jovanovich, 1983), 93–116, esp. 105–106.

2. In her foreword to Calvin Hernton's *The Sexual Mountain and Afro-American Women Writers: Adventures in Sex, Literature, and Real Life* (New York: Doubleday, 1990, xxi), Gloria Wade-Gayles quotes Hernton as asking: *Why do women carry two loads and men only one?"* He is referring to *"at least two"* struggles women wage—against racism and sexism. [His emphasis]

3. See Deborah G. Plant, "Narrative Strategies in Zora Neale Hurston's "Dust Tracks on a Road," *Sage* VI.l (Summer 1989): 18–24, for an excellent revision of previous readings on Hurston's "accommodationist" attitude.

4. Gates is referring to Hurston's description of Janie's consciousness, although Hurston uses it for other characters, such as Joe Starks.

5. The sudden violence of language and tone of extreme outrage against Nanny exhibited by Janie in this passage seem excessive and unwarranted, given that Hurston had taken care to depict Nanny as convention-bound and materialistic. Nevertheless, Nanny had done the best for her granddaughter, according to her lights. Thus Hurston led readers to sympathize with Nanny's predicament. However, Hurston here gives readers a dilemma. They can change their opinion of the grandmother, which they would tend to resist, since Hurston has not hitherto led readers to view Nanny as "hateful" in any way. Or readers can lose some of the vast reservoir of sympathy she had garnered for Janie when Janie expresses "hatred" of her grandmother and reads her motives in marrying her off to Killicks in the worst possible light. This shocks readers. Up to this moment in the text, and beyond, Janie displays a large compassion for and tolerance of her loved ones' flaws and weaknesses: for example, those of her husband, Tea Cake, when he steals money from her, flirts with another woman, beats her, etc. I see in this passage not only evidence that Hurston is transposing her hatred for her maternal grandmother onto Janie, but also evidence as to where Hurston was for the ten missing years of her life that she concealed from posterity. I believe that Janie's marriage to old Logan Killicks and subsequent incarceration on his farm is autobiographical. In *Dust Tracks*, Hurston maintains that this was her sister's fate. My guess is that it may have been hers: that Hurston's suppressed resentment and bitterness for

this waste of her youth took form in her decision to erase those ten years from her life as if she had never lived them. Marrying a man who was almost that much younger may also have been part of Hurston's eradicatory "repayments" to herself for wasted living. Again, this may well be reflected in Janie's unwarranted "overdetermined" outburst against her wasted youth in the form of an expose of her grandmother.

6. Mann's data supports hooks, Guy-Sheftall, et al. on the patriarchal nature of the Black home and family, even during slavery. This is contrary to Moynihan et al. My opinion is that here the African world view dovetailed with the European/European American world view about the relationship between the sexes and the role of women in general. Otherwise, it would not have been perpetuated without difficulty. The clue is in the fact that any attempt to shift paradigms in their basically African world view in *any* area of life, for example, in relation to gender, has always been and will continue to be bitterly fought openly or covertly by African men in the diaspora. An example is the intense barrage of persiflage and calumny launched by them against Alice Walker when she attempted to do so.

References

Baker, Jr., Houston. *Modernism and the Harlem Renaissance*. Chicago: University of Chicago Press, 1987.

———. "Zora Neale Hurston's *Their Eyes Were Watching God*." In *Zora Neal Hurston's* Their Eyes Were Watching God. Ed. Harold Bloom. New York: Chelsea House, 1987.

Bambara, Toni Cade. "Salvation is the Issue." *Black Women Writers: 1950–1980: A Critical Evaluation*. Ed. Mari Evans. New York: Anchor, 1984.

Barkley Brown, Elsa. "Africanamerican Women's Quilting: A Framework for Conceptualizing and Teaching Africanamerican Women's History." *Signs* 14.4 (Summer 1989): 921–929.

Ferguson, Sallyann H. "Chesnutt's Genuine Blacks and Future Americans." *MELUS* 15.3 (Fall 1988–1989): 109–120.

Gates, Henry Louis, Jr. "Review of *Dust Tracks on a Road*." *The New York Times Book Review*. April 21, 1985, 43.

Gilbert, Sandra M. and Susan Gubar. *The Madwoman in the Attic: The Woman Writer and the Nineteenth-Century Literary Imagination.* New Haven, CT: Yale University Press, 1979.

Guy-Sheftall, Beverly. *Daughters of Sorrow: Attitudes Toward Black Women, 1880–1920.* Brooklyn: Carlson, 1990.

Haile, Barbara J. and Audreye E. Johnson. "Teaching and Learning About Black Women: The Anatomy of a Course." *Sage* VI.1 (Summer 1989): 69–73.

Holloway, Karla F. C. *The Character of the Word: The Texts of Zora Neale Hurston.* Westport, CT: Greenwood Press, 1987.

hooks, bell. "Feminism and Black Women's Studies." *SAGE* VI.1 (Summer 1989): 54–58.

Hurston, Zora Neale. *Dust Tracks on a Road.* Ed. and intro. Robert Hemenway. Urbana: University of Illinois Press, 1984. First printed, 1942.

———. *Their Eyes Were Watching God.* Intro. Sherley Williams. Urbana: University of Illinois Press, 1978. First printed, 1937.

Krasner, James. "The Life of Women: Zora Neale Hurston and Female Autobiography."*Black American Literature Forum* 23.1 (Spring 1989): 113–126.

Mann, Susan A. "Slavery, Sharecropping, and Sexual Inequality." *Signs* 14.4 (Summer 1989): 774–798.

Plant, Deborah G. "Narrative Strategies in Zora Neale Hurston's *Dust Tracks on a Road.*" *SAGE* VI.1 (Summer 1989): 18–23.

Sadoff, Diane. "Black Matrilineage: The Case of Alice Walker and Zora Neale Hurston." *Signs* 11.11 (1985): 4–26.

Walker, Alice. *In Search of our Mothers' Gardens.* San Diego: Harcourt, Brace, Jovanovich, 1983.

CELIE IS SHORT FOR CINDERELLA: ALICE WALKER AND AMERICAN SUCCESS MYTHS

The influence of Zora Neale Hurston on Alice Walker has been more than amply and justifiably acknowledged by many critics. But Alice Walker herself has striven so nobly for the reclamation of Hurston's reputation from oblivion that it has perhaps diverted critical attention to some extent away from her own equally extraordinary accomplishments. To begin with, exposure to Hurston's life and written work enabled Walker to appreciate her mother's oral tales and those of other relatives and members of her African American community, thereby providing a lifeline of continuity between her and her African ancestry. Before this time, until Walker first came upon Hurston when she was researching her first short story, "The Revenge of Hanna Kemhuff" (based on a story her mother had told her in which voodoo was involved), she had already absorbed and internalized the European/European American literary tradition and all its cultural mythologies and trappings. But once she discovered Hurston, these great white antecedents lost their hold over her. A part of Walker achieved a distance from European American culture—that "double consciousness" which DuBois had first named and is so much a part of many hyphenated American psyches.

In the process of finding Hurston, Walker clarified the precise source of her dissatisfaction: that her ancestry, her experiences, her perspective, her potential as a young Black Southern female, were all considered worthless in the eyes of the culture's gatekeepers, personified for Walker in her traditionalist professors at Howard University and at Sarah Lawrence. For these traditionalists, African American literature was a "specific," a "particularistic" literature, "lacking in universality," as Richard Long and Eugenia Collier put it sarcastically. As such, it languished, hopelessly peripheral, in contrast to what traditionalists deemed the monumentally significant subjects and themes of European/European American canonical literature. Long and Collier concede that there are universal themes such as "love, death, and nature, for example." But they argue that "any extensive treatment of such themes outside of lyric poetry has to be circumstantial, set in a given time and place. And no given time and place are universal." With justified indignation they demand to know: "What is inherently universal about Dante's ten heavens and limbo, about Homer's libations to the gods and his funeral pyres of heroes, about Shakespeare's feudal kings? The answer is, very little. Or Melville's whaling ship or Mark Twain's river towns? The answer is nothing" (1985:5).

The moment when Walker finally uncovered and recovered Hurston's life and work is as historic for African American literary history as the moment when Harriet Jacobs put her pen to paper to tell the Black woman's side of the slave narrative. Writes Walker: "What I had discovered, of course, was a model. A model, who, as it happened, provided more than voodoo for my story, more than one of the greatest novels America had produced—though, being America, it did not realize this. She [Hurston] had provided, as if she knew someday I would come along wandering in the wilderness, a nearly complete record of her life. And though her life sprouted an occasional wart, I am extremely grateful for that life, warts and all" (*Mothers' Gardens* 1984:12).

At the moment she discovered Hurston, it all came together for Walker. She began to come from her own center of experience. She realized that she had all along possessed a specifically gendered, classed, racially, and ethnically cultural grounding. Further, this grounding afforded her an aesthetically viable alternative to her prior models. So it came about that Walker achieved distance from her previously cherished models, including even William Faulkner and her beloved Flannery O'Connor.

Walker was not, however, divorcing herself from previous models as if she were an isolated unit who in judging them had found them wanting. She approached them now as a trained

African American and European American writer addressing writers of another group while noting their commonalities and differences. Walker for the first time realized that she was a member of another community, as well as the European/ European American community, with as (en)viable a culture and world view as any on earth. This can be seen when she writes: "A shack with only a dozen or so books is an unlikely place to discover a young Keats. But it is narrow thinking, indeed, to believe that a Keats is the only kind of poet one would want to grow up to be. One wants to write poetry that is understood by one's people, not by the Queen of England. Of course, should she be able to profit by it too, so much the better, but since that is not likely, catering to her tastes would be a waste of time" (*Mothers' Gardens* 1984:18).

Finding Hurston, Walker came home to her mother(s), to herself. In her writing, from that point on, she could cut through "the master script" or "master agenda," as Morrison and Gates define what I call "the European American myths." Walker learned precisely how those mythologies related to her and her community; not only in the United States, north, south, east and west, but also in Africa, and throughout the globe. Walker was free from that point on to take up the European American white male-as-norm prescribed myth for herself and her Othered group and do with it what she liked.

Walker's "fairy godmother" first appeared to her, appropriately enough, as Walker tells us, not on the kitchen hearth, but in a book, in a "footnote to the white voices of authority." Zora Neale Hurston turned out to be none other than the ancestral model with whom Walker had been desperately seeking to connect. From this point on, she tells us, she has never again written without yielding herself up in the act of writing to "The Word," the *nommo*, the conduit through which the ancestors speak. "Well, I don't really hear voices, you'll be happy to know," she informs Claudia Tate defensively, "But sometimes I have something like visitations, and I know they come from what is Indian in me, and I don't necessarily mean Indian blood. . . . I like that. I like these visitations popping into my mind" (Tate 1990:179).

Her joy in discovering Hurston's "prior existence," as Walker puts it, stimulated so profound a transformation in her consciousness that she has never written since without gathering "up the historical and psychological threads of the life my ancestors lived, and in the writing of it" feeling "joy and strength and my own continuity. I had that wonderful feeling writers get sometimes, not very often, of being *with* a great many people, ancient spirits, all very happy to see me consulting and acknowledging them, and eager to let me know, through the joy of their presence, that, indeed, I am not alone" (*Mothers' Gardens* 1984:13). This is the meaning of her epigraph to *The Color Purple* when she writes: "I thank everybody in this book for coming. A.W., author and medium." This is the meaning to the pun in the signifying title of her collection of essays, *Living by the Word* (1987).

Walker also sees Hurston as the ancestral "godmother" for her people as well as for herself: "Zora was committed to the survival of her people's cultural heritage," Walker argues. In the approximately ten years between the time Walker found Hurston and her writing of *The Color Purple*, she developed her own repertoire of devastating signifying techniques (bitterly ironic, as well as simultaneously and scathingly humorous) to subvert the European American male success mythology, techniques that Hurston and African and African diaspora people have employed for thousands of years. Two incidents stand out as key components of this repertoire. One was when Walker read *Mules and Men*, which she considers "perfect":

> The "perfection" of which I immediately tested on my relatives, who are such typical black Americans they are useful for every sort of political, cultural, or economic survey. Very regular people from the South, rapidly forgetting their Southern cultural inheritance in the suburbs and ghettos of Boston and New York, they sat around reading the book themselves, listening to me read the book, listening to each other read the book, and a kind of paradise was regained. For what Zora's book did was this: it gave them back all the stories they had forgotten or of which they had grown ashamed (told to us years ago by our parents and grandparents—not one of whom could *not* tell a story to make you weep, or laugh) and

showed how marvelous, and, indeed, priceless, they are. This is not exaggerated. No matter how they read the stories Zora had collected, no matter how much distance they tried to maintain between themselves, as new sophisticates, and the lives their parents and grandparents lived, no matter how they tried to remain cool toward all Zora revealed, in the end they could not hold back the smiles, the laughter, the joy over who she was showing them to be: descendants of an inventive, joyous, courageous, and outrageous people; loving drama, appreciating wit, and, most of all, relishing the pleasure of each other's loquacious and *bodacious* company. (*Mothers' Gardens* 1984:84–85)

The second incident occurred when Walker belatedly realized that her parents and community had trained her in this tradition all along, from the time she was a child:

Both of my parents were excellent storytellers, and wherever we lived, no matter how poor the house, we had fireplaces and a front porch. It was around the fireplaces and on the porch that I first heard, from my parents' lips—my mother filling in my father's pauses and he filling in hers—the stories that I later learned were Uncle Remus stories. . . . Joel Chandler Harris is billed as the creator of Uncle Remus. Uncle Remus told the stories of Brer Rabbit and Brer Fox, all the classic folk tales that came from Africa and that, even now in Africa, are still being told. We, too, my brothers and sisters and I, listened to those stories. But after we saw *Song of the South*, we no longer listened to them. They were killed for us. In fact, I do not remember any of my relatives ever telling any of those tales after they saw what had been done with them. (*Word* 1988:29, 26)

In *The Color Purple*, Alice Walker transformed the myth altogether with her devastating innovations—by creating an entirely new definition and scenario for herself and her group. Before analyzing the nature of her historic achievement, however, I will first describe the mythological elements, primarily in Hurston's *Their Eyes*, which Walker utilized, expanded on, transformed, and transcended, to shape that achievement.

As I have noted, Cinderella has been an especially potent myth for restricted females for centuries; it promises relief and release forever from kitchen and household drudgery, from constriction within the small confines of small rooms. Some day Cinderella will meet a prince of a man. He will seek her out, appear to her, and take her away from this dungeon that is her life to a gay and glittering world far, far away; to wealth, status, and a carefree existence.

In this formula is the "fairy godmother," the *dea ex machina*, the one who makes all of this possible in the first place. With a few waves of her magic wand, she creates Cinderella's elegant ensemble and Cinderella's transportation to the gala event where she will meet and evoke in Prince Charming his undying love.

As I maintained in the previous chapter, Hurston, in *Their Eyes Were Watching God*, modified the Cinderella myth to suit her own heroine's situation and to signify *against* the traditional myth. This offers another dimension of pleasure for Hurston's readers who are conscious of this myth. For example, Tea Cake takes Janie not to a palace, but to muck. A second dimension of the joke, however, is that paradoxically *that* is where the couple is happiest and where they live an idyll: their palace is a shack. Side by side they toil by day in the rice swamps of Florida. They party by night, but in lieu of the traditional royal balls, they engage in gambling, dancing, and feasting. Tea Cake also picks guitar with the "Bahamans" and their other African diaspora neighbors.

In the original, Cinderella is beautiful but has no other special traits (unless her despair and crying a good deal because she is forced to work in the kitchen as a scullery maid can be considered a trait). The same was true for Janie, so long as she was married to Logan Killicks or to Joe Stark, who used her in his general store as his slavey. One of the ways by which Tea Cake reveals himself as Prince Charming is his promise to Janie to release her from her drudgery at the store the very first time she sets eyes on him.

A life of drudgery was Nanny's, too. As I pointed out in Chapter Four in relation to Jacobs and *her* slave owners, Nanny's owners are so many wicked stepsisters and evil stepmothers who get to go to the ball every day at the expense of *their* drudges.

Improving on reality, however, Hurston's heroine Janie gets to go to "the far horizon" and back, until at the end she is content to live with her memories. How many Black (or white) women could afford such a luxury in real life, in most times and places, when women's lives literally depended on the good will of men? The paradox is that Hurston was the product of post-Reconstruction mythology, which combined the Cinderella myth for Black women with a white male success model for Black men. Thus the most romantic of women's myths was made even more romantic by fantasizing that Black women were neglected Cinderellas whose Prince Charmings would eventually come. Then, somehow, their material needs would be adequately supplied if the couple worked very hard. Indeed, Tea Cake does. He supports them adequately through gambling and working the muck. Janie works at his side, not out of material need, but to be with him.

To Walker, Hurston has played a variety of roles. Hurston first waved a magic wand for her when, through reading Hurston, Walker discovered and re-visioned her own culture. This literary wand of Hurston's waved into being a profound transformation from the white mindset into which Walker had been molded all her student life. She realized that Hurston was *her* fairy godmother, whom she had been seeking all her writing life.

In *The Color Purple*, Walker does complex signifying (like so many riffs) on the concept of "fairy godmother" in relation to Hurston. Hurston's role in the novel is not only as Black godmother to the author herself, but to her heroine, Celie, and to Walker's people, as well.[1] This is consciously and perversely ironic, in view of Walker's awareness that Hurston herself had a white "godmother," Cynthia Osgood Mason, whom she shared with Langston Hughes, among other Black artists. "Godmother" was Hurston's own term for Mason and what she frequently called her.

Zora Neale Hurston serves as Walker's model for Celie's fairy godmother and for Celie's Prince Charming in the person of the bodacious Shug Avery (as in "Shug a very," or "Shug Every";

either meaning "A Whole Lot of Sugar," or "Every Kind of Sweet In One"). Shug Avery is one of the greatest characters in African American literature. Like Shug, Alice Walker tells us, [Hurston]:

> Tended to marry or not marry men, but enjoyed them anyway—while never missing a beat in her work . . . [She was] maddeningly indifferent to other people's opinions of her. With her easy laughter and her Southern drawl, her belief in doing "cullud" dancing authentically, Zora seemed—among these genteel "new Negroes" of the Harlem Renaissance—*black*. No wonder her presence was always a shock. Though almost everyone agreed she was a delight, not everyone agreed such audacious black delight was permissible, or, indeed, quite the proper image for the race. (*Mothers' Gardens* 1984:88, 89)

Also, Walker has in her possession "a photograph of [Hurston] in pants, boots, and broadbrim hat . . . given to [Walker] by her brother, Everette. She has her foot up on the running board of a car—presumably hers, and bright red—and looks racy" (*Mothers' Gardens* 1984:88).

As Walker treasures her photograph, so Celie/Cinderella treasures hers of Shug Avery. Even before she has met her, Celie is shown fantasying over an announcement of the imminent arrival of her Prince Charming/fairy godmother combined in Shug. The pose, attitude, and "red" color (which is associated with Shug), are all like that of Hurston's photograph: "Shug Avery standing upside a piano, elbow crook, hand on her hip. She wearing a hat like Indian Chiefs. Her mouth, open showing all her teef and don't nothing seem to be troubling her mind. Come one, come all, it say. The Queen Honeybee is back in town. Lord, I wants to go so bad. Not to dance. Not to drink. Not to play card. Not even to hear Shug Avery sing. I just be thankful to lay eyes on her" (*Purple* 1982:33).[2]

Shug's car is the pumpkin that takes Celie and Squeak, another, lesser Cinderella to Shug's palace in Memphis. And Grady, who is indeed a rat, serves as their chauffeur/footman. Walker is here signifying on the biographical aspects of the term "fairy godmother" in relation to Hurston and Mason and as embodied in her photograph of Hurston so proudly showing off *her* "pumpkin." This was the Chevrolet two-seater that Hurston's "fairy godmother" gave her as part of her scholarship to go to the "ball," which was for Hurston to be held at Eatonville, Florida, and environs. Hurston was to drive there to meet what would turn out to be *her* Prince Charming: African/African American diaspora culture and folklore.

For Celie, Shug Avery serves as both fairy godmother and Prince Charming combined, another subtle use of signifying by Walker. She does so by appropriating and subverting the concept of a male Prince Charming by depicting a woman in the role, instead. Shug is to Celie, the Cinderella figure, exactly what a traditional Prince Charming is to Cinderella. Shug sweeps Celie off her feet and away to personal, sexual, psychological, and physical freedom from her kitchen drudge slavery. Simultaneously, Shug is Celie's fairy godmother, her *dea ex machina*. Shug literally takes Celie in her car to live for a while in her mansion in Memphis, Tennessee. At the end of the novel, Shug returns to Celie, and in *Temple of My Familiar* (1989), readers discover that they live together "happily ever after" until Shug's passing.

In Shug's occupation lies Walker's conviction that Hurston shares certain of her essential qualities of character, more with blues singers than with writers:

> Zora Neale Hurston, Billie Holiday, and Bessie Smith form a sort of unholy trinity. Zora *belongs* in the tradition of black women singers, rather than among the "literati," at least to me. There were the extreme highs and lows of her life, her undaunted pursuit of adventure, passionate emotional and sexual experience, and her love of freedom. Like Billie and Bessie she followed her own road, believed in her own gods, pursued her own dreams, and refused to separate herself from "common" people. It would have been nice if the three of them had had one another to turn to, in times of need. I close my eyes and imagine them: Bessie would be in charge of all the money: Zora would keep Billie's masochistic tendencies in check and prevent her from singing embarrassing anything-for-a-man songs, thereby preventing Billie's heroin addiction. In return, Billie could be, along with Bessie, the family that Zora felt she never had. (*Mothers' Gardens* 1984:91–92)

Walker did more than "close her eyes and imagine them" as she wrote in 1979. She went on to create them all combined in the person of Shug Avery, Celie's godmother and Prince Charming. Shug is a Bessie-Billie type singer possessed of Hurston's personality, character, attitude, and life-style, but depicted as a "blues" singer rather than a writer.

In *The Color Purple*, Walker also mused on and resolved Hurston's ambivalent response toward the American success myth of upward mobility, which presumably constituted the source of the good life for men and women. Hurston's tragic end as a pauper haunted Walker, so much so that she reversed the trajectory of Hurston's life in planning that of her Cinderella's/Celie's life: "*Being broke made all the difference*, Walker mourns about Hurston, "Without money of one's own in a capitalist society, there is no such thing as independence. This is one of the clearest lessons of Zora's life, and why I consider the telling of her life a cautionary tale. We must learn from it what we can" (*Mothers' Gardens* 1984:90).

So it is that Walker starts Celie out as the lowest possible of Cinderellas in every way and ends with her very successful, not as in the realities of Hurston's later life, or as Hurston fantasies it in *Their Eyes Were Watching God*, in accordance with the traditional European fairy tale. Walker instead gives her ending a Black signifying and womanist twist. Celie doesn't go off to transcendence with Prince Charming, as in the European myth. Nor does she go off as Janie goes off with Jody Starks first and with Tea Cake later, only to end disappointingly for some readers when in a static trance she restricts herself primarily to her bedroom, dreaming forever after of her good times with Tea Cake.

In *The Color Purple*, everybody important in the text eventually ends up on Celie's front porch. This ending reflects another instance of Walker's signifying on Hurston's placing the center of community life in Eatonville on the Clarkes' front porch. Walker's ending for Celie does more, however, than signify on Hurston's ending for Janie. It heralds a new era in American literary history and African American women's literature. Walker reverses all former paradigms and creates a unique trajectory for her Black heroine's life. Celie's story marks the first time a Black heroine successfully reverses and appropriates the prevailing work ethic, an ethic conceived of and hitherto reserved for privileged white European American men and which was appropriated by Washington for Black men. Mr.____ (before his transformation), subscribes wholeheartedly to this myth and sums it up well when he pulverizes Celie: "You black, you pore, you ugly, you a woman. Goddamn, he say, you nothing at all" (*Purple* 1982:187).

In terms of Walker's own biography, this is exactly *her* observation about the way European American culture felt about her until she found Hurston. In refutation, Walker shows her Black heroine as gradually working her way up through her own talents. In doing so, Walker consciously violates all the racial, class, and gender taboos set up against Black women by European American culture.

The male myth became the universally accepted paradigm for Americans after Benjamin Franklin's definitive treatment of it in his *Poor Richard's Almanack* and *Autobiography*. Every American home had its Bible and Franklin's works on the shelf until the early twentieth century. Moreover, from 1895 to sometime around the Great Depression, Washington's mediating influence expanded this mythology to include Black males. Thus, over time, all men, Black and white, arrogated this myth to themselves as theirs by right of masculine privilege.

In *The Color Purple*, both Celie's real and fictive father seem to be created by Walker as characters out of the eighteenth-century Gothic novel convention in which appearances belie reality; where, for example, evil parent figures are shown to be impostors; where at the denouement, the real hero(ine) comes into his/her birthright; where the hero(ine) is ultimately revealed as the truly noble heir(ess) to a truly noble father. So in the course of events, Celie is revealed as the true daughter of her ambitious, upwardly mobile, decent, hard working, loving and devoted father.

Walker, in creating Celie's mythical father, also follows Hurston's recounting of her own father's pursuit of the American success myth in the persons of Joe Starks in *Their Eyes Were Watching God*, and John Pearson and Joe Clarke in *Jonah's Gourd Vine* and *Of Mules and Men*. Celie's father is obviously based on Walker's familiarity with all three characters' lives, for he becomes successful in the same manner as his predecessors.

After arriving as a stranger in town, Celie's father achieves success through ownership of a general store, buying farmland and property, marrying well and for love. Suddenly, however, his successful, upwardly mobile life is snuffed out. Envious white "business men" (in their off-hours members of the KKK) lynch him as an example for other would-be Black Ben Franklins. This is a terrorist tactic designed to discourage other Black men from presuming to pursue "the American dream" which the KKK have reserved for themselves. By their definition, only they are American, and therefore only *they* deserve access to and identification with American success myths.

In Alice Childress's earlier treatment of this motif in *A Short Walk* (1979), which may have influenced Walker, the heroine's aunt is forced to flee precipitously to unknown parts after her ambitious and successful husband is murdered by jealous white business competitors. However, in Hurston's more optimistic version, the widow inherits after her successful husband dies of natural causes (although Joe believes Janie has hoodooed him).

At this juncture, Walker creates Alphonso, a negative *doppelganger* to Celie's father. In a contrast to Celie's father's fate, Alphonso also comes into town as a stranger, but lives off and uses what his predecessor had built up. Ultimately this youthful appearing villain (one of Satan's characteristics) dies appropriately *in flagrante delicto*. Walker cannot resist signifying on his death, for the recognition he undeservedly gets and the respect shown him by the way he is buried were tributes which both Hurston and Celie's father were denied, but deserved.

Walker nobly took it upon herself to erect to Hurston a "plain gray marker . . . pale and ordinary, not at all like Zora," but at that time she was "not rich." The marker reads: "Zora Neale Hurston/'A Genius of the South'/Novelist Folklorist/ Anthropologist/ 1901–1960" (*Mothers' Gardens* 1984:107).[3] But there the similarity ends. Here is what the grateful townspeople have erected to Alphonso, whom Shug describes as a "bad odor passing through":

> About a mile before us got to town us come up on the entrance
> to the colored cemetery. Shug was sound asleep, but something
> told me I ought to drive in. Pretty soon I see something look
> like a short skyscraper and I stop the car and go up to it. Sure
> enough it's got Alphonso's name on it. Got a lot of other stuff
> on it too. Member of this and that. Leading businessman and
> farmer. Upright husband father. Kind to the poor and helpless.
> He been dead two weeks but fresh flowers still blooming on
> his grave. . . . Finally she [Shug] yawn loud and stretch herself.
> The son of a bitch still dead, she say. (*Purple* 1982:216)

In Alphonso, Walker fleshes out an extremely minor
character described in Hurston's *Their Eyes Were Watching God*.
Hurston in that work tells the readers about a character who is a
reverse or negative double to Tea Cake. But, unlike Tea Cake,
this young man, Who Flung, is an evil gigolo who uses a
deluded older woman, Annie Tyler, for his own evil ends
(material gain, of course). Similarly, Alphonso marries Celie's
distraught, dazed mother (who never recovers from the trauma
of her husband's lynching and her sudden widowhood).

Alphonso, whom Celie only knows as Pa (a cruel travesty
of the name in this context) usurps his predecessor's property
and wealth. This is very much like the infamous Murdstone of
David Copperfield, and, of course, the wicked stepmother in the
Cinderella myth. Pa, in Walker's hands, not only usurps his
predecessor's role and status in the community and in bed, he
also turns into a contemporary man-monster image: the father
figure who abuses his position in the household to impose sex on
his predecessor's child, Celie.

Walker depicts Pa as freely abusing, terrorizing, and
raping every young female in his reach (or attempting to) until
his sudden, richly deserved death on his third child-wife. It is
only then that the rightful heir(ess), the verbally, emotionally,
and sexually abused heroine, Celie, discovers the identity of her
real father. Celie, as well as her absent sister, Nettie, were all
along meant to be the beneficiaries of his wealth, primarily real
estate, in the form of farm, store, and a fine home.

Such an incantatory, iconographic image of wealth was a
crucial element in Booker T. Washington's advocacy of the "self-
help" philosophy for Black men that Washington incorporated

into his program for Black economic viability. This was to be achieved through efficient farming and ownership of one's own home and farmland. This would result in small business entrepreneurship. Walker uses the same format in depicting her father's method of achieving success, and the same elements comprise his success.

Despite its creative twist (from male agency to female), Walker's plot resolution has been criticized. Both Pa's sudden convenient demise and Celie's coming into an inheritance as a result seem far-fetched and awkward, too obviously fairy tale in quality. Walker objects to this criticism. But however she justifies Celie's miraculous inheritance, she is perhaps not so influenced by post-Reconstruction reality as she staunchly maintains. It appears, rather, that she is influenced by her readings in English and African American literature and her own unique experience as a writer. Nevertheless, the criticism seems valid, since Walker is here basing her far-fetched inheritance motif, when all is said and done, primarily on Hurston's fantasy-sourced solution of inheritance through widowhood for Janie Crawford, and hoary European myths like the Cinderella myth.

I agree with Walker's contention that Hurston in *Their Eyes* "wrote what is perhaps the most authentic and moving black love story ever published" (*Mothers' Gardens* 1984:35): one of the "sexiest, most 'healthily' rendered heterosexual love stories in our literature" (*Mothers' Gardens* 1984:88). Subliminally, Hurston's incredible message would seem to be like Jane Austen's: If a strong, self-assertive woman follows her own desires and remains true to herself, then economic self-sufficiency will somehow automatically accrue as a by-product. This would seem to be the case when Hurston depicted Janie ending up with a nice home, mortgage-free, and with sufficient money in the bank. All this enables Janie to live out her days in a golden afterglow of fulfillment in love, having once in her life known the love of a real man, Tea Cake.

Living by this philosophy, relying on others, on white and Black men and women to support her, Hurston lived haphazardly. For a while she lived successfully on the largesse of white female "godmothers," such as Cynthia Osgood Mason and Fannie Hurst. In return, she became an exotic toy for Hurst and a vehicle for Mason to further indulge her "primitivist" fantasies about Blacks. Later in her life, she was a servant and maid in less privileged encounters with white employers.

On this count, Walker eloquently defends Hurston, perhaps because she has had personal experience with poverty: "Without money, one becomes dependent on other people, who are likely to be—even in their kindness—erratic in their support and despotic in their expectations of return. Zora was forced to rely, like Tennessee Williams's Blanche 'on the kindness of strangers.' Can anything be more dangerous, if the strangers are forever in control? Zora, who worked so hard was never able to make a living from her work" (*Mothers' Gardens* 1984:90), Walker reasons in justification of her literary foremother's taking "largess from whites."

Still, given the poverty of most Blacks in the early twentieth century, Walker's response to this criticism strikes me as inadequate, even though it perhaps inadvertently reveals the enduring influence of Washington's mediated version of the American success myth. Walker's father was not a Bookerite, but an ardent follower of DuBois in his youth, at least in terms of prioritizing the right to vote, whereas Washington prioritized primarily land wealth. This may be why Walker does not acknowledge Washington's key role in disseminating his visionary program to his people, which she utilized in her novel. Nor does she acknowledge that Washington is identified with the advocacy of this vision, namely, the purchasing and owning of land as key sources of stability for one's self and one's children, despite the fact that she maintains that this was Celie's father's admirable intent. Nor does Walker acknowledge that millions of Blacks followed Washington (perhaps Celie's father was one of them), read his publications, were proud of his principalship of Tuskegee Institute, and that he orated before huge audiences to capacity and overflow throughout the country. Instead, Walker bases her defense on historical reality, "the post-Reconstruction era," but not on a realistic situation in that context:

> Carl Dix . . . expressed concern over the way so many of Celie's problems seemed to be solved by her receiving a house and

business left to her by her father (who had been lynched when she was a child). He correctly argues that the inheritance of private property is not a viable solution in terms of the masses of poor people and wishes that this aspect of Celie's existence could have been more progressive. I understand this criticism and feel it does indeed project our thoughts forward into the realm of better solutions for the landless, jobless, and propertyless masses. However, I also feel that for Celie's time—the post-Reconstruction era in the South, whose hallmark was the dispossession of blacks—this solution was in fact progressive; it spoke eloquently of the foresight of her father in his attempt to provide for her in a society where black people's attempts to provide for their coming generations were brutally repressed. (*Word* 1988:92)

Virginia Woolf predicated in "Shakespeare's Sister" that if the great playwright had had a sister who had attempted to leave home, she wouldn't have gotten very far, for obvious reasons. The same thing would have happened to any young Black (or even white) pubescent girl if she had gone on the road by herself, as Shakespeare and Booker T. had done; or on the boat as Franklin had done. This is why Hurston puts Janie on the road, but with a protector, Joe Starks. At the end, in a daze, she is protected only by her highly publicized final widowhood and the extreme means by which she had been forced to achieve it. That is, by killing her rabidly insane husband who was trying to kill her. This is how Janie comes to travel unescorted back up to Eatonville from the muck. Despite dressing herself in baggy overalls (in contrast to the bridal finery she had worn on her way out of town), Janie does not entirely succeed in de-sexing her body. As she passes on the way to the home she had inherited from her previous husband, the eternal Eatonville porch sitters scrutinize her closely and spread lies about her afterward.

However, the revisionary Walker sets *her* heroine, Celie, out on an internal road of self-discovery via her protector and beloved, Shug Avery. Shug is conceived as a minor goddess figure who comes and goes freely without the mediation of men. As for Pa, he is the opposite—one of the few truly devilish villains without external excuse or justification in African American literature. The way Walker has created Pa, he has no excuse environmentally. That is, his character has not been deformed by white brutalization. According to Hurston and Walker subtly and to Malcolm X not so subtly, whites are peripheral to their separatist scheme of things. Walker makes this clear in her oblique critique of Richard Wright and his followers for considering whites *too* significant:

> It is interesting to note, too, that black critics as well as white, considered Miss Hurston's classic, *Their Eyes Were Watching God*, as *second* to Richard Wright's *Native Son*, written during the same period. A love story about a black man and a black woman who spent only about one-eighteenth of their time worrying about whitefolks seemed to them far less important—probably because such a story should be so entirely *normal*—than a novel [*Native Son*] whose main character really had whitefolks on the brain. . . . Wright died in honor, although in a foreign land. Hurston died in her native state a pauper and, to some degree, an outcast. (*Mothers' Gardens* 1984:35)[4]

Walker also maintains this perspective in her own works, as she makes clear in a recent interview: "I can't think of any twentieth-century black woman writer who is first and foremost interested in what white folks think. I exempt Phillis Wheatley and all the nineteenth-century black women writers who *did* have that problem. Twentieth-century black women writers all seem to be much more interested in the black community, in intimate relationships, with the white world as a *backdrop*, which is certainly the appropriate perspective in my view" (Tate 1990:180–181).

In Walker's works, and *The Color Purple* is no exception, whites enter the Black world only on occasion, usually to oppress Blacks cruelly, for no rhyme or reason. Whites, however, are not presented as having the power to *internally* brutalize, mutilate, or deform any Black.

Thus it is that Sofia may be physically beaten and mutilated because of her proud, unbending spirit, but the whites never succeed in brutalizing *her*, only in embittering her. Squeak (Mary Agnes) is raped, but only in the flesh by her own white uncle. As sheriff, he is the chief (mis)representative of law in the town. He and his wife are responsible for crushing Sofia into the shell of her former self. Only the sheriff's daughter and Sofia's charge, Eleanor Jane, is the rare exception. She is well-meaning, kind, large-hearted. Unfortunately, she is also a fool: dense and insensitive because so self-centered. She adores Sofia, but more as a giant cuddly Mammy doll than as a three-dimensional human being.

Because of Eleanor Jane's crucial interventions in the past on her behalf (which have prevented Sofia from greater torture and beatings than she would otherwise have had to endure), Sofia puts up with her. Clearly, Walker uses Eleanor Jane as a symbolic representation of some acutely observed foibles of "bleeding heart liberals."

To return to Pa, the mean, low-down critter! Has there ever been a man who was bad *and* Black in his very nature in African American women's literature before Hurston? Though Hurston reveals wife beating in her work as a traditional African-sourced cultural construct for masculine status, she seems, nevertheless, to accept it and justify it. She does so both when recollecting it in her own marital experience (as what we would today call a battered wife), as well as in her work, in "Sweat," for example. Walker, in treating spousal abuse, follows Hurston, but unlike Hurston, she is openly judgmental. Further, she has no precedent in any of her foremother's works for the crusading attitude she has consistently taken, especially against sexual molestation of children (which Hurston does not address).[5] Contrary to widespread belief, however, it was not Alice Walker who first exposed this subject in print, but Ralph Ellison in *Invisible Man* (1947). However, Ellison treats Trueblood sympathetically, from the Black father's, the male's point of view, not from the outraged mother's or even the pregnant daughter's. In *The Invisible Man*, the sharecropper's seduction of his daughter is shown as accidental (a tragic by-product of poverty, cold, and overcrowded conditions) while Trueblood is asleep.

Walker is here signifying on two counts on European mythology, rather than on Hurston. Going as far back as Harriet Wilson's *Our Nig* (1854), and Jacobs's *Incidents* (1861) (in which Jacobs even tackled white slave owners' sodomizing of Black male slaves), no female freedom narrative writers or any African

American women writers before Walker ever depicted African American *males* abusing children. If we wish to examine African American writing tradition to find influences on this subject in Walker, we would have to turn to male writers for the earliest depictions of Black men as rapists and abusers of Black women. We would have to start with Richard Wright's *Native Son*.

Readers are all too familiar with Bigger Thomas's gratuitous rape and murder of his Black mistress Bessie (by hurling her down a shaft). The white media place much more emphasis on Bigger's incineration of the drunk white girl whom he had already suffocated to death. Innocently trapped in Mary's bedroom, Bigger fears (rightfully so) that he will be destroyed if she reveals his presence there. Wright is here signifying on white inhumanity to Blacks. They do not care about Bessie's murder, only about the white girl's.

The point of view is always external. Both women are objects, similarly weak fools who are used as symbols to further strengthen the evidence Wright brings to bear in *his* political case against whites. For him, *they* are on trial for creating the genocidal environment which has victimized Black men as personified by Bigger Thomas and twisted him into becoming a murderer. Wright influenced Ellison and then Toni Morrison, who dealt with the subject in *The Bluest Eye* (1970), when she depicts a drunken father, also the mutilated product of a devastatingly hostile environment, raping his daughter, who goes mad as a result.

Wright's and Ellison's handling of sexual abuse as opposed to Morrison's lies in point of view. Morrison, for example, shows the impact of the rape on the child, from the female and female victim's point of view, as well as that of the white and Black community and the perpertrator. Wright and Ellison do not. Ellison, in *Invisible Man*, takes the rape as an opportunity to show how the community's whites treat it as a propaganda field day against Black men. They are titillated and thrilled that Trueblood has committed this crime against nature because it proves all their cherished stereotypes about Black men.

Ellison also makes it an opportunity to signify against the typical New England descendent of Puritans in the person of the

"Northern philanthropist" Norton. This is to signify to readers not only that they do not love their fellow (Black) men, but also are in no way superior to those to whom they condescend. In fact, Ellison depicts all whites in the novel as lower on the scale of life. As for Norton, he is guilty of the same crime as Trueblood. But unlike Trueblood, who committed incest accidentally due to his environment, Norton's depravity is intrinsic. He is in incestuous love with his daughter. Ellison also makes the rape an opportunity to draw a complex portrait of Trueblood and a comic strip character out of his wife (when she hurls the frying pan at her husband's head in response to her daughter's pregnancy). Not once in all this signifying did Ellison choose to take the opportunity to depict what the victim *herself* thinks and feels about it.

Morrison, on the other hand, devotes the whole book to the victim, how and why she lost her mind from the child's point of view and that of her parents, all of whom she makes three-dimensional and believable. There are signifying elements in all this, but Morrison does not see the situation as having comedic overtones, as Ellison does, only tragic ones. Similar to Morrison's treatment of the subject, but autobiographical rather than fictional, is Maya Angelou's *I Know Why the Caged Bird Sings* (1970). Vivian Baxter's boyfriend, Mr. Freeman, who is in a position of stepfather to eight-year-old Marguerite (Maya), rapes her after many incidents of actual abuse (as does Celie's stepfather, "Pa" in *The Color Purple*).

Angelou's precedent obviously influences Walker here. Like Freeman, Alphonso, a respected businessman, knows that he would lose standing in the community if he told the truth about how Celie came to be "used goods." Sadly, Celie's mother, as in so many cases of child abuse, believes her husband's lie at Celie's expense, just as Mrs. Flint had at Jacobs's expense. Neither wife gets the story from the victim. Even if she did, would she believe it?

Mr._____ also believes Pa without question. Later, when Nettie tells the noble and high-minded Rev. Samuel about Mr._____'s abuse of Celie, although he does believe it, the minister refuses to interfere in what he considers euphemistically (for men) a family matter, a domestic dispute. Women would not so term it. Here Walker is being historically accurate about religious and official authorities' traditional response to domestic violence.

Until now, feminist and womanist critics alone have dared to object to such gratuitous violence when displayed by African American male characters in canonical texts by African American male writers, as I illustrated in the examples of Wright and Ellison. Recently, however, the front has begun to crack. Calvin Hernton has written a full-length work on this issue in which he courageously and publicly "calls out" hallowed names in *The Sexual Mountain and Black Women Writers* (1989). Just two stunning instances out of many *are* Richard Wright and Ralph Ellison. I quote Hernton's work at length because of its historic significance:

> The male authors have portrayed male heroes and male protagonists almost exclusively, and the complexity and vitality of black female experiences have been fundamentally ignored.
>
> Consider, for example, the depiction of black women in the two most acclaimed black novels of the twentieth century. In *Native Son*, Richard Wright portrays Bigger Thomas's mother and sister "realistically" as decrepit nagging bitches. Bigger's girlfriend, Bessie Mears, is a pathetic nothing. Mary Rambo, the black female in Ralph Ellison's *Invisible Man*, is a symbolic mammy figure. . . .
>
> Black men write a lot about the "castrating" black female, and feel righteous in doing so. But when black women write about the incest, rape, and sexual violence committed by black men against black females of all ages in the family and in the community at large, and when black women write that black men are castrators and oppressors of black women, black men accuse the women of sowing seeds of "division" in the black community; the women are accused of promoting animosities not only between the sexes in general but between males and females in the black family itself. In other words, when the women tell the truth about men and refuse to accept the blame for what men have done to them, the men get mad as hell. They get "hurt." They try to discredit and invalidate the women.

Black male writers, for example, band together and write about the comraderie [sic], competition, cooperation and brotherhood of black men in the struggle for manhood. This is viewed as manly and fitting by the men. But when black women write about the conflicts, joys, problems and sisterhood of black women in their struggle for self-esteem, black men brand the women "feminist bitches." (1987:46)

Without in any way diminishing Hernton's historic accomplishment, the truth of the matter is that he is not saying anything new and/or different. For example, the distinguished poet and novelist Margaret Walker (who was also Alice Walker's professor at Jackson State College, as well as a biographer of Richard Wright), has made the same point. "The black male writer has largely imitated his white counterparts, seeing all black characters and particularly females as lowest on the socioeconomic scale: as slaves or servants, as menial, marginal persons, evil, disreputable and powerless. . . . Black women have as much status in this regard as white women (who really don't have much either). . . . I do not, however, feel comfortable with the kind of treatment black women have received." Margaret Walker's perspective, in addition, is economic (which bears on Black male response to European American success mythology, as well as on Richard Wright's outlook): "If we understand the underlying philosophy of white racism, and its development as a buttressing agent of slavery and segregation and if we see these social institutions as necessary for the development of Western world capitalism, then we would know why these subhuman roles have been assigned to blacks. But why blacks feel they should imitate such castigation of black characters is harder to answer" (Tate 1990:202–203).

Because Hernton's forthright and passionate stand comes from a Black male critic, this subject may at last be given the serious consideration it deserves. Most ironically, the center of the storm, Alice Walker, has all along made similar observations, equally eloquent, which may now finally be given some weight. For example, as when she argued that some Black men are handicapped by "an apparent inability to empathize with black women's suffering under sexism, their refusal even to acknowledge our struggles; indeed, there are many black men who appear unaware that sexism exists (or do not even know what it is), or that women are oppressed in virtually all cultures, and if they do recognize there is abuse, their tendency is to minimize it or to deflect attention from it to themselves." This is the root cause, Walker concludes, for the uproar over both the book and the film, *The Color Purple*: "A book and movie that urged us to look at the oppression of women and children by men (and, to a lesser degree, by women) became the opportunity by which many black men drew attention to themselves—not in an effort to rid themselves of the desire or tendency to oppress women and children, but, instead, to claim that inasmuch as a 'negative' picture of them was presented to the world, they were, in fact, the ones *being* oppressed." What caused Walker the most suffering, what she found "nearly crushing," was the hypocrisy underlying all the vilification: "to realize there was an assumption on *anyone's* part that black women would not fight injustice except when the foe was white" (*Word* 1988:79–80).

Equally importantly, Walker has always maintained that she violated for many of these Black male critics yet another, even more sacrosanct taboo than publishing works in which Black men are depicted as sometimes oppressing their women. In using Hurston as model; in having Hurston represent not only Celie's fairy godmother, but her Prince Charming, as well; in combining all three into the character of the bodacious Shug Avery, Walker has outdone even her outrageous foremother. Another woman acting as a *dea ex machina* and sweeping the heroine off her feet simultaneously? A female *modus operandi* simultaneously for Celie's psychological, spiritual, psychic journey to independence in life, as well as sex and love? Bypassing men altogether? Walker reinforces my point that *therein* lay the real source of the ferocious attack launched against *The Color Purple* and its author:

> It is not the depiction of the brutal behavior of a black male character that is the problem for the critics; after all, many of us have sat in packed theaters where black men have cheered (much as white racists have cheered at images depicting blacks being abused) when a black woman was being terrorized or beaten, or, as in one of Prince's films, thrown in a garbage dumpster. Rather, it is the behavior of the women characters

that is objectionable; because whatever else is happening in the
novel and the film (and as is true more and more in real life),
women have their own agenda, and it does not include
knuckling under to abusive men. Women loving women, and
expressing it "publicly," if they so choose, is part and parcel of
what freedom for women means, just as this is what it means
for anyone else. (*Word* 1988:91)

Walker thereby violates an even more powerful taboo than
Jacobs had in her day when she dared to describe for white
women what Black women had to put up with under slavery in
supposedly decent Christian homes. Walker violates an even
more powerful taboo than Hurston had when, for the first time
in American literary history (let alone African American
literature), a twenty-five-year-old man falls in love with and
marries a thirty-eight-year-old woman and continues to live with
her in a working and viable relationship! Hurston dared to
depict a Black woman as seeking to satisfy her needs *as a*
woman. Hurston has Janie make this quest without guilt or
apology or psycholo-gizing, and without it ending in personal
and societal tragedy for herself *on those grounds*. In contrast, in all
other previous work, for example in Jacobs's *Incidents in the Life
of a Slave Girl*, and Nella Larsen's *Passing*, and *Quicksand*, when
their heroines try to break out of culturally prescribed systems of
repression for women they are made to suffer the torments of the
damned (and this goes for white women as well).

In capping on Hurston's exploration of this subject as part
of her Cinderella story, Walker violates a greater taboo. In fact,
many of her signifyings are examples of wildly perverse,
rebellious, even outrageous wordplays on taboos for Black
women. For instance, the success at business which Walker
permits Celie is initiated at Shug's nurturing suggestion. Celie
rises to become a small business entrepreneur, successful enough
to support her extended family, in keeping with Washington's
model. However, his model was for a Black man!

At the very end, perhaps too late to generate a change in
readers' perception of him as a brute, Mr._____ is transformed
from a frog into a prince of a porch philosopher, meditating on
the nature of gender and what it means to be fully human. All
this while sewing pants for Celie's business. He even wants to

remarry her. Economic upward mobility has come about for Celie, the female, not Albert, the male. At the end, like a banked fire, *he* (passive, diminished, dimmed) is her appendage.

Initially, Albert appeared seated on horseback in front of Pa's porch as an arrogant, selfish, cruel widower, dependent on a woman for his care, to slave for him like a mule in his home and fields. (Shades of Nanny's famous soliloquy.) Here Walker signifies ironically on auction block memories, on male master's dominion over their female slaves. She does this by using the phrase "on his high horse" in reference to him. For European American white women, this phrase has a seductive association, as well, because it is connected with the happy ending of their Cinderella/Prince Charming myth and its Gothic and romantic escapist variations down to the present day. These include abductions by dark, mysterious, threatening men as exemplified by the likes of Heathcliff, Rochester, or Valentino. In *The Wide Sargasso Sea*, Jane Rhys "caps" on Rochester, hero of *Jane Eyre*. In *her* version, Rochester is responsible for his wife Bertha's madness. Rhys's perspective is revisionary: West Indian and womanist, neither English nor male-centered.

At any rate, these "dashing" men may or may not turn out to have evil intentions toward the objects of their dubious affections. These are all exponents of myths which Walker is debunking in the persons of such truly vicious, battering, rapist-intentioned sadists like Alphonso and Mr._____. Walker also adds to the irony and tension of the phrase's complex use when after Pa offers Celie instead of Nettie to Mr._____, Celie's voice tells the reader that "He's still up on his horse. He look me up and down" (*Purple* 1982:20).

Albert's belated transformation and wilting of machismo comes about as a result of his unadmitted but powerful belief in voodoo. After Celie curses him, he starts to wither away until he changes his ways. This entire episode is based on the famous porch duel between Janie and Joe Starks, when Janie daringly does the dozens on her husband in public. Intimidated by this extraordinary and unprecedented behavior, Starks concludes that Janie hates him and has voodooed him.

In giving Celie financial success, Walker was perhaps influenced by her own financial success story, or perhaps that of a remarkable entrepreneur, Mme C.J. Walker (1869–1919), the hair straightening formula queen. The first Black female millionaire in her own right, *that* Walker (no relation) flourished into the beginning of the Harlem Renaissance. On her death, her daughter A'Lelia Walker (1885–1931), who played hostess throughout the Harlem Renaissance to its "literati," inherited a million dollars.

Our Walker, the successful author, has taken the tradition of inheritance fantasies and carried it one step further into her final innovation of the Cinderella myth. Once again, by doing this she has put her foot in it, violating still another sacrosanct taboo for women, most especially for Black women—that of American male economic success. Without question, for women, this is a myth equivalent in potency to the Cinderella myth. Walker has the temerity to imagine Celie *herself* rising to entrepreneurial success as designer and owner-operator of a medium-sized pants making factory, all from Shug's initial suggestion, or wand waving. Albert and other male characters end up backing the women. Albert assists Celie, who in her own improbable person began as a barely literate cotton-picking farm worker, kitchen slavey, used, abused, molested, raped Black girl. Never before has such a woman with such a loser's profile been depicted in literature as a rewarded heroic; as capable of direct upward mobility, of economic success for herself through her own hard work. Such a trajectory has traditionally been a male perogative only.

Perhaps as a result of the storm of controversy over her violation of so many societal taboos in so many ways, Walker's contribution to African American and American literary history in this regard has been obfuscated. Nevertheless, however one slices it, Alice Walker has made mincemeat of Franklin's and Washington's European American male success myth and the European Cinderella myth.

Several question arise at this point. First, what is the reality of this myth for African American women? What is its relevance for them? Has Walker convincingly conveyed her economic theory of success as a possibility for Black women? How many can become female Ben Franklins or Booker T. Washingtons in their own right, as the author has? Does the book merely offer a fairy tale ending; an inspiring fantasy for Black (and all other) women readers?

Walker's life, I submit, as that of Celie's, seems too romantic a Cinderella *cum* Franklin/Washington success myth to seem representative of reality, although Walker herself in her response to Dix's socialist criticism maintained that she was not capitalist. In fact, she stresses this in her interview with Claudia Tate:

> *C.T.*: Are you drawn toward the folk hero-heroine as the focal point of your work?
> *Walker*: I am drawn to working-class characters as I am to working-class people in general. I have a basic antagonism toward the system of capitalism. Since I'm only interested in changing it, I'm not interested in writing about people who already fit into it. And the working-class can never fit comfortably into a capitalist society (1990:185).

Certainly the success myth cannot be as inspiring a reality for as many African American women as the majority of European American white men have always found it to be. Nor can it even be as inspiring a reality as it was for the millions of Black men who found Washington's mediation of the European American success myth for white men a source of practical improvement in their otherwise often limited lives. In fact, the concept of entrepreneurial success for Walker's Cinderella heroine is the symbolic equivalent to success in marriage to a royal in a never-never land (a difficulty even in real life, according to recent tabloid headlines).

That Celie's success emanates from pants making in a medium-sized factory is straight out of Franklin and Washington. But this success is more related to their "self-help" mythology than is Celie's sudden miraculous inheritance from her mythic father. Walker's use of the first myth, the Franklin/Washington model and program (economic rewards for her Cinderella heroine grounded on the principle of success from hard work) is incongruous when combined with Jane Austen's and Zora Neale Hurston's use of Cinderella fantasies.[6]

Neither Austen nor Hurston lived out these fantasies in their own lives, only vicariously, through the lives of their heroines. But Walker has. This is perhaps how she justifies her truly revolutionary economic romanticism for Black women, on the basis of her own lived realities. When deconstructed, in fact, the name "Celie" signifies on a straitened, i.e., "under-privileged," stringently abbreviated form of "Cinderella." In a scrambled sense, it is also an anagram for the author's own name, Alice.

In college and later, Walker had abortions. Her short story, "The Abortion," devastatingly anatomizes masculine collusion in perpetuating the myth that the personal (when female) is not political. Only what *men* do and experience is political. Walker joined the Southern voting rights movement in Mississippi. She married and divorced a Jewish civil rights lawyer. She was friendly with the Rev. and Mrs. King. She has gone to Africa. In the process, Walker has also gone from a rural Georgia sharecropper's daughter (just down the road, but a world away from Flannery O'Connor's home), to a civil rights activist, to famed author with a secluded studio high up in the California mountains. Blessed with a community of friends of all races and religious orientations, Walker works through social and political causes such as eco-feminism, anti-clitoridectomy, advocacy of natural foods and Native American rights, vegetarianism, and anti-nuclear and anti-war movements in an attempt to save the globe, which she sees as in danger of destruction. Walker's life as she lives it is a commitment to humanity worldwide. It forms a seamless whole with her fearless, cutting edge, trailblazing work as an author. In *Their Eyes Were Watching God*, there is a famous scene which Gates has described as providing a "transformation or reversal of status, [which] is truly the first feminist critique of the fiction of the authority of the male voice, and its sexism, in the Afro-American tradition" (1988:207). What the heroine Janie does to merit such a compliment from the most renowned of living African American critics is to finally call out her husband in public and then take him on and defeat him in a dozens duel.

Jody Starks's shame and humiliation is so complete that he believes Janie has voodooed him. After this duel of wits, he proceeds to shrivel up and die emotionally as well as physically, despite the ministrations of a traditional African medicine man. This system, based on "self-hypnosis" on the part of the believer and chicanery on that of the medicine men (by European American definitions, that is), has been practiced for thousands of years in the diaspora, as well as in Africa. Perhaps the first to describe it in African American literature was Olaudah Equiano (Gustavus Vassa). For a self-proclaimed, highly devout Christian, he is surprisingly positive, even defensive, about African "superstition." Perhaps he is himself signifying on Christians, as I submit Wheatley did. In any event, Walker has the climax of *her* text "cap" on Hurston's quoted earlier, with the addition of a direct voodoo curse (Walker calls it "juju").

Walker's heroine, Celie, also ultimately bests her husband, Mr._____, with the use of *nommo*:

> I curse you, I say.
> What that mean? he say.
> I say, Until you do right by me, everything you touch will crumble.
> He laugh. Who you think, you is? he say. You can't curse nobody. Look at you. You black, you pore, you ugly, you a woman. Goddam, he say, you nothing at all.
> Until you do right by me, I say, everything you even dream about will fail. . . .
> Whoever heard of such a thing, say Mr._____. I probably didn't whip your ass enough.
> Every lick you hit me you will suffer twice, I say. Then I say, You better stop talking because all I'm telling you ain't coming just from me. Look like when I open my mouth the air rush in an' shape words.
> Shit, he say. I should have lock you up. Just let you out to work.
> The jail you plan for me is the one in which you will rot, I say. . . .
> I'll fix her wagon! say Mr._____, and spring toward me.
> A dust devil flew up on the porch between us, fill my mouth with dirt. The dirt say, Anything you do to me, already done to you. . . . I'm pore, I'm black, I may be ugly and can't cook, a voice say to everything listening. But I'm here.
> Amen, say Shug. Amen, amen. (*Purple* 1982:187).

In the film, Celie forks her second and third fingers, pointing them threateningly at him, which substantiates

Mr._____'s conviction that he has been "jujued." It also has the
same result as in the case of Jody Starks, only Mr._____
experiences a transformation and mends his ways, literally,
because he begins to sew! This is only one of Walker's many
humorous tongue-in-cheek punnings or doublings of meanings,
and all can be subsumed under the rubric of signifying.

When Celie meets her fairy godmother cum Prince
Charming, Shug Avery, Walker signifies on the potent European
American myth in delightfully subtle ways. Her glitzy outfit is a
takeoff on the fairy godmother's magnificent raiment, and the
epithet that Celie gives her, "Queen Honeybee" is linked with
Bruno Bettelheim's interpretation of the fairy godmother as a
queen bee symbol whose power both gives pain through her
mortal sting (her wand), and pleasure (honey), in Celie's case,
love and passion. Further, when Celie terms Shug "evil," with
admiration, it is in the sense of "bad," meaning outrageous,
strong, sassy, spirited, bodacious, blues woman for whom
community conventions and ru(o)les are irrelevant.

In a celebrated section of the text, Shug and Celie do a
take-off on Platonic dialogue in which Shug meditates,
sermonizes, and answers her disciple's questions on the nature
of God. Walker also signifies here on Emerson's macho "rugged
individual" transcendentalism, designed and meant for white
men only. Shug begins the challenge session against the white
male God and the white male hegemony by signifying on the
transcendentalists' "universalist" language and assumptions,
which include their denial of female (right to sexuality). But it is
Celie's "cap" of her mistress's (pun intended) parody of
Emerson's famed eyeball passage in his "Essay on Nature,"
which provides closure to the session:

> It ain't something you can look at apart from anything else,
> including yourself. I believe God is everything, say Shug.
> Everything that is or ever was or ever will be. And when you
> can feel that, and be happy to feel that, you've found It. . . .
> She say. My first step from the old white man was trees.
> Then air. Then birds. Then other people. But one day when I
> was sitting quiet and feeling like a motherless child, which I
> was, it come to me: that feeling of being part of everything, not
> separate at all. . . . I knew just what it was. In fact, when it

happen, you can't miss it. It sort of like you know what, she say, grinning and rubbing high up on my thigh. . . . I think it pisses God off if you walk by the color purple in a field somewhere and don't notice it. . . .

Well, us talk and talk about God, but I'm still adrift. Trying to chase that old white man out of my head. I been so busy thinking bout him I never truly notice nothing God make. Not a blade of corn (how it do that?) not the color purple (where it come from?). Not the little wildflowers. Nothing. . . . Still, it is like Shug say, You have to git man off your eyeball, before you can see anything a'tall.

Man corrupt everything, say Shug. He on your box of grits, in your head, and all over the radio. He try to make you think he everywhere. Soon as you think he everywhere, you think he God. But he ain't. Whenever you trying to pray, and man plop himself on the other end of it, tell him to git lost, say Shug. Conjure up flowers, wind, water, a big rock.

But this hard work, let me tell you. He been there so long, he don't want to budge. He threaten lightening, floods and earthquakes. Us fight. I hardly pray at all. Everytime I conjure up a rock, I throw it. (*Purple* 1982:178–79)

In her own life, the author has had, through *The Color Purple*, the last laugh on her traditional professors who, she points out bitterly, "directed" her "toward a plethora of books by mainly white male writers who thought most women worthless if they didn't enjoy bullfighting or hadn't volunteered for the trenches in World War II" (*Mothers' Gardens* 1984:6). Walker has the last laugh, as well, on the white, middle-aged, racist Northerner to whom she remembers she once confided while in college that she "hoped to be a poet. In the nicest possible language, which still made me as mad as I've ever been, he suggested that a 'farmer's daughter' might not be the stuff of which poets are made" (*Mothers' Gardens* 1984:18). She also has the last laugh on a group she defines as her "Northern brothers" who "will not believe me when I say there is a great deal of positive material I can draw from my 'underprivileged background'" (*Word* 1988:20).

Ultimately, in *The Color Purple*, Walker has the last laugh on any racist and sexist assumptions about the possibility of success for her characters and for herself. Unfortunately, all that such readers perceive in both the author and her text are racially and sexually "disadvantaged" characters: manifestations of lack rather than celebrations of a complex world view. *The Color Purple* is clearly such a celebration, not least in Walker's appropriation and subversion of European American male success mythology to express a womanist perspective instead.

Notes

1. I am aware that as long ago as 1982 the connection between *The Color Purple* and the Cinderella myth was made by Trudier Harris. However, she does not ascribe the fairy godmother role to Shug, as seems logical, but to Nettie.

2. See Calvin Mercer, "Walker's Critique of Religion in *The Color Purple,*" *SAGE* VI.1 (Summer 1989): 24–26. Mercer agrees that Shug's arrival in Celie's life is providential, not, however, in terms of a Cinderella myth, but in terms of religion. "Although it is never made explicit in the novel, Shug can easily be interpreted as a savior figure for Celie. Significantly God drops out of the picture as expressed in her second letter to Nettie. . . . One cannot overestimate the importance of Shug's arrival for Celie's spiritual struggle"(24).

3. Since that time, Hurston's birth records have been found. They reveal that she was born in 1891. She had concealed ten years of her life.

4. During Hurston's lifetime, Wright and Hughes could not abide Hurston's topics, and, to them, the embarrassingly Negroid characters she loved to write about. Walker, as much as she adores Hughes especially, sides with Hurston on this issue. For both women authors, whites and white culture and history are peripheral in and to their lives and to be avoided whenever possible by Blacks. It is noticeable that both *Their Eyes* and *The Color Purple* give only minimal clues about the historic periods covered in them in terms of European American time divisions.

5. Perhaps this is the case because she was especially sensitive to this subject, having herself been wrongfully accused of molesting an eleven-year-old boy.

6. It may be recalled in this regard that Jane Austen in the early nineteenth century modified the traditional Cinderella myth into a more

realistic English economic mythology: the heroine married into land wealth instead of royalty.

References

Gates, Henry Louis, Jr. *The Signifying Monkey*. New York: Oxford University Press, 1988.

Hernton, Calvin. *The Sexual Mountain and Afro-American Women Writers*. New York: Anchor Books, 1987.

Hurston, Zora Neale. *Dust Tracks on a Road: An Autobiography*. 2d ed. Ed. and intro. Robert Hemenway. Urbana and Chicago: University of Illinois Press, 1984.

————. *Their Eyes Were Watching God*. 1937. Foreword Sherley Anne Williams. Urbana and Chicago: University of Illinois Press, 1978.

Long, Richard A., and Eugenia Collier, eds. *Afro-American Writing: An Anthology of Prose and Poetry*. 2nd ed. University Park: Pennsylvania State University Press, 1985.

Tate, Claudia, ed. *Black Women Writers at Work*. New York: Continuum, 1990.

Walker, Alice. *The Color Purple*. New York: Harcourt Brace Jovanovich, 1982.

————. *In Search of Our Mothers' Gardens: Womanist Prose*. New York: Harcourt Brace Jovanovich, 1984.

————. *Living by the Word: Selected Writings 1973–1987*. New York: Harcourt Brace Jovanovich, 1988.